Web Design Studio Secrets®,
2nd Edition

DEKE MCCLELLAND, KATRIN EISMANN, AND TERRI STONE

WEB DESIGN STUDIO SECRETS®,

2ND EDITION

IDG BOOKS WORLDWIDE, INC.

AN INTERNATIONAL DATA GROUP COMPANY

Foster City, CA ▲ Chicago, IL ◆ Indianapolis, IN ▼ New York, NY

Web Design Studio Secrets®, 2nd Edition

Published by
IDG Books Worldwide, Inc.
An International Data Group Company
919 E. Hillsdale Blvd., Suite 400
Foster City, CA 94404
www.idgbooks.com (IDG Books Worldwide Web site)

Library of Congress Card Number: 00-100827

ISBN: 0-7645-3455-6

Printed in the United States of America

10 9 8 7 6 5 4 3 2 1

1K/SS/QT/QQ/FC

Distributed in the United States by IDG Books Worldwide, Inc.

Distributed by CDG Books Canada Inc. for Canada; by Transworld Publishers Limited in the United Kingdom; by IDG Norge Books for Norway; by IDG Sweden Books for Sweden; by IDG Books Australia Publishing Corporation Pty. Ltd. for Australia and New Zealand; by TransQuest Publishers Pte Ltd. for Singapore, Malaysia, Thailand, Indonesia, and Hong Kong; by Gotop Information Inc. for Taiwan; by ICG Muse, Inc. for Japan; by Intersoft for South Africa; by Eyrolles for France; by International Thomson Publishing for Germany, Austria and Switzerland; by Distribuidora Cuspide for Argentina; by LR International for Brazil; by Galileo Libros for Chile; by Ediciones ZETA S.C.R. Ltda. for Peru; by WS Computer Publishing Corporation, Inc., for the Philippines; by Contemporanea de Ediciones for Venezuela; by Express Computer Distributors for the Caribbean and West Indies; by Micronesia Media Distributor, Inc. for Micronesia; by Chips Computadoras S.A. de C.V. for Mexico; by Editorial Norma de Panama S.A. for Panama; by American Bookshops for Finland.

For general information on IDG Books Worldwide's books in the U.S., please call our Consumer Customer Service department at 800-762-2974. For reseller information, including discounts and premium sales, please call our Reseller Customer Service department at 800-434-3422.

For information on where to purchase IDG Books Worldwide's books outside the U.S., please contact our International Sales department at 317-596-5530 or fax 317-596-5692.

For consumer information on foreign language translations, please contact our Customer Service department at 800-434-3422, fax 317-596-5692, or e-mail rights@idgbooks.com.

For information on licensing foreign or domestic rights, please phone +1-650-655-3109.

For sales inquiries and special prices for bulk quantities, please contact our Sales department at 650-655-3200 or write to the address above.

For information on using IDG Books Worldwide's books in the classroom or for ordering examination copies, please contact our Educational Sales department at 800-434-2086 or fax 317-596-5499.

For press review copies, author interviews, or other publicity information, please contact our Public Relations department at 650-655-3000 or fax 650-655-3299.

For authorization to photocopy items for corporate, personal, or educational use, please contact Copyright Clearance Center, 222 Rosewood Drive, Danvers, MA 01923, or fax 978-750-4470.

ABOUT IDG BOOKS WORLDWIDE

Welcome to the world of IDG Books Worldwide.

IDG Books Worldwide, Inc., is a subsidiary of International Data Group, the world's largest publisher of computer-related information and the leading global provider of information services on information technology. IDG was founded more than 30 years ago by Patrick J. McGovern and now employs more than 9,000 people worldwide. IDG publishes more than 290 computer publications in over 75 countries. More than 90 million people read one or more IDG publications each month.

Launched in 1990, IDG Books Worldwide is today the #1 publisher of best-selling computer books in the United States. We are proud to have received eight awards from the Computer Press Association in recognition of editorial excellence and three from Computer Currents' First Annual Readers' Choice Awards. Our best-selling ...For Dummies® series has more than 50 million copies in print with translations in 31 languages. IDG Books Worldwide, through a joint venture with IDG's Hi-Tech Beijing, became the first U.S. publisher to publish a computer book in the People's Republic of China. In record time, IDG Books Worldwide has become the first choice for millions of readers around the world who want to learn how to better manage their businesses.

Our mission is simple: Every one of our books is designed to bring extra value and skill-building instructions to the reader. Our books are written by experts who understand and care about our readers. The knowledge base of our editorial staff comes from years of experience in publishing, education, and journalism — experience we use to produce books to carry us into the new millennium. In short, we care about books, so we attract the best people. We devote special attention to details such as audience, interior design, use of icons, and illustrations. And because we use an efficient process of authoring, editing, and desktop publishing our books electronically, we can spend more time ensuring superior content and less time on the technicalities of making books.

You can count on our commitment to deliver high-quality books at competitive prices on topics you want to read about. At IDG Books Worldwide, we continue in the IDG tradition of delivering quality for more than 30 years. You'll find no better book on a subject than one from IDG Books Worldwide.

John Kilcullen
Chairman and CEO
IDG Books Worldwide, Inc.

*Eighth Annual
Computer Press
Awards ≥1992*

*Ninth Annual
Computer Press
Awards ≥1993*

*Tenth Annual
Computer Press
Awards ≥1994*

*Eleventh Annual
Computer Press
Awards ≥1995*

FOREWORD

The design and creation of Web pages has gone through several revolutions since it began as a way for scientists to distribute physics papers. First came the dull, text-heavy pages with basic gray backgrounds. Then came the slow, graphics-intensive sites with cryptic interfaces inspired by Myst. Now we are finally seeing the types of pages that let people easily do what they wanted to do from the beginning: Find the information and software they need quickly and conveniently.

Let's face it: Most of the Web sites in the world are there to deliver either a commercial or editorial message. While some sites focus on creating an "experience" and others on community or self-expression, the real business of the Web designer is (and should be) getting the right message across to the right audience. One of the hottest industry terms these days is "usability." This is a refreshing change. After years of obsession with Java, plug-ins, and other bleeding-edge technologies, we have settled into a time where the priority is on making pages that load quickly, can be searched, and can be found easily on Yahoo! and AltaVista.

This book is a great example of the trend away from the previous gee-whiz design focus, and the trend toward getting results. At our Web Design events, we've worked hard to achieve the same kind of results that Deke McClelland, Katrin Eismann, and Terri Stone have with this book. In *Web Design Studio Secrets*, Deke, Katrin, and Terri have assembled a collection of some of the industry's top Web design professionals to tell how they create great Web sites. A great site is one that meets the needs of the organization sponsoring it while creating an interesting and useful (and sometimes fun!) destination for the browser.

It's not about technology. It's about teamwork, communication, and understanding the needs of the client while facing the reality of a 28.8 world. This book shows how to do it right.

Steve Broback
President
Thunder Lizard Productions

Steve Roth
CEO
Thunder Lizard Productions

PREFACE

Web design is a bit like chess. Just because you know the basic rules doesn't mean you know the game. Sure, the bishop moves diagonally and the rook moves up and down, but how do you exploit these moves to confound your opponent and win the game? Granted, GIF and JPEG are the universal image formats on the Web, but how do you use these formats to produce attractive, fast-loading graphics?

The best way to get a feel for how chess is played is to watch the game in action. With a little observation, you get the hang of it. If you're inclined toward serious study, you can master the game. The same holds true for the world of online design. Browse through a few sites, check out the source code, and you begin to get a feel for how the Web works. If you're serious about making a living or establishing a firm presence on the Web, you can study the ways of those who have come before you and devise new and better techniques based on theirs.

This book is for serious students of online design. Chapter by chapter, we peer over the shoulders of 15 of the most capable professionals working on the Web. And they tell it all, from basic HTML and image manipulation to high-end production techniques and eventually marketing your site to the masses. Their stories are instructional, packed with tips and tricks; enlightening, based on years of hard-won experience; and inspirational, rife with ideas and approaches that you can start implementing into your site immediately.

But most importantly, the stories are real. Every artist covers a highly focused topic that he or she eats, drinks, and breathes on a daily basis. Don't expect a bunch of meandering artist profiles to cure a celebrity fix until the next issue of *People* magazine arrives. Each chapter features a successful artist crawling out of the trenches for a moment to explain in detail how to use HTML as a design tool, how to make your site easy to navigate, how to script buttons that highlight, how to create animated GIF and Flash files, how to design effective database-driven sites, and much more.

A FEW BORING DETAILS

Throughout this book, we assume that you already know your way around the Web. If the World Wide Web is completely new territory to you, we urge you to consult a primer and come back to this book in a couple of months when it will make more sense. We'd love to sell you a book, but we'd rather you get up to speed and learn in the most efficient manner possible.

This book is aimed specifically at designers, but even designers have to write and edit code when creating content for the Web. So in and amongst the bright colorful artwork, you'll come across occasional lines of HTML and JavaScript code. It just can't be helped.

That said, we're big believers that designers should have to focus on code as little as possible. To this end, we have tried to pull out only the code that is pertinent to the techniques that the artist is demonstrating. This makes the medicine more digestible without over-simplifying the source code so it doesn't make sense.

If you want to dig deeper and examine the source code for yourself, we provide many of the original HTML files on the CD at the back of this book. Feel free to open the files in your favorite text or HTML editor and scan away.

FROM CRAFTSMAN TO ARTISAN

Web Design Studio Secrets is about the art of online design. It's like an intense three-week apprenticeship program at a leading design house, except that you don't have to leave the privacy of your home or office, and your mentor won't ask you to fetch him a cup of coffee and a bagel when business is slow. Assuming that you're moderately familiar with how to create a Web page and you're looking to upgrade your talents, expertise, and general level of sophistication, then you're good to go.

CONTENTS AT A GLANCE

CONTENTS

CHAPTER 3
CREATING WEB GRAPHICS   39

CHAPTER 4
BASIC HTML AS A DESIGN TOOL   53

CHAPTER 5
DYNAMIC HTML AS A
DESIGN TOOL   83

CHAPTER 6
CONSTRUCTING PAGES USING
TABLES   93

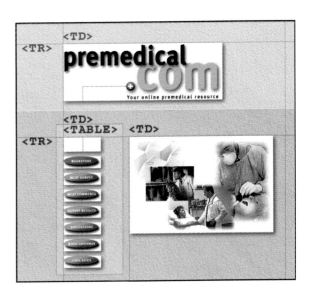

CHAPTER 7

DESIGNING TYPE FOR THE WEB   109

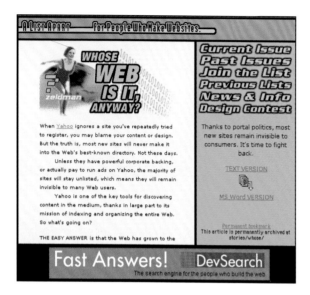

CHAPTER 8

CREATING ROLLOVERS WITH JAVASCRIPT   121

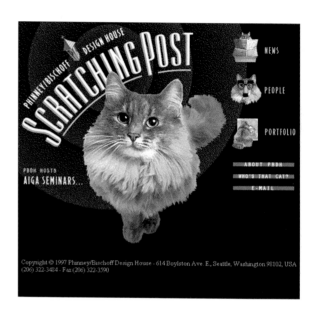

CHAPTER 14
IMMERSIVE ONLINE IMAGING   209

CHAPTER 15
ANNOUNCING YOUR WEB SITE   233

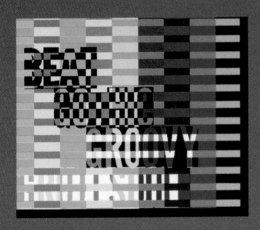

PART I
GENERAL TECHNIQUES

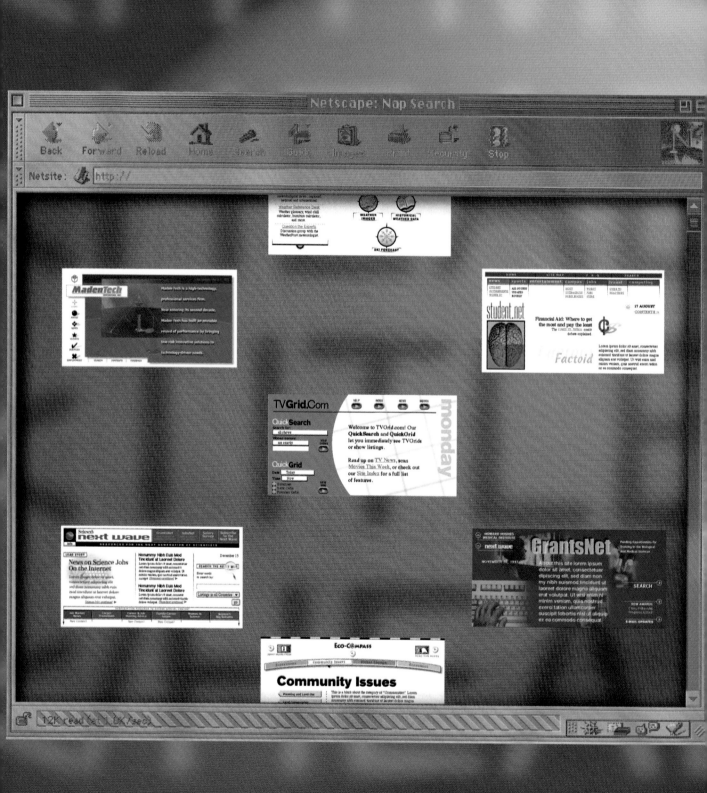

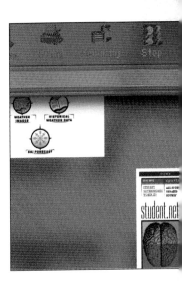

CHAPTER 1
DESIGNING FOR THE WEB

The Web presents a sizable challenge to even the most skilled graphic designers. In order to be successful in Web design, you must understand the added dimension of the medium. Many of the rules and techniques of traditional print composition still apply, but there are additional issues to consider and techniques to master. The challenge is to take traditional design skills and experiences and reshape and apply them with an understanding of how the Web works.

The most successful design is the one the viewer doesn't even notice.

TRACY KEATON DREW

WHERE TO BEGIN?

Tracy Keaton Drew studied graphic design before desktop computers were even used as tools of the trade. As Apple Computer, Aldus PageMaker, and Adobe PostScript were spawning desktop publishing in the mid-to-late 1980s, Tracy was working as the in-house designer in a large printing company. "I learned that to create the best design, you had to understand as much of the process as possible. I would talk to the strippers, the pressmen, the bindery. Everything that I learned in those areas was relevant to my design. When I began designing for the Web, I learned HTML. Understanding how HTML works improves my design, allowing me to better control the final appearance of the Web site. Getting into the code is much more interesting and easier than most designers think.

"Most importantly, Web designers need to understand the language of interaction. Your designs are no longer static and they are no longer two-dimensional.

You need to learn what the viewer reacts to, what attracts them to a site, and to structure the site so the viewer can find the information, service, experience, or product quickly and easily."

GETTING TO KNOW YOUR CLIENT

"Before I pick up a pencil or launch Photoshop, I always interview the client about the purpose and audience of the Web site. The more information that I can start with, the better my design proposal will be. As you can imagine, a client who is unsure about what they want can be a nightmare to work with. One part of a Web designer's role is to help the client define the objectives of the site. For instance, some clients want links to everything on the opening page: links to the mission statement, worldwide factory locations, client lists, a complete product catalog, job openings, all the way through to a picture of the board of directors! Step back and help your client see what information is most important and relevant to the people they wish to attract to the site."

GETTING TO KNOW YOUR VIEWERS

Just as in traditional graphic design, designing for the Web requires defining your target audience and what appeals to them. You need to have a feel for your target viewers' experience using the Web, their likely patience, age, and gender, as well as whether they are at your Web site for entertainment, information, and so on. This will help you establish the tone and personality of your site. "For example, in the case of the FreeLoader site, the client wanted to appeal to a young audience, so I decided the site had to have a slightly irreverent look. The banners are playful through the use of a hand-written font with mixed upper- and lowercase letters (1.1)."

Taking the time to technically "define" your viewers also includes determining their likely access speed, preferred computer platform, browser, and level of computer experience. "With the millions of people on the Web, you may wonder how you can define the ideal viewer. But the reality of the matter is, a Web site doesn't have the same reach that, say, a Super Bowl commercial does. The Web actually narrows your general audience." Once a Web site is up, the server can be configured to supply specific statistics including the speed at which people are accessing the site, whether they are accessing it from home or work, and how long they are staying in the site. This information allows you to do some fine-tuning and can serve as a reference for future site-design projects.

From a technical point of view, understanding the end-viewer in terms of computer platform, preferred browser, and access speed will influence your decisions about the size and complexity of the design, thereby influencing download time and the viewer's

ARTIST:
Tracy Keaton Drew

ORGANIZATION:
Keaton Drew Design
1728 Q Street, NW
Washington, DC 20009
202/518-0853
tkdrew@tkdrew.com

SYSTEM, MACINTOSH:
Power Mac 8500/333
Mac OS 9.0
5GB storage/352MB RAM

SYSTEM, PC:
IBM Aptiva M71
Windows 95
1GB storage/16MB RAM

CONNECTIVITY:
56.6 Kbps modem dial-up

PERIPHERALS:
NEC MultiSync x2 17-inch monitor, Wacom ArtZ tablet, Agfa Studio Star scanner, Connectix Color QuickCam

PRIMARY APPLICATIONS:
Adobe Photoshop 5.5 and Illustrator 8.0, Macromedia Dreamweaver 2.0, HTML Editor, Macromedia Fireworks 2.0, Adobe

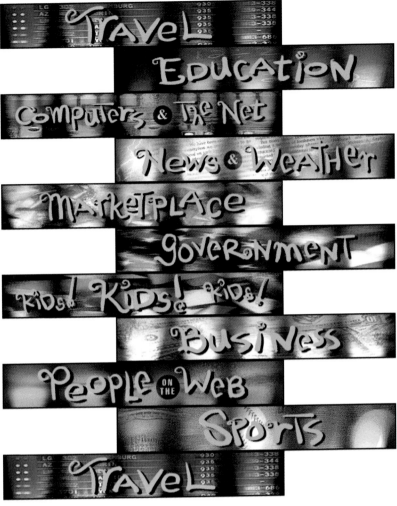

Travel
Education
Computers & The Net
News & Weather
Marketplace
Government
Kids! Kids! Kids!
Business
People on the Web
Sports
Travel

1.1

ImageReady 2.0, Netscape Navigator versions 3–5, and Internet Explorer versions 3–5

WORK HISTORY:

<u>1984</u> — While studying traditional graphic design, saw a computer-enhanced Kodak ad and had the revelation to learn and work with computers — although there weren't any computers at the school.

<u>1986</u> — In-house graphic designer for printing company and learned that "to be a good designer I had to know what was going on behind the scenes."

<u>1987</u> — Acquired first Macintosh.

<u>1989</u> — Beta tested Adobe Photoshop.

<u>1990</u> — First job as an independent contractor at *The Washington Post*. News artist during the Gulf War, and DTP specialist to assist in electronic pagination of first weekly section.

<u>1992</u> — Six-month internship at the Kodak Center for Creative Imaging in Camden, Maine. "I came to the Center as a print-oriented graphic designer and left as a multimedia and interface designer."

<u>1993–95</u> — Design Director for "Digital Ink," *The Washington Post* online.

<u>1996</u> — Founded Keaton Drew Design. Clients include *The Washington Post*, the American Association for the Advancement of Science (*Science Magazine*), Student.Net, MediaOne, and Maden Tech. Teaches Web design courses at George Washington University.

FAVORITE PLEASURE:

Movie soundtracks — "I especially love soundtracks that were composed for a specific movie. It's the classical music of our time."

NOTE

FreeLoader was one of the first Web sites to use push technology, allowing viewers to configure their computers to automatically log on to the site and download the latest FreeLoader issue complete with huge graphics (1.2 and 1.3).

experience. "Always design with a specific audience in mind. Organize and support the information through clear design, avoiding distracting elements."

The GrantsNet.org Web site helps graduate and postdoctoral students studying the biological and medical sciences to find positions and grant money in their respective fields (1.4). The site needed to balance speed, simplicity, and clarity to quickly and easily give the viewer the essential information (1.5). The search engine was the most important aspect of this site (1.6). Most of the pages returned in searches are dynamically generated from databases of text and graphics. "In addition to designing the graphical interface, it was important that I could write the

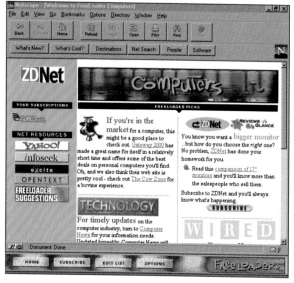

1.2

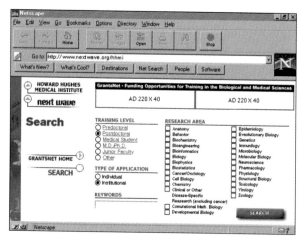

1.4

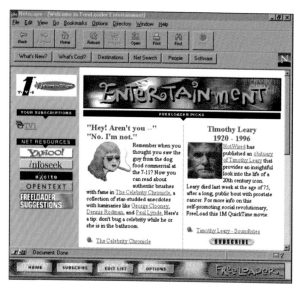

1.3

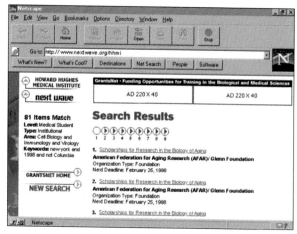

1.5

HTML and JavaScript since I was creating 'templates' that the Webmaster would be using to maintain the site and the database."

NEW GAME, NEW RULES

To avoid the "lost in interface" dilemma, Web designers need to distill information and categories carefully, underscoring the information with a consistent interface. Everything that goes into the user interface, from colors, controls, behaviors, navigation in and between screens, interactivity, and metaphors used, influence a viewer's experience. "Designing a Web site is similar to designing a mini-application; the viewer doesn't separate her experience from the design. If the design is poor and confuses the viewer, then the site has failed, no matter how relevant the information. The most successful design is the one the viewer doesn't even notice."

WHO IS IN CONTROL?

We all revel in the control that sophisticated software offers — from pixel-level image retouching to the ability to precisely fine-tune the word spacing of an important document. Designing for the Web requires an emotional 180-degree turn. You do not have the control that you're used to having over how the final result will look. You have no control over leading, letter spacing, and fonts when designing for 2.0 and 3.0 browsers. Further, you don't know for sure what computer platform, color depth, browser type, or version your viewers are using (unless you're developing an intranet), and all of these variables affect how content is displayed on the screen. "I always check a site throughout the design process on both

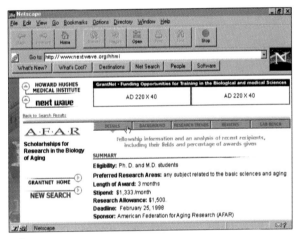

1.6

SELECTING FONTS

When it comes to selecting fonts, the rules are different for the Web than they are for print. "Blocks of serif 'body' text are easier to read in print, because the serif of one letter leads your eye gracefully to the next letter. Serifs help give type distinctive shapes, thereby increasing readability. But on the Web — or more accurately, on the screen — type is made up of pixels, and not continuous lines. If you were to count the number of pixels that are required to create a 10-point lowercase serif Times *h* and a 10-point lowercase sans serif Helvetica *h*, the difference is 20 versus 17 pixels. You can begin to see that serif fonts are more complex due to the nature of how they are displayed on the screen. In the illustration (1.7), Times, the serif font, is on the left and Helvetica, the sans serif font, is on the right. The smaller the typeface, the fewer pixels there are to display the letter. So there are fewer pixels, but you still have to add one or two pixels on either end of an ascender or descender because it's 'serif' and because of the low-resolution pixel display of computer monitors — it's getting messy. The bottom line? Sans serif fonts with a high x-height are the most legible onscreen."

1.7

Mac and PC. What happened with the Next Wave site is typical. The PC version (1.8) displays the pop-up boxes differently and has more white space above the navigation bar, while the Macintosh version shows the entire navigation bar (1.9)."

DESIGNING UP OR DOWN?

After identifying your audience, the next step requires a judgment call: Design to the lowest common denominator (LCD) or assume that your viewers have more advanced hardware and software? The decisions made at this stage will influence page weight and screen size. "Most of my clients request that I design for the average user. It's debatable what 'average' really is anymore, but I define average as someone who has an 8-bit color 15-inch monitor and uses either Netscape Navigator or Internet Explorer, usually version 4.0 (although I check my designs on 2.0, 3.0, and 5.0 browsers, too). They use 28.8 dial-up service and leave the default browser navigation options available (toolbar with text/icons and URL

indicator), which dictates the size of available screen real estate."

SPEED ISSUES

"I used to design the home page to look as nice as possible, thinking that it was like a magazine cover and should make a great first impression. I tried to keep the total page weight — HTML document plus graphics — under 35K. But I have come around to thinking that's still too big. (Being a Web designer is a dynamic process.) The novelty of using the Web is wearing off. The vast majority of people on the Web are looking for specific information — and they want it quickly! There are exceptions to every rule, but a great general rule of thumb is to keep the top level Web page under 20K, which at 28.8 bps would download in approximately ten seconds. I've read usability studies on Jakob Nielsen's site at *www.useit.com* that indicate a user's attention wanders after waiting more than ten seconds. I encourage any designer who makes the leap to the Web to read as much as possible about usability issues. This is as important as learning about color, balance, scale, repetition, etc."

An example of a site that needed to load quickly is *www.islandpress.com* (1.10). As a nonprofit environmental publisher, Island Press wanted their site to have a natural and serene look and feel. The icons, which look like woodcuts, and the simple yet graceful arch for the main navigation bar help create a

1.8

1.9

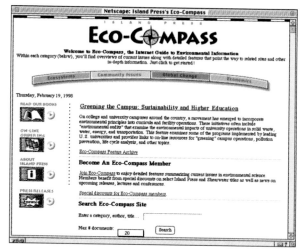

1.10

hand-made low-tech atmosphere. As viewers go deeper into the site, details such as the small red triangle under the active topic (1.11) help them to easily orient themselves (1.12). As the information becomes more specific, the subsectional navigation clearly indicates the path that the user followed, how they got there, and how they can return to higher levels.

1.12

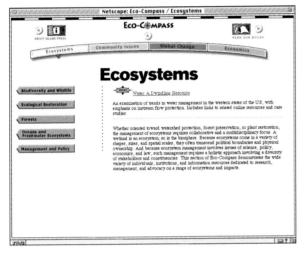

1.11

"As a designer, you are used to working with the 16.7 million colors that a 24-bit system offers. You've even adapted to working within the limitations of color printing. Well, here you go again. Another reduction of your palette, but this time it is even more radical. You get 216 colors! The 216 color Web-safe palette is a compromise between browsers, computer platforms, and monitors. The established norm is an 8-bit monitor, but Macs and PCs do not use the same 256 color palette. They share only 216 colors and the remaining 40 colors vary between platforms. If you design with the Macintosh 256 color palette, your work will look great on a Macintosh. But the great majority of the people surfing the Web are using PCs, and the remaining 40 colors will dither on their machines. This can cause undesirable results." Designing with a Web-safe color palette ensures that the majority of viewers will see colors that are consistent with your intention.

"I have to admit that I get tired of seeing the same gray-blue color on everyone's Web site. If I need a different tone of blue or if the 216 Web palette doesn't have the color I'm looking for, I'll use BoxTop's ColorSafe plug-in, which creates a tiled non-dithering version of the color." (See the ColorSafe folder on the *Web Design Studio Secrets* CD-ROM.) Using the ColorSafe filter is the same as defining a pattern in Photoshop and then using the Fill command with that pattern to fill an area of the image. ColorSafe actually makes a 2×2 pixel tile of alternating tones to fool the eye into seeing one color (1.13). ColorSafe also converts RGB values to hexadecimal values and allows you to save your unique palette where you can name the colors anything you like. One word of caution though, this technique creates large GIF files.

SITE NAVIGATION

The global and subsectional navigation throughout a site should give viewers confidence that they know where they are and how to get where they want to go. Navigation quickly becomes intuitive when you use consistent treatment, placement, weight, and behavior for the site navigation. At the top level, the home page, the global navigation offers the viewer essential choices. For example, on the *www.student.com* site, the global navigation includes "About Us," "Contribute," "Help," "Search," "Site Map," and "Ad Info." These are the choices the viewers should have available to them at every level of the site. When a viewer is browsing a specific area of the site, a second level of navigation appears—one that reflects the specific content at hand.

On Keaton Drew Design's Web site, the initial page reads quickly (1.14). The following portfolio pages (1.15) enable the viewer to see examples of Keaton Drew Design projects. Note the simple primary navigation that appears consistently on all pages, and the subsectional navigation (the individual portfolio pieces) that enables the viewer to nonlinearly navigate throughout a category (1.16). It requires no further explanation and is intuitive to use.

TIP

"A shortcut to adding up all the files to determine your page weight is to use an HTML validator such as the CSE HTML Validator (*www.htmlvalidator.com*). This tool automatically checks your HTML to see if it is 'clean.' It will check pieces of code that you paste in or an entire page that is publicly available on the Web. It's a great tool that helps me optimize my files and, subsequently, my design."

1.14

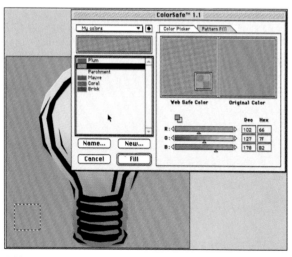

1.13

1.15

REAL ESTATE: KNOWING YOUR SCREEN SIZES

"As I begin to think about laying out a page, I start with a screen shot of an empty Web browser that is set using the default options. There is a common misconception that 640 × 480 pixels is a Web standard. That is a convention that remains from multimedia design and is not appropriate for Web design because it does not take into account how much monitor space the actual browser interface takes up. The viewing size of a default Netscape Navigator window on a Macintosh (1.17) is approximately 580 × 315 pixels and on a PC it's 635 × 314 (1.18).

"It is surprising how many people do not resize their browsers or, even worse, surf the Web with the entire browser toolbar visible."

LIMITING SCROLLING

On the home page of a Web site, a viewer should not be required to scroll at all — all the important information should be within the monitor-safe rectangle. The viewer should understand where they are, what the site is about, what they are about to see when they delve deeper, and most importantly, how to use the site. "The initial page of a Web site is like the cover of a book — it gives you an impression of what is in the book and offers you a navigational scheme to explore the site, but it doesn't spell out every chapter like a table of contents would."

Just because viewers can scroll doesn't mean they want to scroll. One Web usability study (*www.useit. com/alertbox/9605.html*) has shown that a large majority of people will select an option that appears above the scroll line before they will scroll down to see what else is on the page.

The length of the page is just as important as the width. "Browsers and platforms influence the length of the page. PCs running Internet Explorer stretch pages, so I have to be careful to make sure that important information isn't lost at the bottom of the page." Of course viewers expect to scroll the deeper they get into the site. You expect that you may have to get through six screens worth of text before you finish reading an article, for example.

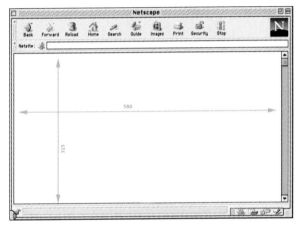

1.17

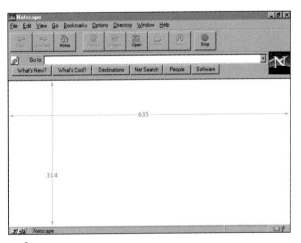

1.18

1.16

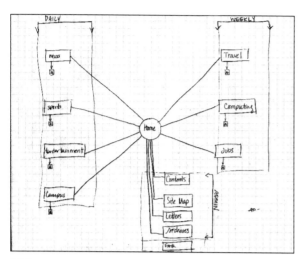

THE DESIGN PROCESS

"I always begin a site by planning out the site structure, either on paper (1.19) or with NetObjects Fusion. If I see certain areas are too content-heavy or one-sided, it is an indication that the structure isn't working. If one area has too much information and another one is sparse, I go back to the drawing board to find a better way to organize the information.

"Island Press wanted their Web site to be a useful electronic resource for booksellers, professors, and people conducting environmental research via the Internet. Originally, the site was called Island Press

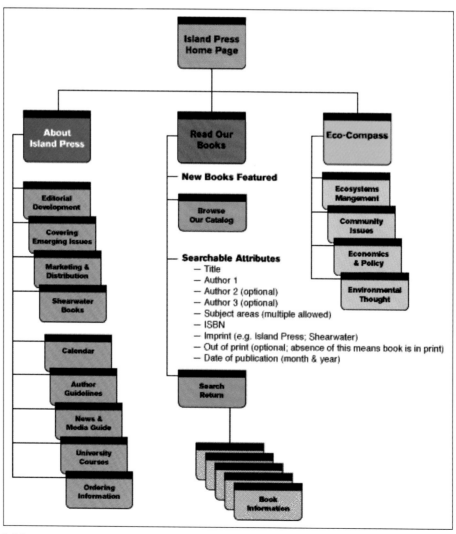

Books. It included a section called 'Eco-Compass,' which featured book reviews and resources for varying environmental topics. The first site map shows the original structure (1.20). I suggested elevating 'Eco-Compass' to become the top level, or home page, for the site to distinguish the site areas more clearly (1.21).

"Rather than having a home page that just links to subcategories, we reorganized the information so that the top level contained a timely and resourceful feature summarized and presented along with the other important options that a user might be looking for.

"After a site's scaffolding is in place, I begin to storyboard each screen in the most fundamental way (1.22). I've found that if I begin to show a graphic design direction in these early sketches, the client almost always gets hung up on not liking a color, rather than looking at what choices are available on each screen (1.23).

"After all the information structure is defined, and all content and navigation is applied to each screen in the structure, I begin to work on the visual appearance of the screen. My first step in establishing the graphical look and feel is to design the navigation elements."

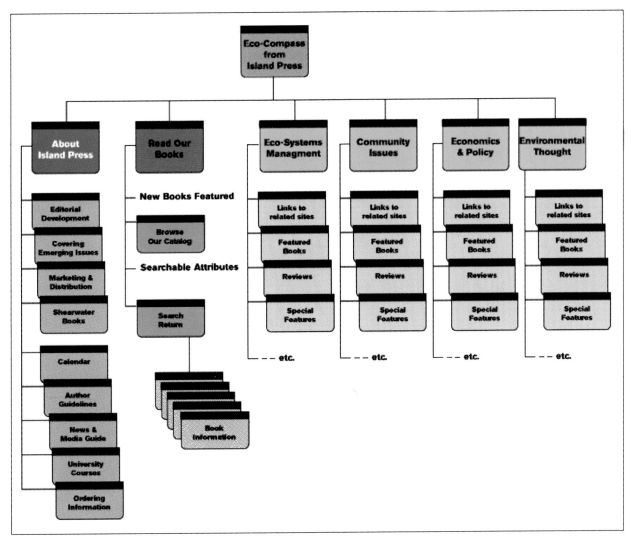

1.21

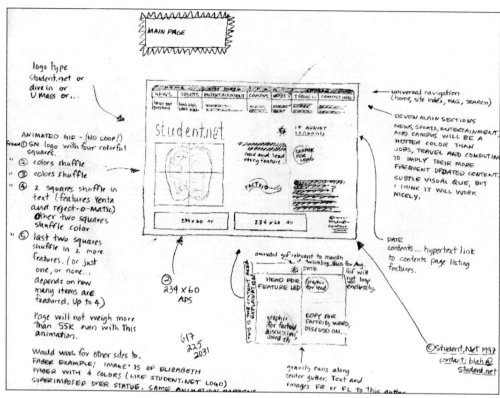

1.22

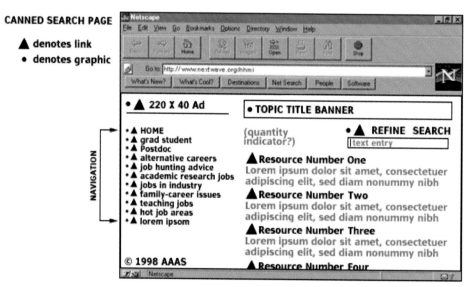

1.23

DESIGNING BUTTONS

"I keep the style of navigational aids simple. I don't use cute names for buttons. I generally don't use pictures for buttons, and I strive to keep the text of the button to one — no more than two — words. Rather than saying 'In a Nutshell', the word 'Info' or phrase 'About Us' is more successful. It is very tempting to design cute little icons for each site, but this can backfire on you. Clarity and brevity are the key. If an icon needs an explanation, or can't be summed up and accompanied by one word, then bag it. This is especially important if the site will be accessed by an international audience. An analogy that I like to use is the up and down arrows on an elevator panel. The buttons need no description such as the wordy 'How to go up to a higher floor in this building.' The arrow or the word up are sufficient. It works. (For an interesting study on icons as buttons, see *www.useit.com/papers/sun/*.)

"After designing the navigation elements, I begin to work in even more detail, trying to work out the design treatment, layout, and placement of the navigation (global, sectional, and subsectional) (1.24 and 1.25)."

PHOTOSHOP AS A PAGE LAYOUT TOOL

"I use Photoshop to create my designs and get approval for concepts. I live by layers, guides, grids, and actions. I start with my screen shot of an empty browser. I use a PC screen shot if my client uses a PC, and a Mac screen shot if they are on a Mac. By hiding and revealing various layers, I can design any number of screens easily within the same file. To proof the design, I flatten and save the different screens, use the screens as comps (posted on the Web) for client approval, and print them out later to use as I write the HTML.

"I use Macromedia Fireworks and Adobe Image-Ready to slice my comps, but I still use Photoshop to create a master layout sketch that notes the width and height of all cells and tables. Not only do I find this invaluable for myself when I have to edit a layout (which I still do by hand), but my clients, who generally take care of updating their own sites, appreciate having documentation of the layout for their use.

"Back in the pre-Fireworks and ImageReady days, I used to dissect my comps in Photoshop and write HTML tables by hand. I came up with the following

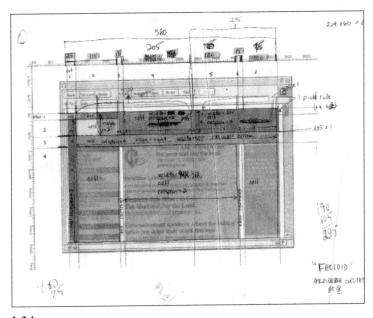

1.24

production technique, which makes the whole process a breeze."

1. Start with an empty layer in Photoshop on top of a comped screen.

2. Use the guides to draw accurate marquee selections that will represent each cell of each table (1.26).

3. Illustrate the rows, columns, spanning rows and columns, and the individual cells.

4. Make each table cell a different color (1.27), and then, using the magic wand tool and the Info palette, select each cell by the exact width and height (1.28).

5. Check the math to make sure that all the cells add up to the width of the table.

6. Next, write the actual table in HTML using a text editor (1.29).

7. During this process, try to create as many cells as possible that won't require an actual graphic by using hexadecimal background colors instead of graphics. You can add these as you're writing the HTML.

8. "Once you have the colored grid, by dropping the layer opacity down to 50 percent (1.30), you can see through to the active layer. With the magic wand set to zero tolerance and no antialiasing, you can select (1.31), copy, and paste the elements quickly into new documents (1.32).

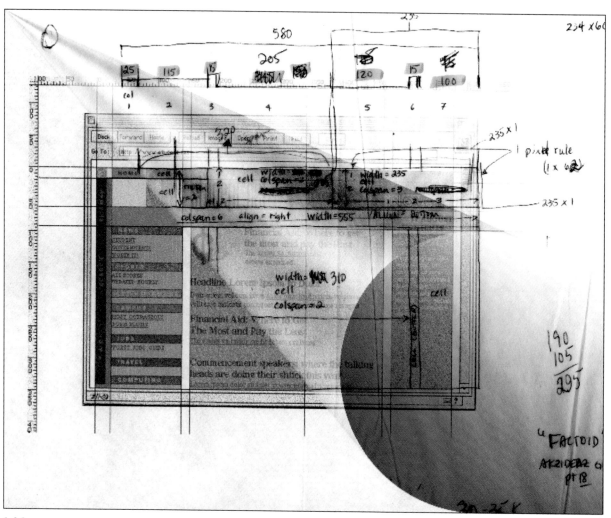

1.25

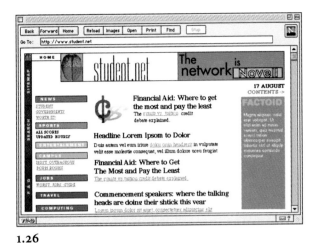

1.26

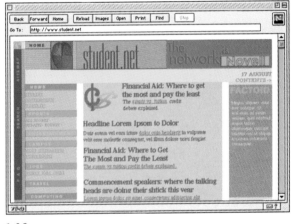

1.29

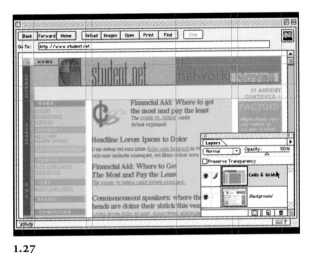

1.27

1.30

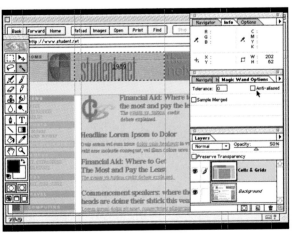

1.28

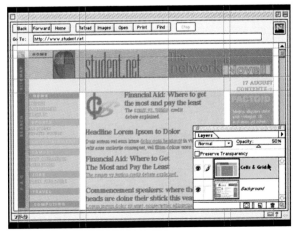

1.31

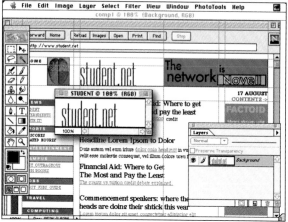

1.32

BUTTONS IN ACTION

Designing buttons is a snap when working with layers and actions. "When I use JavaScript rollovers for my buttons, each button has to be in three states: not clicked, mouse over, and mouse click. I start by copying one of the buttons from the layered Photoshop comp and making that my working document (1.33). Whenever I drop in new text, Photoshop creates a new layer, and by working with layer transparency I can see if the word is properly aligned. Creating the different states of the button can be made into an Action item (1.34 and 1.35)."

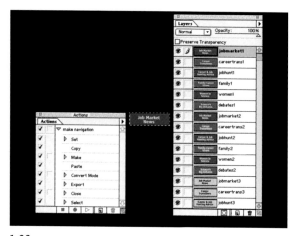

1.33

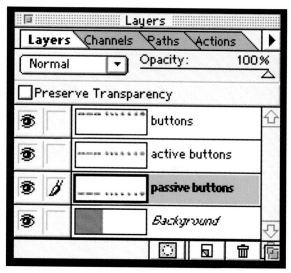

1.34

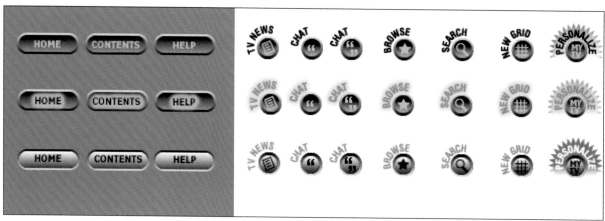

1.35

ENGAGING THE VIEWER

Refreshing your Web site regularly will entice viewers to return. Viewers like getting something back from a site: a sense of community, downloadable goodies, chat rooms, e-mail that actually gets answered, and most importantly, accurate and up-to-date information. "*The Washington Post* weather site challenged me to find a new approach to show world, national, and local weather (1.36) so that viewers could find up-to-the-minute weather information. As a reference site, the most important thing was for people to be able to access information quickly and easily. The client also wished to include graphical displays of weather data to support visual scanability (1.37). It was quite a balancing act."

ACTIONS IN ACTION

Working with the Photoshop Actions palette requires an understanding of what is and what is not actionable and a good grasp of the Photoshop command keys. In Photoshop 5.0, working with Actions became much clearer and almost every tool and menu item is actionable. After building the buttons in the layered file, use Tracy's action to separate the files out into individual files. To use Tracy's action, start by loading the action Nav_butt.atn into your Actions palette. Start the action at the top of the layer stack and work your way down.

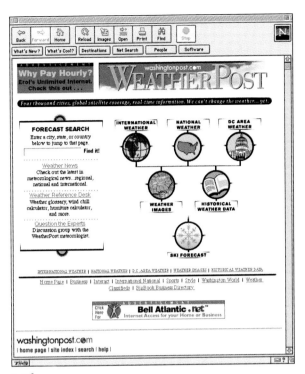

1.36

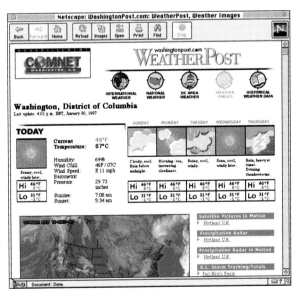

1.37

THE BOTTOM LINE

"In pricing out my Web design work, I follow the basic guidelines in *Pricing, Estimating & Budgeting* by Theo Stephan Williams, *Graphic Artists Guild Handbook : Pricing & Ethical Guidelines (9th Edition)* by Graphic Artists Guild, Rachel Burd (Editor), and *Web and New Media Pricing Guide* by Jp Frenza and Michelle Szabo. I calculate my costs: rent, equipment investment and depreciation, health insurance, my salary, and vacation to define my bottom line. Since I wear many different hats — designer, programmer, illustrator, project manager, site implementer, and tester — I've assigned each role a specific hourly rate. From the very first time that a client calls, I monitor every moment that goes into that job: phone calls, doing research, writing and presenting proposals, graphics production, and designing and implementing the site. This also helps me if I ever get into a tight deadline situation and I have to hire outside help. What the client doesn't see is how I have broken down the hourly rates. I did do that once and it turned into a slice and dice game. The client kept saying, 'Can't we trim this part or cut back on that part?' and it turned into a nightmare scenario.

"Doing Web design is so much more intensive on the back end than traditional design work. Keeping up to date is an ongoing process — sometimes I envy print designers. I mean, Quark doesn't change that much that quickly! The Web is constantly changing, and it requires a lot of time just to keep up with the changes in technology, so that you can deliver the best product possible. I spend a lot of time reading books and magazines, going to conferences, and surfing the Web, and that changes my hourly rate. But my clients don't flinch because I deliver the most up-to-date product possible."

FROM START TO FINISH

"Writing a proposal and design document is the most important step of any design project, especially since every project has different parameters. The design document includes the production schedule, budget, and job checklist of what has been completed. I use the design document to keep myself and the client on schedule. The client needs a schedule too since they are responsible for providing content in the form of images, text, logos, and so on.

"During the design process, I create a client viewing area on my Web site (1.38). I only give the URL to the client, and that way we can exchange ideas about the work in progress without having to have time-consuming face-to-face meetings. Clients love this way of working since they can see my progress (1.39) and add their input about their sites (1.40).

"Designing a Web site is rarely a cut-and-dry process. It's not like designing a glossy marketing brochure where once the job has gone to press the designer is done and can move on to the next project. Clients will want you to update or maintain the site. If not planned for, this can really eat into your profit margin. I often include future expenses, such as updating the site, as a line item on the project estimate. That way the client is aware that changes and maintenance will be a cost and we can discuss that before the budget is finalized. I always budget in at least four hours with the Webmaster to teach him about how and why I laid out the site as I did. Those four hours are always worth it for the site, the client, and my own sanity!

"The best thing about designing for the Web is that there aren't any hard or fast rules, and we are all learning as we go. The only way to learn it is to do it and enjoy the process."

1.38

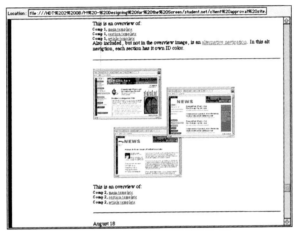

1.39

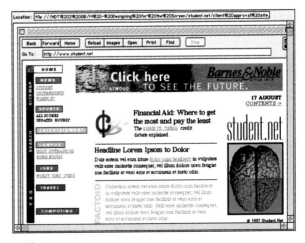

1.40

CHAPTER 2
MAKING YOUR SITE EASY TO NAVIGATE

I n print media, navigation is an issue that both receives and warrants little attention. Most of the basic navigational protocols were developed long before any of us were born. If a sentence halts abruptly at the end of a page, the reader has only to turn to the next page to locate the remaining words. To help readers find the information they're looking for, the thoughtful designer provides a table of contents or, for a more complex document, an index. If a story jumps from one page to a nonsequential page later in a periodical, the reader can expect to see a short line offering guidance, such as "Continued on page 116." In the most extreme cases, a book might include footnotes along with a comprehensive bibliography to inform readers where they can go to further their knowledge.

Unfortunately, few of the navigational techniques you may have learned as a page designer are applicable to the Web. The rules of print navigation are based on the assumption that the pages are bound together in a sequential order. But electronic pages float freely; any order assigned to them is purely arbitrary. The default home page — *index.html* — isn't the first page in any traditional sense, whether the pages are arranged by size, date created, or alphabetical order. When you come right down to it, a site is nothing more than a random assemblage of unrelated documents. So as a designer, you begin from a point of absolute chaos.

The question then becomes, how do you ensure that your arbitrary ordering of information makes sense to your visitors? Do you work from a single navigation page and gradually spread out more and more

In my opinion, carefully planned information architecture is the basis of sound navigation and user interface design.

CHRIS GOLLMER

23

links like the branches of a tree? Do you create multiple button groupings that are available from every single page so any piece of information is just a single click away? Do you set up a network of navigational aides, including a site index, a help page, and a search option? Where do you begin, where do you stop, and how much can you tweak it when it comes time to add yet more pages to your site?

To find out the answers to our questions, we turned to Chris Gollmer, a guy who's spent the better part of a decade making a living at making Web sites easy to navigate.

MAXIMIZE ACCESS, MINIMIZE CLICKS

Gollmer's guiding principle is simple. "It's all about creating a positive user experience. People go to a site for a reason — maybe they're looking for information on a specific subject or they want to buy a product. When designing a navigation system and user interface, everything we do needs to contribute to making it easy for visitors to get what they came for — efficiently — so they leave the site with a smile."

According to Gollmer, the key is to provide maximum access to information with a minimum number of clicks. "One goal we work toward is to give visitors access to any page in just two or three clicks. Obviously, as the amount of content in a site grows, that becomes more and more difficult. If you followed the two- or three-click rule for a really large site, for example, you'd end up with navigation elements overloading the visual design space, and no room for content. The important thing is to understand your visitors' needs and make the navigation system serve those needs as much as possible."

Why not just create a site map that includes a link to every page? "If a site is well-organized and the navigation system is designed correctly, you don't need a site map. The site map *is* the navigation model and the user interface. By glancing at the navigation elements and interface, the user should be able to quickly understand what the main components of the site are and what type of content hierarchy lies behind."

DIGITALTHINK: DEVELOPING PATHS TO LEARNING

A good navigation system is always important, but on a learning-based site it's downright critical. When we first met Gollmer, he had just completed one of the first versions of the Web site for the online training firm DigitalThink (*www.digitalthink.com*, 2.1) — a version that helped launch the company into the corporate market. This version of the site design also won a couple *CIO WebBusiness* 50/50 awards, and a Gold Invision award from *NewMedia Magazine*. Since that's where Gollmer cut his teeth, that's where we'll begin.

ARTIST:
Chris Gollmer

ORGANIZATION:
gelDesign
2710 16th Street
San Francisco, CA 94103
415/575-4860
www.gelDesign.com
chrisg@gelDesign.com

SYSTEM:
Power Mac G3/400
Mac OS 8.6
6GB storage/192MB RAM

CONNECTIVITY, ISP:
OC-3, GlobalCenter

SERVER ENVIRONMENT:
Unix

PERIPHERALS:
21-inch Mitsubishi Diamond Pro monitor

PRIMARY APPLICATIONS:
Adobe Photoshop, Adobe Illustrator, Adobe ImageReady

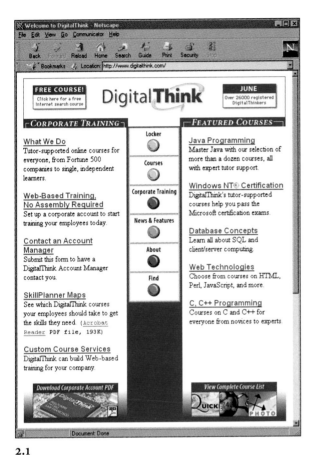

2.1

"When it comes to learning online, time is really of the essence. You need to present information in the most efficient way possible, so visitors don't have to wade through a lot of content that isn't important to the lesson at hand." Efficiency requires planning.

"In the beginning, I started very linear and just wrote everything down. I made diagrams and mocked up a basic organizational chart in Word. No graphics, just text. The whole time I was working closely with the Webmaster and an instructional designer. We spent weeks just making sure the user could get around. Once you get the network of paths figured out and mock up the site in plain-gray HTML pages, then you can add all the bells and whistles. That's when you assign the look and feel, not before. In my opinion, carefully planned information architecture is the basis of sound navigation and user interface design. It's all a very simple structure until we know it works."

WORK HISTORY:

1978 — Mother enrolled Chris in his first oil painting class when he was in first grade.

1990 — Enrolled in Design, Architecture, Art, and Planning school at University of Cincinnati.

1993 — Learned about focused graphic design and the competitive nature of business working for industry-leading marketing and design firm SBG Partners.

1996 — Joined up as first member of the creative staff at Web-based training company DigitalThink.

1999 — Cofounded gelDesign, a multi-disciplinary design and technology firm based in San Francisco.

FAVORITE ICE CREAM FLAVOR:

Ben & Jerry's Chubby Hubby ("It sounds bizarre, it looks bizarre — but when you taste it, it's just unreal.")

CANDY-COATING THE INTERFACE

Even the bells and whistles were designed to help students get around. "When it came time to design the main navigation buttons, we came up with a sort of colorful candy treatment. We called the first-tier round buttons 'skittles' (2.2) and the second-tier square buttons 'chiclets' (2.3). The buttons are soft and colorful. We got a lot of positive feedback because they weren't high-tech looking. People seemed to think they made the site easier to use. They're also easy to spot because of the bright colors."

Gollmer also used color to identify the main sections of the site. "The colors of the skittles tell you where you are. Red is always help or search, dark blue is company background, purple is for the large corporate accounts, light blue is the course catalog. Your locker, which is your gateway to all your courses, is always orange. Green is the news section, and yellow takes you back to the home page.

"We had to stick with a few bright primary colors because of all the different platforms and monitor settings. Each color had to be really unique and easily identifiable. We did a lot of testing to find seven colors that we could separate very well regardless of what kind of screen you're looking at. We ended up with a rainbow palette. In the worst-case scenario, with a really dark, low-contrast monitor, the blue

started looking a lot like the purple, and the orange looked like the red. But even then, users were able to distinguish the colors well enough to get around."

THE HOME PAGE SETS THE STANDARDS

Smack dab in the center of the DigitalThink home page Gollmer placed a column of colored buttons, the main navigational skittles (2.4). "Centering the navigation bar was a tough sell at first. Everyone wanted to go with left-to-right buttons across the top or top-to-bottom buttons down the left side, following traditional Web standards. The problem was, we had two primary audiences that we had to address equally. There's the corporate training audience, then there are the home users who just want to take a Photoshop course. We found that the corporate trainers who come through with 100 or so employees at a time wanted a dedicated part of the site designed for them. So we used the navigation buttons to split the corporate stuff on the left from the individual course information on the right.

"Running the navigation section down the center of the home page was always a topic of debate. With the Web as a publishing medium still in its infancy, I think these kinds of design experiments need to happen in order to explore new possibilities in usability.

2.2

2.3

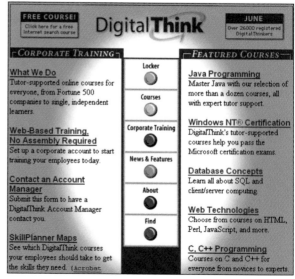

2.4

The Web is more of a two-way street than print. In print, the designer controls the layout and delivery of content almost exclusively, but with the Web the user has a fair amount of control over how the content will be displayed. For me, one of the most interesting aspects of this design experiment was to see how the users would react to center navigation." And how did they? "This turned out to be one of DigitalThink's most popular home page designs."

To find out what any one of the buttons does, you just move your cursor over it (2.5). The buttons were created using the JavaScript `onmouseover` command. (For complete information on making interactive buttons, see Chapter 8.)

"When you mouse over a button, you get more information about a specific area. The button title changes from black on white to white knocked out of a blue stripe. And the skittle shows through somewhat transparent in the background. That way, you know it's still there and you can click it if you want to. I think it helps point you in the right direction. It also saves you time by briefly explaining where you're going before you go to the trouble of loading the page."

THE TWO-TIERED APPROACH

"In the early days of the site, we just had the round skittles at the top. As we started expanding, we developed subgroups within each group. We decided to add this gray bar below the skittles so we could increase the number of buttons and tie the new, second-tier chiclets in with the first-tier skittles. The gray bar accommodates up to six chiclets in all (2.6). But we still leave the gray bar in there even when there are no chiclets (2.2). I think consistency is really important. It's something that users feed on. If you change the navigational elements from one page to the next, you're going to confuse people.

"We made a big effort to integrate the colors from the skittle buttons into the pages. The balloon in the upper-right corner of the page — which is modeled after the DigitalThink logo — changes colors to demonstrate the section you're in (2.7)." The gradient along the bottom of the spot illustration on the left side of the page also changes to reflect the key color.

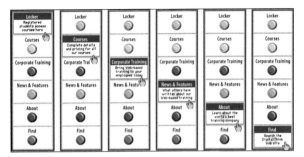

2.5

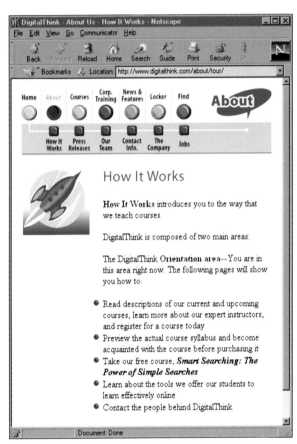

2.6

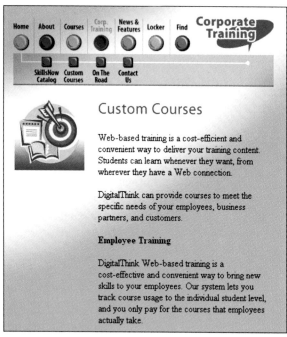

2.7

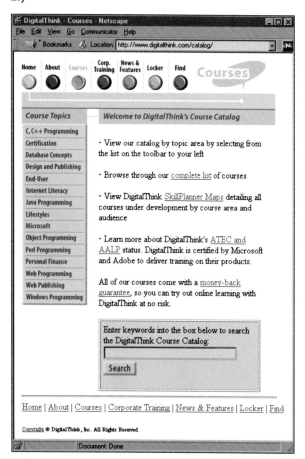

2.8

"That's a subtle treatment and I doubt some people even notice it. But it does give you a sense of where you are in the site, and I think that's worth emphasizing and re-emphasizing in as many ways as you can. Too much consistency is usually better than not enough."

The beauty of the two-tiered approach is that it establishes an obvious hierarchy to the site structure. It also allows a user to switch to a completely different section of the site without backing out of the current section. "This goes back to my two- or three-click principle. You should be able to move quickly to anywhere in the site you choose, without having to look at certain pages over and over again."

SPECIALTY NAVIGATION

The skittles and chiclets served as the interstates and freeways of the DigitalThink site, binding together the main areas and letting you jump from one page to another in a matter of seconds. But if you're interested in touring DigitalThink's specific courses — which are, after all, the real purpose of the site — you have to get off the freeway and make your way into the suburbs. And when touring the garden district, you need a new map.

The Course Catalog

The one section of the site that was too large to fit the standard navigation model was the course catalog. "Setting up the standards for the course navigation was the toughest task because there's such a wide range of information relating to each course. We just couldn't squeeze it into the chiclet model. So we had to come up with something different that felt like an extension of the main navigation system and not a complete departure.

"To start with, I divided the page in thirds, with the major course topics on the left, the specific course information on the right, and an empty margin in between (2.8)." The thing to keep an eye on here is the blue bar that stretches across the top of the two columns. Gollmer used the bar to show students where they are and where they've been. In some cases, the blue bar even offers a way back.

"If you clicked one of the topics, like Design and Publishing, you'd see all the design and publishing courses offered (2.9). Then if you looked at the blue bar at the top, it would still say Course Topics on the left, but on the right it would say Design and Publishing. If you then clicked one of the course titles, such as Illustrator Fundamentals, the right half of the page would contain a description of the course, just as you'd expect (2.10). But up top in the blue bar, it would say Design and Publishing on the left, which is where you were, and Adobe Illustrator Classroom in a Book Series on the right, which is where you are. The Design and Publishing heading is actually a clickable button so you can back out. So you can go anywhere inside the Illustrator Fundamentals area—check out the training objectives, view the syllabus, read the instructor bio—and then back out to Design and Publishing in just one click.

"I call this the 'bread crumb trail' approach. If I can't show you all parts of the course catalog at once, I can at least make sure you can get back out to the last course topic in one step. And the main skittles are still there at the top of the page in case you want to switch to a different section of the site."

The Student Locker and Remote Control

Every student who signs up for a DigitalThink course gets a locker (2.11). This is where registered students sign in and gain access to their courses. "Originally, we called this area the home room. Then we decided to call it the locker. It seemed to be a good metaphor for most students, and it represents a secure area to keep all of your 'stuff.'

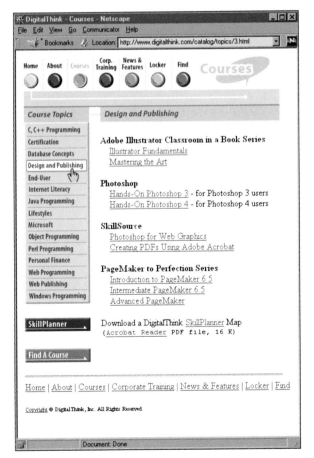

2.9

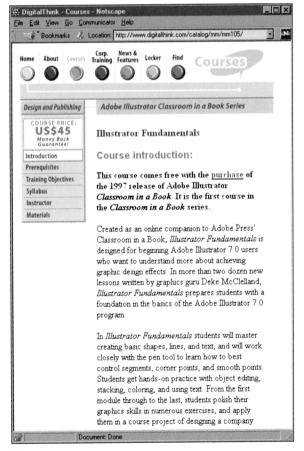

2.10

"Once you enter your locker, the skittles and chiclets go away and you see a yellow toolbar on the left side of the window (2.12). This element is only seen by registered students. From then on, as you study the lessons and take the quizzes, this toolbar is always with you. That way, you can concentrate on your course without being distracted by all the other areas of the DigitalThink site.

"I went through a lot of different looks for the toolbar (2.13). But then I finally settled on a remote control look (2.14). I actually went to a few big electronics stores to see what different remote controls looked like and decide what worked and what didn't." Gollmer finally arrived at two versions of the remote control–style toolbar (2.15). The first appeared in the locker area and the second followed you as you worked inside the courses. "The differences between the two toolbars reflect the context that you're working in. In the locker, you need access to orientation and setup functions. In the courses, you need to be able to talk to tutors and classmates. But the basic concept stays the same.

"We decided to make the center Locker button look really different from the others because we wanted students to be able to get back to home base easily. The shape and angle of the button matched the balloon in the DigitalThink logo, just for a little extra continuity. The orange buttons were a bit more recessed to make them blend in with the yellow background. This showed that the buttons had a lower priority within the content hierarchy."

2.11

2.12

Moving Through the Course

Developing the course navigation model was a collaborative effort, involving input from instructional designers, graphic designers, and programmers. The end result was nothing short of straightforward. "Once you enter a course, things become more linear. The courses are arranged into lessons, so Lesson 2 comes before Lesson 3. You have to work through it in a prescribed order, just like a traditional course.

"The buttons that let you go forward and backward were built into the banner art at the top of the page. We used to custom design each banner with the navigation buttons integrated into the art. But we found that some students had problems finding the buttons. The banners looked great, but they became too much fluff and not enough function.

"So we had to come up with a standardized system where the forward and back buttons are separated from the banner art that's specific to each course (2.16). We ended up going with the corporate DigitalThink blue and yellow as a starting point. And since the arrows were so important for getting through the course, we made them really jump off the page so students didn't miss them.

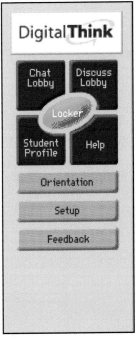

2.15

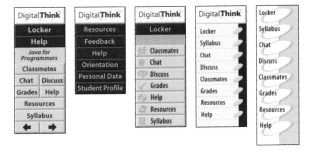

2.13

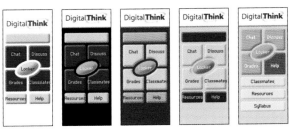

2.14

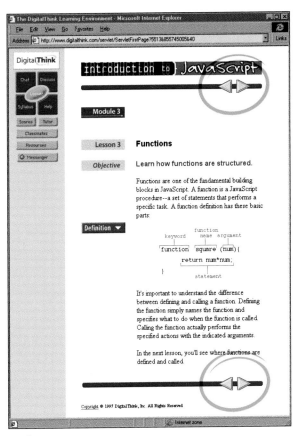

2.16

"Frankly, this is a lesson that we learned through trial and error. Personally, I liked the old way better with the buttons folded into the banner art. But it just wasn't working. A lot of people were trying to use the forward and back buttons built into their browsers. And of course that doesn't work because the browser's forward button doesn't let you go places you haven't been yet. So we had to come up with something that students would see again and again in every single course they take."

In addition to myriad buttons, Gollmer employed static navigation elements. You can't click them, they merely show you where you are. "Every course is divided into ten or so modules, which are subdivided into several lessons. You always need to know where you are in the course, so each page includes a dark blue tag to tell you what module you're in and a light blue tag for the lesson (2.17). The tags are a static form that grew out of the margin buttons. The only difference is that the tags are flat where the buttons

are beveled, like the yellow Audio button in the figure. There's another interesting design element in this figure: Notice the old style banner with the arrows integrated within the art. The arrows are almost camouflaged because of the graphical nature of the subject matter (Adobe Illustrator).

What if you want to jump forward or backward to a different module in the course? "Clicking the Syllabus button brings up a separate window that lists every module and lesson in the course (2.18). Just click one of the links to go right to that page. That might not be something a user would think of automatically, but we explained how it works in the orientation section."

DEUTSCHE BANK: MORE THAN A PRETTY INTERFACE

One of Gollmer's favorite projects was also one of his most complex. "Deutsche Bank came to gelDesign

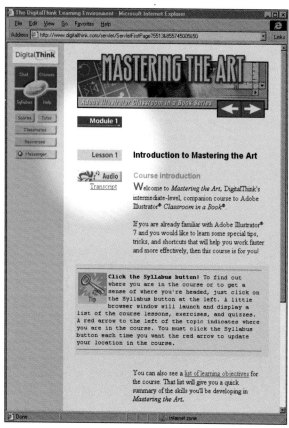

2.17

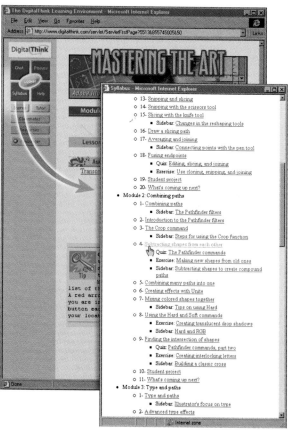

2.18

looking to make their training offerings available to employees online. They had converted a printed version of their training catalog into a Web site on their intranet, but it lacked an actual interface, so the information was nearly impossible to find. Our challenge was to work within their corporate standards system to create a unique and dynamic design that made the training experience more accessible to the company's thousands of North American employees."

SITE TREES AND SKETCHES

As always, the first step was to plan. Gollmer began by working with the gelDesign technology team to lay out a site tree diagram (2.19). "This step in the process is very important. You need to understand the information architecture and determine how that will influence the navigation and user interface design." Next, Gollmer put pencil to paper and sketched out some general ideas for different page levels (2.20). "This helped categorize the groups of information that would be involved in the user interface design. I also reviewed and discussed the sketches with the client and design team to identify concepts for further refinement."

THE SPLASH PAGE

The first page (or splash page) introduces employees to the variety of training opportunities available and sets the tone for the rest of the experience that awaits them (2.21). "This is the screen that users see when entering the site for the first time. The image of the snowboarder is actually one of six different images that rotate within a loop using animated GIF technology. Since this site is part of Deutsche Bank's intranet, there are fewer bandwidth restrictions, so we had more flexibility when it came to file sizes."

Navigation-wise the splash page couldn't be simpler. Your only option is to click the Enter Here button to move to the training portal page. "Just to be safe, we designed the page with a flowing curve that forces the user's eye to follow the blue line from the 'Get A Jump Start' headline down and around the training options to the Enter Here button. This also frames up the right side of the page and visually contains the imagery on the left."

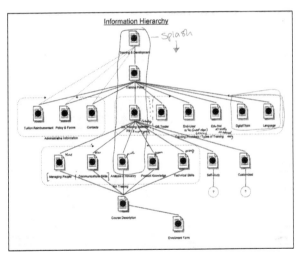

2.19

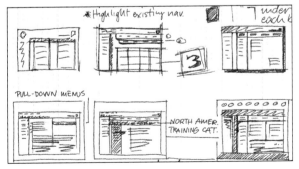

2.20

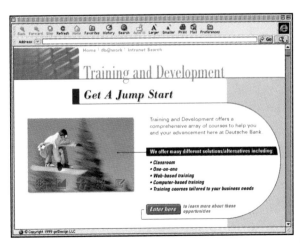

2.21

THE TRAINING PORTAL

Once you enter the site, your options expand dramatically. Gollmer used a gray bar along the top and right side of the page and a thin black rule along the left side to divide the page into three sections (2.22). From the left column, you can access the main intranet home page (Home), the training site home page (Training Portal), or the training catalog (North American Training Catalog) with a single click. "The thin black line on the left is a Deutsche Bank corporate intranet standard, so we had to use it. As a compromise, we came up with the idea to extend the gray bar to point to the Training Portal link, so users can easily go back to the starting point for the North American training experience from any page."

The silver buttons in the right column lead to general training departmental information that is consistent throughout the site. "We defined the 'Special News' area as an internal advertising space of sorts for Deutsche Bank. At this level—when you're just entering the site—the space is used to promote new courses and training providers, but we don't want

users to leave the site just yet. Once you have navigated deeper into the site and chosen a specific course, then the option to leave the training portal (if applicable, depending on the course selected) is presented."

The main column in the center of the page gives you two ways to access the five main training areas. First, you can click a colored button to the right of the Training Categories heading. "The basic color palette for the different sections of training offerings came from the existing printed catalog, so we were able to pick up on and extend a color system that was already familiar to many employees. We designed the buttons to represent the different sections on an iconic level and included the section names as Tool Tips, so when the cursor is placed over a button, the name pops up in a text box (2.23)." Why not use JavaScript rollovers? "Tool Tips are much faster, and they work better in the tight space of that particular navigation section."

But don't get Gollmer wrong—rollovers can be a highly effective navigation aid, as evidenced by the main navigation in the center of the page (2.24). "Like the old DigitalThink home page with the center navigation, the rollovers give users a way to read a description of each section without having to load a new page. They also add a more dynamic look and feel to the static page while enticing users to explore the main categories of training offered. The blurred icon behind each description is another subtle device used to visually link each color within the color

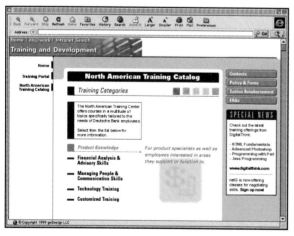

2.22

2.23

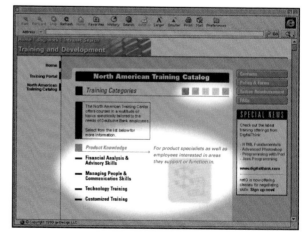

2.24

system to its corresponding icon. The colored buttons in the upper portion of the screen are faded out until the rollover for the corresponding category is activated. This makes the various buttons 'turn on' when the category titles are investigated below," as shown in the figure.

VIEWING COURSE OPTIONS

Clicking a training category takes you to a page that lists all the course offerings for that category. The important thing to note here is the color scheme introduced with the training category navigation system. Each of the five colors is used throughout its respective section in colored boxes, subheads, buttons, and so on. "The secondary color coding makes it easy for users to keep to track of where they are. If the subhead bars are green, as in this example (2.25), you're in the Product Knowledge section. If they're pink, you're in Financial Analysis & Advisory Skills — and so on. This is similar to the original DigitalThink site design. We picked up on this again because it proved so successful in helping the user visually sort and digest a multitude of course listings."

What if you want to switch to another training category? "Just click the appropriate button to the right of the training category subhead. The button for the section you're in appears dimmed, so that's not an option. Also, the dimmed icon appears in the graphic to the left of the section title to reinforce the relationship between a category and its color. Because of the

complex content hierarchy, we had to use numerous subtle visual cues and links to solidify this system throughout the entire experience."

The actual course listings are straight HTML links. To get information about a particular course, you just click its name to go to a course description page.

LEARNING ABOUT A COURSE

Let's say you're a Deutsche Bank employee. You're on a course description page and reading about the objectives. You decide it's not quite what you're looking for, so you want to skim through the list of course offerings again. Thanks to Gollmer, you don't need to go back to the course offerings page within each section. Instead, you can just peruse the list in the Select Course pop-up menu located immediately below the training category subhead near the top of the page (2.26).

"In addition to allowing us to list a large number of courses within a very confined space on the page, the pop-up menu makes it fairly simple for the Deutsche Bank internal staff to add and delete courses as necessary over time. This kind of pop-up menu can be tricky to implement when surrounded by other graphics and text, so it's best to keep things simple. In this case, the only other element that appears near the menu is the Select Course graphic. We tried to make the graphic match the height of the pop-up menu to achieve a horizontal striping effect for this level of navigation within the overall system. Since these

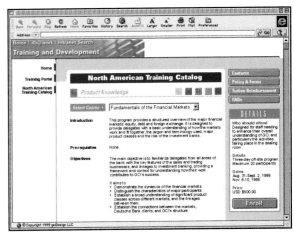

2.25   2.26

devices are dependent upon the user's operating system, we had to compromise on the size of the graphic. Our project parameters identified 99 percent of the Deutsche Bank training audience as PC users, so that's what we designed for."

Another significant navigational element on the course description page is the Enroll button near the bottom-right corner. "This button links to a back-end registration system that we created specifically for Deutsche Bank to streamline the registration and approval process. Obviously, the Enroll button is very important in completing the user's experience, so making it easy to find was critical. By making the button the only beveled element that is color coded and placing it within the 'advertising space,' I think it achieves some sort of prominence. Just to be certain, we made the type raised with a drop shadow to make it really pop."

It's also worth noting that even here, three levels down in the site, you still have access to all the main navigation options.

RGA TECH: THREE SITES IN ONE

Before we said goodbye, we asked Gollmer about a site he designed that *isn't* training-based. "RGA Tech (*www.rgatech.com*) wanted to present their two subsidiaries, RGA Associates and RGA Consulting, with equal emphasis within one site. To accomplish this,

we created a three-tiered navigation system that used subtle color coding (blue for RGA Associates and green for RGA Consulting) to clearly brand each company under the umbrella of the parent company, which is gray (2.27)." The colors fade into one another above the gray corporate section using black as the common color.

The color coding also makes it clear which section of the site you're in. For example, if you click I Want a Job under RGA Associates, the subnavigation that appears is blue. If you click I Need Contractors under RGA Consulting, the subnavigation is green. Even within this three-tiered system, any page on the site is accessible within just two clicks.

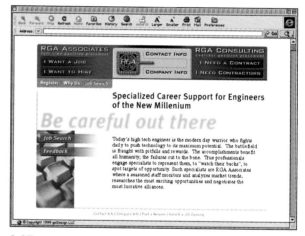

2.27

Does the new interface and navigation scheme work? If the proof is in the bottom line, the answer is a resounding yes. "Since we launched the new RGA site, the number of applicants and interested employers has more than doubled."

THE ULTIMATE TEST

Gollmer warns his fellow designers that what seems obvious to them may not make a lick of sense to the end user. "When you're putting together Web graphics and other elements, you're working with the artwork day after day. You always see the buttons, you know what they do. It seems so obvious, it never occurs to you someone else might not get it."

The ultimate test comes when you put the site in front of the user. "If you want the best feedback you can get, ask an average person who's never seen your product and doesn't know anything about your navigation system to go through your site. You'll recognize very quickly what does work and doesn't. We offer usability testing as a phase in our project timelines. After we release a site to a client, we get user feedback, measure the success, and then make revisions. The reality is, it's really rare that you get things perfect the first time around when designing for the Web.

"Navigation design has a purpose — to create a positive user experience. If the purpose isn't being met, then it needs to be fixed. You can't expect to take your beautiful design and put it on a pedestal. It has to do its job; otherwise, it's history."

CHAPTER 3
CREATING WEB GRAPHICS

B oil down many Web sites to basic building blocks and you get just two elements: text and images. They may not have the same appeal of zippier new kids on the block like DHTML and Flash, but if the text and images suck, your site sucks. This book won't tell you how to write for the Web; however, if you want to make the most professional images, you've bellied up to the right bar.

Ironically, the familiarity of Web images can be a designer's downfall. "I've made a billion of these," you mutter. "I know everything." But software and hardware are always changing, and with Web years racing along at a much faster clip than the calendar above your desk, your techniques may be due for a gold watch and retirement party.

Valerie Casey's many responsibilities keep her up to the minute. She's a senior designer at San Francisco's vivid studios, where she specializes in visual and interaction design and online branding strategies. Not only does she know her stuff, she shares it with others by teaching classes in Web design at San Francisco State University and the University of California at Berkeley. Her students are always eager to know how to create the best Web graphics. Essential to that task is understanding how to use color on the Web.

I always recommend indexing to the adaptive palette.... That's the key to making your images look professional, sleek, and well-thought out, and it's an easy thing to do.

VALERIE CASEY

COLOR ON THE WEB

The color palette is an important principle to grasp. Every image is composed of a certain number of colors; put 'em all together and you have the image's palette. Although the palettes of some image formats can be made up of thousands, even millions of colors, low-end monitors recognize only 256 colors. Feel like the walls are closing in on you? The claustrophobia continues, because the always-feuding Windows and Macintosh platforms share only 216 of those 256 colors. This meager offering is called the Web-safe palette, or Color Look-Up Table (CLUT).

"Always create your graphics with the Web-safe palette," advises Casey. Image editors such as Photoshop include Web-safe palettes (3.1), but Casey dislikes the standard numerical organization. "There's a palette on the Visibone site (*www.visibone.com*) that organizes colors by hue and saturation (3.2)," she notes, "and that's much more useful." Saving to any palette, including the Web-safe palette, is called *indexing*.

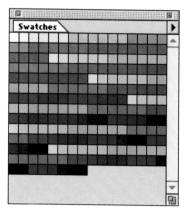

3.1

BIT DEPTH

The 256-color straitjacket is thanks to the GIF image format, which can include only 256 colors, and to low-end monitors. A computer screen uses pixels to display information, and each pixel has a specific number of bits of information about the Red, Green, and Blue colors in that pixel. That number is called the *bit depth*.

Monitor bit depths are 8, 16, and 24. Eight bits equal 256 possible colors, 16 bits equal 65,536 colors, and

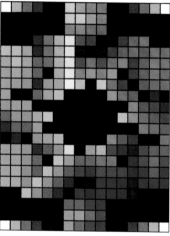

3.2

ARTIST:
Valerie Casey

ORGANIZATION:
vivid studios
510 Third Street, Suite 200
San Francisco, CA 94107
415/512-7200
www.vivid.com
www.valcasey.com
valerie@vivid.com

SYSTEM:
Power Mac G3
Mac OS 8.6
4GB storage/96MB RAM

CONNECTIVITY:
T1

PERIPHERALS:
17-inch Sony 200SF monitor

PRIMARY APPLICATIONS:
Adobe Photoshop, Adobe Illustrator, Adobe ImageReady

24 bits serve up 16,777,215 colors. (That's 16 million to you math dropouts.) Although you can never allocate more than 8 bits to a GIF, it's important to remember that as bit depth goes up, so does file size.

It doesn't take long to weary of the 256 colors imposed by 8 bits. The good news: Though GIF has an 8-bit ceiling, other file formats such as JPEG and PNG offer wider horizons, and monitor technology is catching up to the possibilities. "Fewer and fewer people have 8-bit monitors," says Casey. "I researched a range of retailers and manufacturers, including Dell, Gateway, and CompUSA, and found that in the last eight months they've been shipping 16-bit monitors as a standard."

Still, you want to make your GIFs as attractive as possible and spare the poor schmoes with the crappy monitors. Dithering can help.

DITHERING

Dithering is a trompe l'oeil technique that uses a checkerboard of like-colored pixels to give the illusion of a wider range of hues. This illusion lets low-bit images seem to display out-of-palette colors.

But don't assume that dithering is always a great idea. "Adjusting the dithering amount in an image influences the file size. The more an image is dithered, the greater the file size."

With earlier optimizing techniques, you could specify only yes or no to dithering. Now, with products such as Adobe ImageReady and Macromedia Fireworks, you can spec degrees of dithering and check out the image-quality and file-size consequences on the fly. You'll have to test to find the best compromise, but if the file size doesn't become prohibitively large, Casey recommends a 100 percent dither. She experimented with several possibilities before finding the right balance for the car Web site OpenAuto.com. The first example (3.3) shows the original image. The next two examples (3.4, 3.5) both use the Web-safe color palette, but the highlights in Figure 3.4, which has 100 percent dithering, aren't as "blown out" as the highlights in Figure 3.5, in which dithering is 50 percent. The last two examples (3.6, 3.7) both use the adaptive palette, which is explained in the next section. Figure 3.6 has a 100 percent dither; Figure 3.7, 50 percent. Dithering makes less difference in quality when you index to the adaptive palette. Note how much more realistically the adaptive palette figures render the car hood, despite the fact that the number of colors is the same as in the Web-safe palette figures.

"If you set dithering at 100 percent and you optimize to an adaptive palette, you won't see any dithering on a 16-bit or 24-bit monitor. I always recommend indexing to the adaptive palette." So what exactly is an adaptive palette? Read on.

WORK HISTORY:

1977 — Moved to the United States from Ireland. First memory of loving ABBA's outfits.

1983 — Fixated on Legos and the smell of crayons.

1994 — Graduated college with English and Psychology degrees, which later proved beneficial in relating to clients.

1994 — Did odd jobs to support continued work on independent films and photography. Can still make a killer cappuccino.

1995 — Fell in love with Photoshop.

1996 — Designed first Web site to distribute own creations. Hooked by the potential and equality of communication, started to design for others.

FAVORITE TYPE OF WOOD:

"I'm an environmentalist and a vegetarian, so I don't like to encourage wood use, but my favorite tree is the Oak."

3.3

3.4

3.5

3.6

3.7

ADAPTIVE PALETTE

In any image-editing program worth its salt, you can specify a custom, or adaptive, palette that samples colors from an image's true spectrum. If you instead index to a Web-safe palette, the colors in your final optimized palette may not be the actual colors in your graphic, even when you used Web-safe colors.

"You can create a better, smoother graphic for people with higher-end monitors if you index to an adaptive palette," says Casey. It used to be the common practice to always index to the Web-safe palette, but the spread of 16- and 24-bit monitors now makes the adaptive palette more feasible. "The people with better monitors see a better graphic, and the people with 8-bit monitors see the same thing they'd see either way. That's the key to making your images look professional, sleek, and well-thought out, and it's an easy thing to do." Casey's Web design class primer at *www.valcasey.com/webdesign* demonstrates the difference a palette makes (3.8, Web-safe palette; 3.9, adaptive palette).

"Of course," she warns, using an adaptive palette means that "you need to test more rigorously across browsers and platforms. Some colors shift unexpectedly in different browsers, such as AOL and WebTV. You could create a graphic with an orange that looks hot pink in a particular browser."

FILE FORMATS

Enough of palettes for now; it's time for the nitty gritty on file formats. The two Web image file formats most widely supported are GIF and JPEG. Both are compressed for faster downloads.

GIF

As you know, GIFs can contain a maximum of 256 colors. GIF compression is *lossless*, which means that it doesn't degrade image quality. (There is a lossy feature for GIFs in ImageReady 2.0, but Casey doesn't recommend it.) Casey says that lossless compression makes for "images that have more integrity across browsers and platforms." Because of the way GIFs are compressed, images with large areas of flat color compress more efficiently.

Unlike JPEG, GIF is capable of animation, as explained in Chapter 11. Another GIF advantage is transparency, which helps you cope with one great limitation of the Web. "Every image on the Web is rectangular or square. It doesn't get any more simple or complex." Fortunately, you can simulate other shapes with GIF transparency; GIFs with transparency are sometimes called *floating graphics*.

Casey steps you through the transparency process using Photoshop 5.0 and later:

1. Choose the background that you want for the Web page on which this graphic will appear. This may be a background tile or a plain Web color. Remember that all optimization should occur after the design is finalized. Make sure the layer you're working with is named something other than the italicized "Background." (The Background layer has specific properties that won't allow subsequent steps.)

2. When you finish creating the main graphic, make a new layer where you'll merge the graphic's layers. With this layer selected, hold down the Option/Alt key while selecting Merge Visible from the Layers palette fly-out menu (3.10). This merges the graphic's layers onto this new layer while keeping your original layers intact. For

workflow ease (and to eliminate the risk of inadvertently altering your source file), copy and paste this layer into a new canvas.

3. Select the magic wand and double-click the toolbox icon to display the magic wand options. (You can also activate the options box by selecting the magic wand and choosing Window ➢ Show Options). In the options box, set the tolerance to 0 and deselect the Anti-aliased check box.

4. Click the background color with the magic wand. You should get a selection that is active all around your image but does not include your image. Now choose Select ➢ Similar to pick up any stray pixels. Make sure your selection doesn't include any part of your graphic except the background color (3.11).

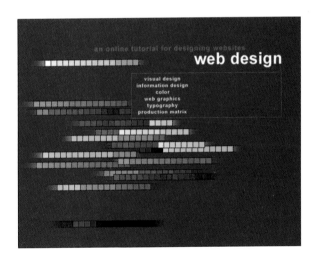

3.9

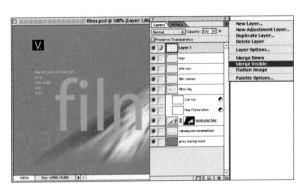

3.10

3.8

5. Delete the selection.

6. Export the graphic as a GIF89a by choosing File ➤ Export ➤ GIF89a. In the GIF89a dialog box, click the Transparency Index Color box (3.12). In the Color Picker, specify the background color you just deleted and click OK (3.13).

7. The GIF89a dialog box appears again with the transparency color back in the image. Select your indexing palette and bit depth (3.14). Choose whether you want the image to interlace as it loads on your Web page. Click OK and then save your image. For consistency, always use the .GIF extension.

Note that ImageReady 1.0 and later uses a slightly different process:

1. Because the application doesn't work well with huge, layered image files, merge them in your image editor. Then open the merged design in ImageReady.

2. Select and delete the area to be made transparent as described in the previous steps, with the addition of deselecting Contiguous Pixels in the Magic Wand Options palette. In the Optimize palette, check the transparency box, go to the Matte box and choose Background Color, and then select the desired file format, bit depth, and dithering specs.

3. Inside the image window, be sure you're in the Original tab, and then click the Optimized tab on your canvas.

4. If you like what you see, choose File ➤ Save Optimized As.

Don't think you can bypass the need for transparent GIFs by creating an image whose background is the same color as a Web page background. You may get a nasty surprise, Casey warns. "Oftentimes background colors referred to in HTML hexadecimal values don't match graphic colors." Just one more way the Web keeps us on our toes.

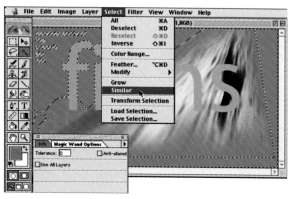

3.11

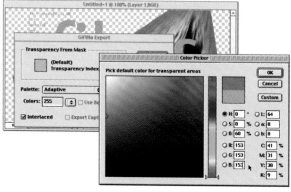

3.13

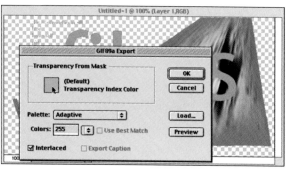

3.12

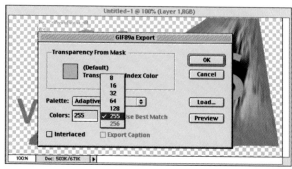

3.14

Optimizing GIFs

There are a few tricks to optimizing a GIF — that is, to making the file size as small as possible while preserving quality as much as possible. Casey's first tip regards gradients: Make them horizontal, not vertical. "A GIF compresses on a horizontal basis. Basically, you're only charged for one pixel if the color is consistent all the way across the row. When gradients shade from left to right or visa versa, every single pixel across the horizontal row will be different, and the file size can get huge."

Second, don't underestimate the number of colors that make up antialiased text. "It's a common novice mistake. They think that because text is created with a single color or a single color background, the image is made up of only two colors. The reality is that images like this — text navigation images especially — have many more colors in the image that make up the antialiasing. I always allocate 16 colors, or 4 bits, for text elements that seemingly have only two colors." Antialiasing is discussed further later on in this chapter.

Casey is also a photographer, and her Web site reflects this. On one page that showcases her photos, she combined type, photos, and a drop shadow and optimized them to form one graphic. The first example (3.15) shows the original image before optimization. The second example (3.16) is the best of the lot: It uses 256 colors and the adaptive palette. The third example (3.17) also uses the adaptive palette, but only 64 colors. Note the slightly more grainy photos

and drop shadows. In the fourth example (3.18), which bumps back to 256 colors but is indexed to the Web-safe color palette, the shadows are only marginally more degraded than in Figure 3.17. The poorest performer is the last example (3.19), which is indexed to the Web-safe palette and uses 64 colors. For this image, the 64-color adaptive palette is the clear winner. Dithering on all examples is 100 percent.

JPEG

The JPEG format was originally developed to transmit high-quality photographs electronically. It's still doing so today.

JPEGs can include 24 bits of RGB color, unlike the indexed, 256 maximum of the GIF. With that many colors, you'll want to compress the file so it's not a bandwidth drain, and there's the rub. JPEG compression actually removes information from an image and is therefore called *lossy*. Image fidelity suffers the more you compress it, eventually resulting in blocky artifacts. Finding the optimum balance between file size and quality can be tricky.

3.17

3.15

3.18

3.16

3.19

Optimizing JPEGs

Casey notes that with JPEG, file size isn't tied so much to the dimension of the image as to the complexity. She manually "smooths out" a complex image while it's still a Photoshop file. "By reducing the areas of strong contrast and detail in the image, the amount of information is less, and therefore the file size is less."

Casey uses two smoothing techniques. She may apply a Gaussian Blur at a low setting to the entire image, although images that depend on detail aren't good candidates for this trick. One of Casey's photographs is a perfect choice for the technique (3.20). "The image is soft and moody," she says, "and it doesn't require a lot of detail to be understood. I

applied a 1-pixel Gaussian Blur and saved it as a 6.0-quality JPEG, which saved about 40 percent in K size (3.21).

"I also hand-paint more complex backgrounds that are secondary information. I would never smooth out, say, someone's face, but I might do it to their shirt." General instructions for this method follow:

1. Locate areas where color seems even (3.22).
2. Zoom in to identify background noise such as artifacts or unnecessary information (3.23).
3. Sample the most common color and make it Web-safe.
4. Paint in the color over the area and soften edges with a low-pressure, big airbrush (3.24).
5. Save the file as a JPEG (3.25).

Casey prefers ImageReady when she's finished prepping the files and is set to optimize JPEGs. "You can play with the settings until you get the ideal file size. It shows you the graphic exactly as it will look in a browser, and it shows you the file size changing as you adjust the slider from low to maximum quality. DeBabelizer also optimizes JPEGs well, but the interface is so badly designed compared to ImageReady

3.20

3.21

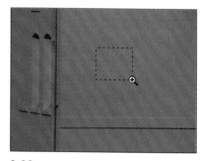

3.22

3.23

that ImageReady is the natural choice. It also helps that its interface is so close to Photoshop that there's almost no learning curve."

In Photoshop, JPEG quality settings range from 1 (most compression) to 10 (least compression). "I never go above 8 quality," Casey states. "File size may be 50 percent more at 10, but in a browser you won't be able to tell the difference between 8 quality and 10 quality."

PNG AND SVG

GIF and JPEG aren't the only image file formats, but they might as well be. PNG is a terrific, lossless-compression format that beats the pants off of GIF. It has full alpha channels, which means graduated transparency. (GIF transparency is either off or on.) It can pack in any number of bits per pixel. And PNG gamma-corrects, so it compensates for differences in brightness between Mac and Windows displays. Sound too good to be true? Here's the catch: You can view PNG images in some browsers, but not fully, not consistently, and not without a plug-in.

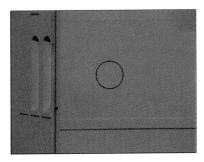

3.24

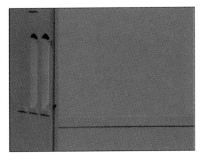

3.25

Prospects are also dim for another contender, SVG (Scalable Vector Graphics), at least in the near future. SVG files can be static or animated and made up of anything vectors can describe. Unlike proprietary, binary Flash (another vector format), open-source SVG appears in an HTML document as editable plain text. SVG is sure to be a hit when it's supported by browsers — just don't hold your breath, unless the color blue suits you.

HOW TO CHOOSE FORMATS

In most situations, choosing a file format is simple. Photographs make good JPEGs. Images with flat colors should be GIFs. But not always.

Casey breaks the rules on several sites, including one for a client and one for herself. Look for the bar at the top of the pages on the FinAid site at *www.finaid.org* (3.26, 3.27). "As you get into the subhead pages, each yellow bar has a little photographic person leaning over the bar. I made those photos GIFs because I wanted them to seamlessly match the yellow bar." You may also want to save photographs as GIFs when you want part of the image to be transparent.

The *www.valcasey.com* home page is another case in point (3.28). Although the background image was originally a photograph (3.29), the large areas of flat color seemingly make it a good candidate for a GIF. However, Casey points out, "a background image has to be really large in dimension so it doesn't tile, and a GIF this big — 1,024 by 768 pixels — wouldn't work."

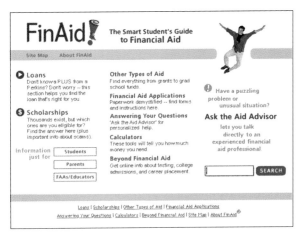

3.26

The JPEG file is 21.3K. When Casey saved it as a GIF, the file tipped the scales at 57.9K.

ANTIALIASING

The resolution of a monitor is vastly inferior to that of the simplest inkjet printer, which can lay down tiny droplets of ink that make curves look curvy. On a monitor, curves are jagged — unless you antialias an image.

Antialiased edges appear to blend into the background. According to Casey, the antialiasing effect is created by placing around the image edge pixels with colors that fall between the image and its background. "With antialiasing, image edges don't look jagged and 'stair-stepped,' even though they're made with square pixels (3.30).

"I antialias all text graphics," she says, "with the exception of some buttons or very small verbal messages on a site. In that case, I use aliased type. At point sizes lower than 8, antialiased text becomes too muddy to be legible." Casey uses HTML text — which is aliased — for long sections of copy.

Despite their smooth moves, antialiased images bring their own troubles. "Antialiasing can add up to 50 percent to the file size," Casey points out. "Also, with antialiased graphics, you have to constantly consider where the image will be placed on the screen because the image includes part of the original background color. If you originally created the graphic on a yellow background (3.31) and then decide later that your Web page background will be white (3.32), the graphic will have a 'halo' or 'cheese' around the edges (3.33). That's very unprofessional."

If you're confused about aliasing and antialiasing, here's a good way to remember which is which: In Photoshop, the pencil tool is aliased and the pen tool is antialiased. Plan ahead and you'll know which to use. For example, Casey believes that the "stair-step aliased look is great for cartoons, flat-color graphics, and imagery that's techy."

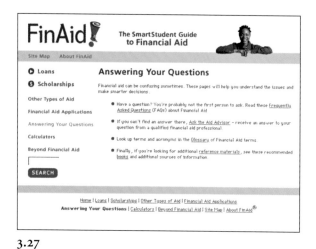

3.27

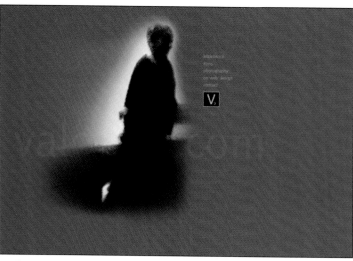

3.28

PLATFORM GAMMA DIFFERENCES

Diversity makes for a richer society, but it's just a pain in the butt for Web designers. You have to keep in mind platform variations in resolution and color palettes, code support that changes from browser to browser, and a host of other variables. Add gamma differences to the pile.

Simply put, images on Macs are lighter than on Windows machines. (More specifically, the Mac gamma is 1.8 and Windows is 2.2.) Statistics say that a majority of Web surfers are on Windows. So if you're a designer on a Mac, you need to account for this difference.

Even though she tests images on Windows and Mac platforms before she launches sites, during the design process Casey relies on a utility called the Gamma-ToggleFKEY. It's a breeze to use: Download it for free from *www.acts.org/roland/thanks/index.html*, install it on a Mac, and toggle to the approximate PC gamma. The toggle maker claims that the utility works in any application, including image editors and Web browsers.

Casey even uses a third gamma setting in the toggle, 2.5, to accommodate lower-end monitors that may display especially dark. She says the 2.5 setting "keeps her honest."

3.29

ALT, HEIGHT, AND WIDTH TAGS

You may think HTML tags have no place in a graphics chapter, but the `<ALT>`, `<HEIGHT>`, and `<WIDTH>` tags can be your friends.

The `<ALT>` tag encloses a description of an image. The description is useful for people with browsers that don't display images. The other two tags describe the image's height and width numerically; with this information, a browser knows how much space to allot and can flow in information that occurs after the image even if the graphic is still loading.

3.30

3.31

3.32   3.33

HOW BIG IS TOO BIG?

Until everybody has a T1 line, bandwidth will remain an issue. That's why it's good to keep individual file sizes small. You also need to keep an eye on how the individual numbers stack up when more than one image appears on a page.

Casey says that the ideal total number of kilobytes per page depends on your target audience. "For the home pages of consumer-oriented sites, the number can be between 30K and 55K, and the inside pages should be between 20K and 40K. I would keep designer's portfolio sites around 50K to 80K per page. People usually view portfolios at work, where they have a faster connection. If your audience is a niche like gamers, you can get away with numbers that are a little higher. They're really goal-driven, they're not just browsing. For some entertainment sites, you can go as high as 130K."

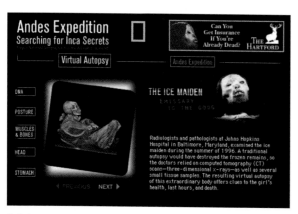

3.34

3.35

Casey designed two sites for National Geographic in 1997, when standard modems were much slower. These intricate visual and interactive sites—Andes Expedition (3.34) and Go West Across America with Lewis & Clark (3.35)—pushed the download envelope without negative consequences. "Pages ranged from 30K to 80K, but these sites were very popular despite the slower download. Users got very involved in the experience—that was our goal. Their expectations for the quick in-and-out that we see on commerce sites simply weren't there."

Another way to make pages load faster is to reuse graphics throughout the site. One example is the FinAid.org logo and tagline pictured earlier in this chapter (3.26, 3.27). "From page to page, the graphics are the same. Even though the placement of the graphics change slightly on the sub page, the user only downloads the graphics once—on the sub pages, the logo and tagline graphics are cached."

IMAGE SLICING

Makers of Webcentric image editors such as Fireworks and ImageReady have touted their skill at image slicing: that is, the automatic segmenting of designed pages into graphics and code (HTML and JavaScript). For all the hoopla, you'd think it was the best thing since, uh, sliced bread.

Casey isn't convinced. "Professional Web design is an accurate science. That's why we use spacer GIFs and hand-coded tables, because we want to make sure we have a known quantity regardless of the browser and platform. I don't like automatic image-slicing functions because it can be hard to get exact pixel dimensions without tedious zooming in and out. You may think you're getting an accurate slice, but you're not.

"After the application slices it," she adds, "it generates the HTML to recreate the image in a table. If the guides aren't exact, the image dimensions won't be exact, and you may have to go back and hand-edit the code."

Casey also dislikes that the image editors' auto-slicing often creates unnecessarily complex tables, which add to a page's K size and are particularly tough to edit. She also cites "non-intuitive and long naming conventions for filenames" as auto-slicing drawbacks.

"I think you're better off drawing your guides, merging layers, and cutting up the images in Photoshop (3.36). Then open them in ImageReady and optimize them there. A WYSIWYG coding program like Dreamweaver can write the HTML and JavaScript that puts the slices together."

Casey does concede a few advantages to automatic slicing, however, including the smart export of Java-Script rollovers. She also points out that it can help people who aren't coders to rapidly prototype a site.

BATCH PROCESSING

It would be nice to have the leisure to optimize every image by hand, painstakingly shaving off bites with the most esoteric methods. Then again, it might drive you nuts. Batch processing is one way to save time — or your sanity.

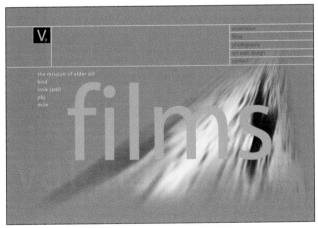

3.36

Batch processing is good for manipulating large numbers of images with similar color palettes. "And it's an easy way to organize the production process," Casey believes. Just choose your batches wisely. "I wouldn't process photographs in the same batch as GIF navigation icons. Some images are going to look better with more colors. A photographic GIF might need 128 colors. Single-color text on a solid background might work with 16 colors. When you batch, you can't make on-the-fly decisions."

Equilibrium's DeBabelizer is the batch granddaddy. "DeBabelizer was the longtime standard because it was the first of its kind," explains Casey. "It has a horrible interface but a very powerful scripting function."

Casey most often uses ImageReady's droplet function to batch. Here are the steps she takes:

1. Load a graphic into ImageReady.
2. Set your optimization options in the Optimize palette.
3. Click the Create Droplet button in the Optimize palette in version 1.0 or choose Create Droplet from the Optimize palette menu in version 2.0.
4. Save the droplet.
5. Drag the droplet onto any image or batch of images for processing.

Casey's only beef is that when you apply droplets, ImageReady places processed images and originals in the same folder. "That's a big workflow pain."

Whether creating Web graphics as a bunch or individually, Casey's goals are to make image creation and download as efficient as possible while maintaining certain quality levels. The tips in this chapter will help you reach these goals as well.

(Thanks to Ryan Shaw for his help preparing this chapter.)

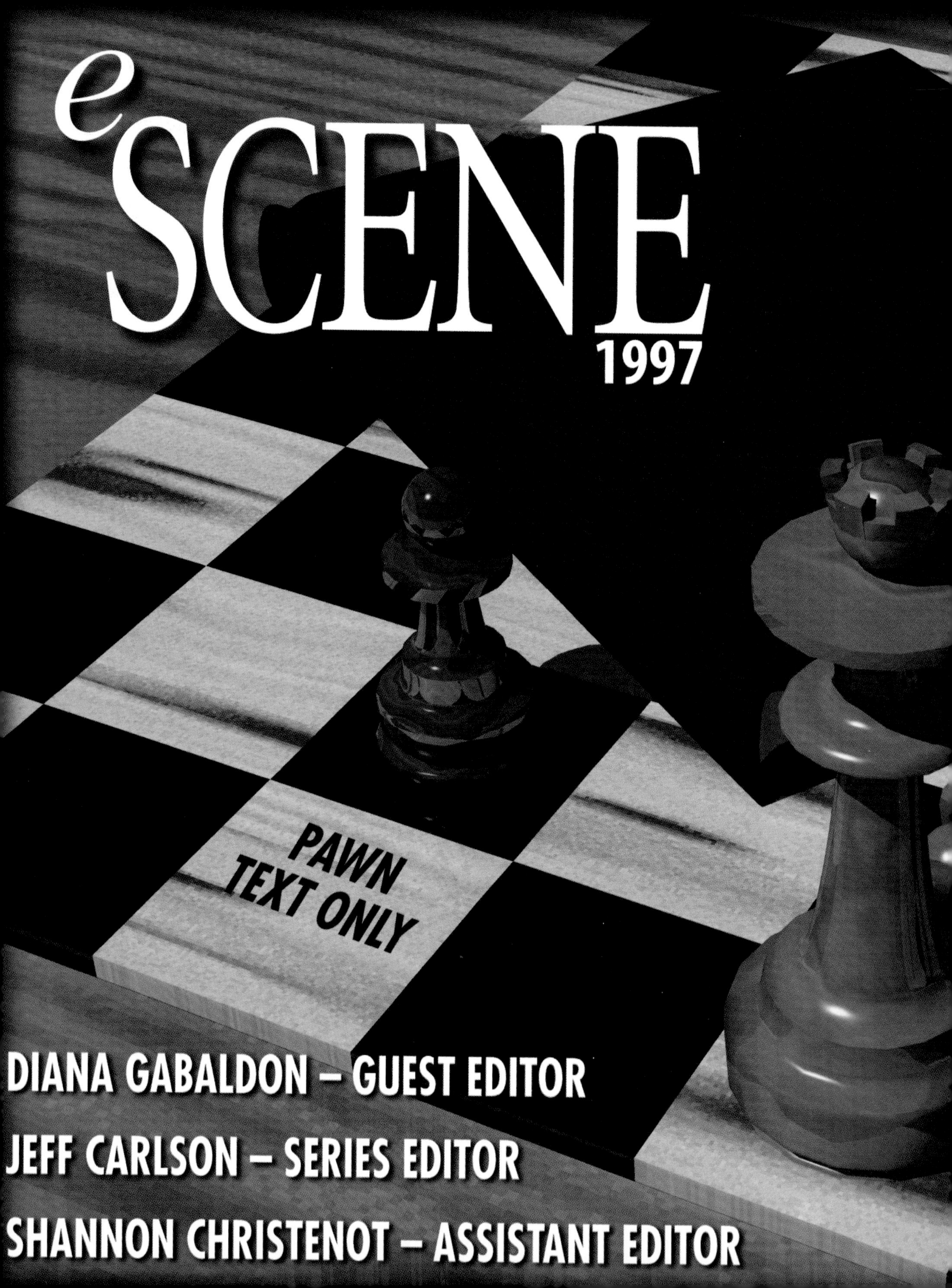

eSCENE

1997

**PAWN
TEXT ONLY**

DIANA GABALDON – GUEST EDITOR

JEFF CARLSON – SERIES EDITOR

SHANNON CHRISTENOT – ASSISTANT EDITOR

CHAPTER 4
BASIC HTML AS A DESIGN TOOL

Every day we work with sophisticated software to edit images, lay out pages, or track finances. Yet, how many people can explain how software really works? The millions of lines of code behind an image-editing program or a database would be gibberish to most of us. On the other hand, HyperText Markup Language (HTML) is a simple text protocol used to structure Web pages — think of it as a translator between the designer's intentions and the viewer's browser.

To design a Web page, you gather images and text, make sketches, and begin to rough out layout and navigation. The design decisions that you make about color, fonts, and image placement need to be expressed in a way that Web browsers, such as Netscape Navigator and Internet Explorer, can understand in order to properly display a Web page. HTML is the go-between, connecting your design and what the viewer sees. It tells the browser what color to use as a background, how large a headline should be, and where to go next when your viewer clicks on a link. Simply put: Design + HTML + Browser = Web site.

Now, that's not to say that every artist and designer must take up hard-core programming as a new career. Rather, understanding how HTML works allows you to take control of your page design with finesse and style. Understanding the possibilities and limitations of HTML allows professional Web designers and Web hobbyists alike to create compelling Web sites that can be viewed by anyone with a browser and an Internet connection.

HTML can be stretched, pulled, and prodded into unexpected shapes for use in Web design, but sometimes you just have to work around its shortcomings as a visual design tool.

JEFF CARLSON

Learning HTML requires a few hours to understand the basic rules and requirements. It's similar to navigating through a large subway system. At first you are hesitant, reading the map at every station, overwhelmed by the colored lines moving underground and backtracking missed connections. Yet within a few days, you are cruising through the subway with the ease of a native, not even glancing at the signs as you catch-up with the daily newspaper of the person sitting next to you.

As Jeff Carlson, principle of Never Enough Coffee creations and managing editor of eSCENE and TidBITS explains, "The best thing about learning HTML is the instant feedback that working with it gives you. When I first started working with PageMaker, we would design pages that looked fine on screen, but when we tried to output them at a service bureau there would be a numbing number of PostScript errors to correct. With HTML, I save the file, preview it in Netscape Navigator or Internet Explorer, and I can see right away if the HTML is working. Believe me, HTML is child's play compared to deciphering PostScript errors!" Jeff Carlson is an artist, author, and a person that finds a personal joy in bending and tweaking HTML to make it do what he needs it to do.

DO I REALLY HAVE TO?

The first time you look at HTML code, your first instinct may be to very quickly close the file. This is understandable, and that feeling of panic is being addressed by a great number of software manufacturers that are announcing WYSIWYG (What You See Is What You Get) tools on a daily basis, promising drag-and-drop simplicity with sophisticated features to make you a whiz bang Web designer overnight. "WYSIWYG tools are good to a point, but I don't know of a single professional designer who doesn't go in and tweak their HTML. Sure, not everyone warms to the idea of hand-coding HTML, but it is really the only way to be a control freak—I mean, designer. Admit it, designers and artists love being in control of the final product."

When the Web was first coming into its own, "there were no professional Web designers or Web layout tools. If you wanted to create for the Web, you had to learn HTML. It was that simple. Now that larger groups are developing sites, there's been a return to the model of compartmentalized job descriptions: designers design, coders code, writers write, and producers . . . manage. Too often, the people that are responsible for making the page work through their HTML skills get very frustrated when the star designer discovers that their design either won't work on today's browsers across today's Internet

<img src="Jeff.Carlson.gif" alt="Hi.">

Photo: Kim Carlson

ARTIST:
Jeff Carlson

ORGANIZATION:
Never Enough Coffee creations
7300 East Green Lake Drive North,
Suite 200
Seattle, WA 98115
206-390-8672
www.necoffee.com
jeff@necoffee.com

SYSTEM, MAC:
PowerBook G3, bronze keyboard
Mac OS 9
4GB storage/192MB RAM
Apple Studio Display 17"

CONNECTIVITY, ISP:
Work: DSL
Home: 56K modem
"The distinction between home and work is very blurred."

PRIMARY APPLICATIONS:
BBEdit 5.1, Adobe Photoshop 5.5, Adobe GoLive 4, Macromedia FreeHand

connections, or that the design will undergo radical shifts before it hits the Web."

When you understand what HTML does and does not do well, you are able to design pages that load quickly and satisfy the designer inside of you. "At the very least, it's very important to know enough about HTML to know what it's capable of, including its limitations. HTML can be stretched, pulled, and prodded into unexpected shapes for use in Web design, but sometimes you just have to work around its shortcomings as a visual design tool. It's definitely better to know the limitations beforehand — or at least know a good work-around for the effect you're trying to achieve — than face hours of frustration."

Fine, it's important to know about HTML, but that doesn't get us past the fact that it's still *code*. What if you're a designer who's more familiar with a Wacom pen than a <WIDTH> tag? Luckily, HTML differs from traditional code in one important way. "HTML is a shared language, so it's necessary for designers to learn it in order to join the Web conversation. People often compare HTML to Adobe's PostScript, pointing out that almost no one hand-codes PostScript anymore now that applications like PageMaker and QuarkXPress do it automatically. But PostScript remains a proprietary, highly technical programming language. HTML, on the other hand, is open, flexible,

and always changing. The best thing about learning HTML is that is doesn't require any expensive or proprietary software. Anyone with a copy of SimpleText or even Notepad can start to create Web pages."

WORKFLOW ORGANIZATION

A little bit of planning before we depart on our cross-country tour of learning HTML will help minimize the number of unexpected pit stops. Let's start with the vehicle that we'll drive throughout this chapter and beyond. As mentioned, you can write HTML with the simplest text editors, such as SimpleText and Stickies on the Mac or Notepad on the PC. Notice we did not include Microsoft Word in that list. Word is a document editor, so everything that makes Word powerful — the capability to use multiple fonts, create outlines, and make your résumé look great — will get in the way when writing HTML because Word marks these attributes in its own format. The vehicle that we will be using for this chapter is free, ubiquitous, and powerful — BBEdit Lite (*www.barebones. com*). BBEdit is the industry standard HTML editing application (on the Macintosh platform), and offers an HTML checker and preview function into any browser installed on your hard drive. On the PC, we recommend Allaire's Home Site 4 (*www.allaire.com*).

WORK HISTORY:

Mid '70s – '80s — Drew dozens of super heroes then couldn't stop drawing *Star Wars* ships after driving two hours from Twin Falls, Idaho to see the movie in Wells, Nevada.

1985 — First experience with Aldus PageMaker 1.0.

1991 – 92 — Internship with the Publications Office at Whitworth College in Spokane, Washington.

1992 — Graduated college with a B.A. degree in English.

1995 — Founded eSCENE, a Web site dedicated to publishing the Internet's best short stories. Learned HTML.

1996 — Managing editor of TidBITS.

1997 — Founded Never Enough Coffee creations. Web site clients include Microsoft, Doug Thomas's Movie Maven, Thunder Lizard Productions, ZAP, TidBITS, and NetBITS. Contributing editor and author for adobe.mag; contributor to *Macworld* magazine, *Adobe Magazine*, and *HOW*.

FAVORITE WEIRD FOOD:

Banana and Egg Sandwiches — Scrambled eggs and sliced bananas on buttered toast. Elvis would have definitely loved this one!

FILE AND FOLDER HIERARCHY

You have mapped out the design of the Web site, gathered all the project assets, prepared all the images to be as small as possible, and the coffee is brewing. Pause a moment and take a look at your hard drive. Is your project neatly organized, or do you have a smattering of floppies, ZIPs, and folders scattered about, each containing bits and pieces of the Web site to be? If the answer to the latter is a sheepish yes, stop and take a few minutes to organize the project's folder and file structure. Create one main folder named "Your Project Title," and inside that create a subfolder named "images". The "ZAP — How Your Computer Can Hurt You" Web site has a simple folder hierarchy: one folder with all the HTML documents and one folder with the images including the opening GIF animation (4.1). (It's best that your Web image folder only contain *final* files.)

"With *eSCENE*, I deliberately offered three versions of the site: graphics-intensive (king) (4.2), minimal graphics (knight) (4.3), and text-only (pawn) (4.4). The folder hierarchy reflected this before I even launched BBEdit (4.5). In this case, designing the site to be viewed in three ways was the same as designing three separate Web sites, and the file hierarchy mimics this. The king, knight, and pawn are really subfolders that required their own images folders (4.6), which helped avoid spidery URLs in relative links such as `<a href"../../bob/eatsfish.html">`. Planning the directory structure in advance helps you avoid wasting time correcting things later. It is easy to move files to a new subdirectory, but that means you'll have to update links

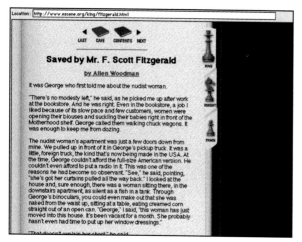

4.1

4.2

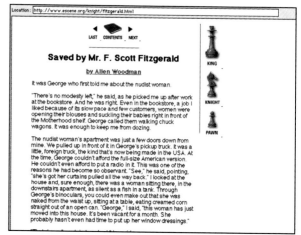

4.3

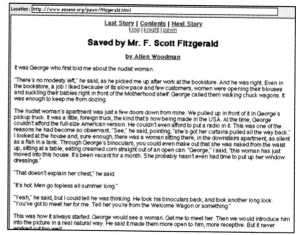

4.4

throughout the site, which is time-consuming. You'll need your time and concentration for better things!"

Finally, be sure to set up a reliable version-tracking system! "I have a copy of the whole Web site structure marked with '.old' or the date at the end of the folder's title on a Zip. If I accidentally apply changes to the wrong file and save it, I can go back and grab a fresh copy from the backup directory." This, of course, is in addition to a regularly scheduled backup system.

NAMING CONVENTIONS AND CONSISTENCY

Naming your files correctly and consistently will help you to avoid problems with some browsers, servers, and within your own workflow, especially if you are working in a production team. A safe rule of thumb is to use all lowercase with the DOS eight-dot-three (8.3) format such as "coffeemn.htm". "Most people do tend to fudge on the 8.3 issue, especially Macintosh aficionados, since 8.3 filenames can be cryptic. To play it safe, check with the ISP that will be hosting the site to see if they have a preference based on what type of machine will be serving the site. Every standard needs to be bent a bit, and you will

notice that most Web designers use the suffix .html rather than .htm when saving their HTML pages."

When naming files and links, don't use spaces. For example, when writing HTML, the filename 'hot_drinks.html' is preferred over 'Hot Drinks.html'. "You won't realize the headaches you'll prevent. It's more universal to use underscores in place of spaces or use no space at all in filenames. Most importantly, develop and use a consistent naming scheme, especially if you are a part of a larger production team."

GETTING INTO THE CODE

The best thing about learning HTML is that the resources can be found on every single Web site that you visit. When you are surfing and find a page that you admire, look at the HTML structure by viewing the page's source (4.7). Notice we said look, not copy and substitute your own graphics into already written code. Writing clean code that structures effective Web sites is an art form. Learn from it and take that knowledge further, knowing that the next person will be looking at your HTML, too (4.8).

As Jeff explains, "In the past, collaboration was key. Looking at people's HTML is how most people initially learned how to design Web sites. Now that the Web is more commercial, people are worrying about having their HTML code stolen. The way I see it, the designer goes into this knowing that her source code will be visible to all. Specialized code, such as JavaScript, should include a copyright notice. Someone may steal your table layout, but it's not the

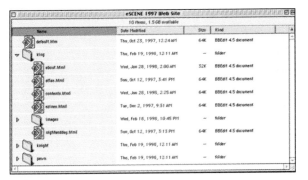

4.5

4.6

4.7

layout that necessarily makes the design succeed. That's just the mortar. It is your design and images that make the table really work.

"If I have a set of Tinker Toys, I can build lots of different things. Someone else can come and use my Tinker Toys to build their own creation, even if they retain 80 percent of my structure and build their own on top of that. I don't own the copyright to those Tinker Toys, just my creation in that particular manifestation. Tinker Toys and HTML are shared tools. Often I'll view a site's source and have the browser window open at the same time (4.9). That way I can scroll through the code to find the part of the site that I like, study the HTML, and be inspired to try new things."

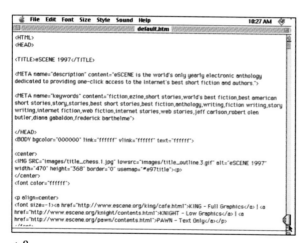

4.8

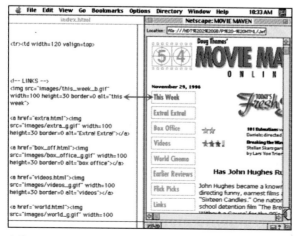

4.9

CLEANLINESS IS NEXT TO ...

To be a happy coder, write HTML that you can skim through quickly by using spacing and line breaks. Browsers will ignore spaces, color (if your HTML editor supports text coloring as BBEdit does), and line breaks. But that doesn't mean you have to, since they will help you organize your thoughts and the structure of the Web site. "I designed the Movie Maven site but I do not maintain it. It was imperative that the Webmaster could easily find the spot to place the latest reviews, so writing clean code with comment tags was essential. From the browser software point of view, both examples of HTML are identical, but from the Webmaster's point of view, the well-spaced version is much easier to get oriented in and work with (4.10, 4.11)."

WHAT EVERY WEB PAGE NEEDS

From the simplest to the most complex, every Web page has certain attributes in common. Notice that HTML tags always appear in pairs. For example, <title>eSCENE 1997</title> translates to "display page name 'eSCENE 1997' stop display page name" (4.12). The angle brackets (<>) are the open or start tag and the forward slash brackets (</>) are the closing tag. Everything has a beginning and everything must end prior to continuing.

In the following few pages, we walk you through the basic aspects of HTML. You can work along in either SimpleText or BBEdit Lite, save the HTML file, and then preview it by opening it with your browser. Consider this a sip of what you can create with HTML. We hope to show you that HTML isn't overwhelmingly complex or cryptic. To create the absolute minimalist page, open a new page in BBEdit or SimpleText and type the following tags:

1. <HTML> — Tells the browser that it is looking at an HTML document to display.

2. <HEAD> — Defines the title of the Web page.

3. <TITLE> — Is the name of the Web page, not the URL. In any site you may have a number of pages: opening page, index, products, reviews, and so on. Each one of those pages can display its own name in the title bar. The <TITLE> </TITLE>

must be enclosed within the `<HEAD>` and `</HEAD>` tags.

4. `</TITLE>` — Closes the page name.

5. `</HEAD>` — Closes the heading section.

6. `<BODY>` — Contains the page's content including text, images, links, and all page formatting.

7. `</BODY>` — Closes body content and attributes.

8. `</HTML>` — Tells the browser that the HTML document has ended. To see what the file looks like, save it and open the file via your browser or use BBEdit's preview function to load the file into your browser. Sadly, the preceding HTML will result in a gray Web page with absolutely nothing on it (4.13)!

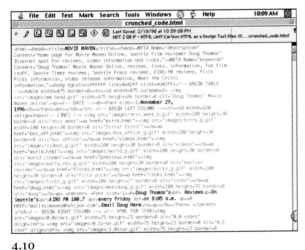

4.10

4.11

`<BODY>` ATTRIBUTES

The body attributes define the most important parts of the Web site, including the color of backgrounds, text, and links, and placement of images, tables, and frames. This is where you will be doing the bulk of your work.

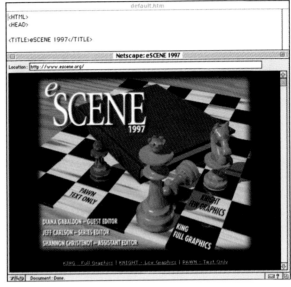

4.12

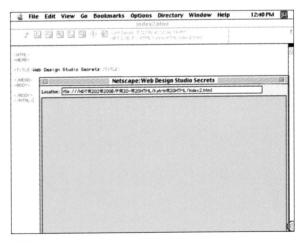

4.13

00FFFF	00FFCC	00FF99	00FF66	00FF33	00FF00
00CCFF	00CCCC	00CC99	00CC66	00CC33	00CC00
0099FF	0099CC	009999	009966	009933	009900
0066FF	0066CC	006699	006666	006633	006600
0033FF	0033CC	003399	003366	003333	003300
0000FF	0000CC	000099	000066	000033	000000
33FFFF	33FFCC	33FF99	33FF66	33FF33	33FF00
33CCFF	33CCCC	33CC99	33CC66	33CC33	33CC00
3399FF	3399CC	339999	339966	339933	339900
3366FF	3366CC	336699	336666	336633	336600
3333FF	3333CC	333399	333366	333333	333300
3300FF	3300CC	330099	330066	330033	330000
66FFFF	66FFCC	66FF99	66FF66	66FF33	66FF00
66CCFF	66CCCC	66CC99	66CC66	66CC33	66CC00
6699FF	6699CC	669999	669966	669933	669900
6666FF	6666CC	666699	666666	666633	666600
6633FF	6633CC	663399	663366	663333	663300
6600FF	6600CC	660099	660066	660033	660000
99FFFF	99FFCC	99FF99	99FF66	99FF33	99FF00
99CCFF	99CCCC	99CC99	99CC66	99CC33	99CC00
9999FF	9999CC	999999	999966	999933	999900
9966FF	9966CC	996699	996666	996633	996600
9933FF	9933CC	993399	993366	993333	993300
9900FF	9900CC	990099	990066	990033	990000
CCFFFF	CCFFCC	CCFF99	CCFF66	CCFF33	CCFF00
CCCCFF	CCCCCC	CCCC99	CCCC66	CCCC33	CCCC00
CC99FF	CC99CC	CC9999	CC9966	CC9933	CC9900
CC66FF	CC66CC	CC6699	CC6666	CC6633	CC6600
CC33FF	CC33CC	CC3399	CC3366	CC3333	CC3300
CC00FF	CC00CC	CC0099	CC0066	CC0033	CC0000
FFFFFF	FFFFCC	FFFF99	FFFF66	FFFF33	FFFF00
FFCCFF	FFCCCC	FFCC99	FFCC66	FFCC33	FFCC00
FF99FF	FF99CC	FF9999	FF9966	FF9933	FF9900
FF66FF	FF66CC	FF6699	FF6666	FF6633	FF6600
FF33FF	FF33CC	FF3399	FF3366	FF3333	FF3300
FF00FF	FF00CC	FF0099	FF0066	FF0033	FF0000

4.14

COLOR

The Web started out as a gray, desolate place. Early browsers used the default gray as the only color. Now, colors have all but eradicated the old gray. As discussed in Chapter 3, working with the Web-safe palette is imperative to avoid banding and dithering. Because browsers can only recognize and display hexadecimal color values, make sure your page and cell backgrounds, text, and active and visited links are valid hexadecimal colors Luckily, most Web editor and graphics software now includes hexadecimal colors. But if you're using older software, look on the *Web Design Studio Secrets* CD for a Photoshop document with 216 Web-safe color patches, complete with hexadecimal values (hexchart.pct) (4.14) that you can use to see and select Web-safe colors.

The body tag defines the color of background, text, and links by enclosing the attributes within the tags brackets, like so: `<body bgcolor="#C6EFF7" text="#000000" link="#00D500" alink ="#299C39" vlink="#8FF6342">`. In this case, the background (`bgcolor`) will be light turquoise, the text (`text`) will be black, an active link (`alink`) will be green, and a visited link (`vlink`) will be a muted red. As you can see in the Netscape Navigator preview from the BBEdit source file, the only thing that has changed about the test Web page is the background color (4.15), even though we defined the color for text and links. The browser, of course, doesn't have anything to display until we add text.

4.15

BACKGROUND

As discussed in Chapter 3, you can create patterned backgrounds on a Web site using small GIF files. These GIF files can be any variation of a rectangle. Working with a very narrow file (4.16) allows you to create backgrounds that mimic a notepad or open book (4.17).

Follow these steps to create the side-strip look that is currently so popular on the Web:

1. Create a new Photoshop file that is 50 by 1,200 pixels. The extreme width ensures that the strip will not wrap around.

2. Do the creative work. "In this case, I started with a blue-and-white file and used the ripple and crystallize filters to break up the edge (4.18)."

3. Index the file and save it into your Projects folder (4.19).

4. To assign this tile as a background, go to the beginning of the body tag and type in `<BODY BACKGROUND="filename.gif>` (4.20).

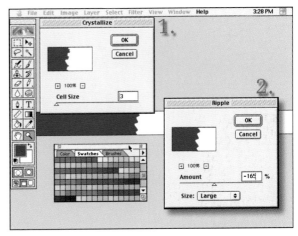

4.18

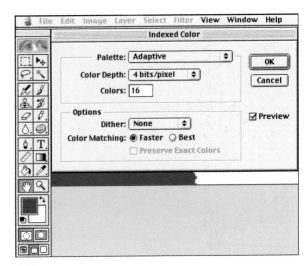

4.19

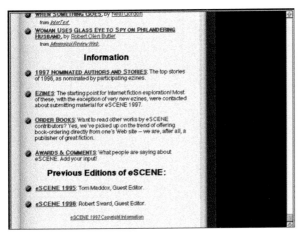

4.16

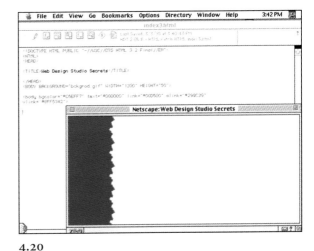

4.17

4.20

THE ESSENTIAL TEXT TAGS

"HTML is a language created to work with text. The fact that one could display in-line images was a nice added bonus. From those basic beginnings, designers have come up with ways to stretch HTML into a vehicle for visual delivery of information, and browser developers contributed by creating tags to facilitate the designers. But it's important to remember that text lies at the root of all HTML. Although the visual limitations of HTML have caused designers to bemoan the lack of control that they have over the final appearance of a Web site, there are ways to use HTML's text foundation to create good design."

<HN>

The headline tag <Hn> tells the browser to display the enclosed text in large type, just like the headline in a newspaper. The lowercase n is reserved for a number between 1 and 6 that denotes the headline size (4.21). Because headings are treated hierarchically (like an outline), 1 is the largest, whereas 6 is the smallest. The following HTML generates these results (4.21):

```
<H1>
The Designer's Guide to HTML
</H1>
```

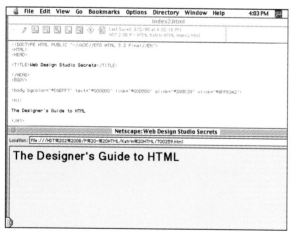

4.21

Keep in mind that due to the way operating systems assume which types of monitor you use, text will usually display larger on the PC platform than on the Macintosh platform. (Macs always assume 72 pixels-per-inch resolution, whereas PCs can range from 90 ppi to 120 ppi, regardless of the actual physical size of your screen.) There is no way to control this except by checking your Web pages on both platforms and fixing extreme problems right away, which is part of the entire Web design process.

<BASEFONT SIZE>

This tag defines the size of the body text, not the headlines of a Web page. The size ranges from 1 (small) to 7 (large). Yes, the sizing is the opposite of the sizing for the headlines.

<FONT FACE>

The <FONT FACE> tag allows you to list which font the browser should use to display the body text. The only caveat is that the font must be installed in the viewer's operating system. To guarantee that the viewer will see a font change, select typefaces that are bound to be preinstalled on his or her system. For sans-serif fonts, you'll usually see <FONT FACE="arial,helvetica"> because Arial (under Windows) and Helvetica (on the Mac OS) are installed by default. Serif font specifications usually read <FONT FACE="times new roman, times">. However, you can include any number of typefaces, depending on what you think viewers may have installed on their systems. The browser will start at the beginning of the list and continue down the list until it finds a font name that matches a font loaded in the operating system.

If your Web site audience includes graphic designers, you can have fun and use creative fonts such as <FONT FACE="caflisch script web,hobo, san francisco,tekton,helvetica,arial"> (4.22). The browser will go down the list and use the first font that it finds installed on the viewer's system. In this example, the first font listed, Caflisch Script Web, was also in the system folder. If the viewer possessed only the default typefaces, the browser would go down the list and finally display the text in Helvetica on a Macintosh and Arial on a PC. In the last example, although Caflisch Script Web is listed in the font face tag, the browser found a font that was listed and in the system folder before it read Caflisch Script Web (4.23).

Microsoft offers a collection of free fonts that are designed to display well on screen: For the Macintosh, go to *www.microsoft.com/truetype/fontpack/mac.htm*; if you work on a PC, go to *www.microsoft.com/truetype/fontpack/win.htm*. Adobe also sells a package of a dozen "Web" fonts that read well on screen. If everyone surfing the Web had at least one of these packages on their machines, the Web would be a prettier and more legible place to be!

For larger sites, or even small sites that change frequently, you should look into specifying font names and attributes using Cascading Style Sheets. For more on CSS and other type technologies, see Chapter 7.

FORMATTING TEXT

HTML was never designed to be an accurate page layout tool such as PageMaker or QuarkXPress. For the most part, accurate spacing and indenting is achieved through hacks and work-arounds, unless you are using Cascading Style Sheets.

`<P>`

The `<P>` tag is unique in that it doesn't require that the tag include "open" and "closed" versions for it to work. To add a double carriage return, just insert `<P>`. Formally, the HTML specifications state that `<P>` and `</P>` be used together (surrounding a paragraph, for example). Although more people and software are implementing the full-tag option, most HTML coders just use `<P>` to make a paragraph break (4.24).

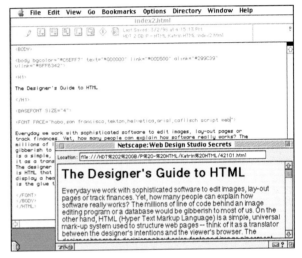

4.23

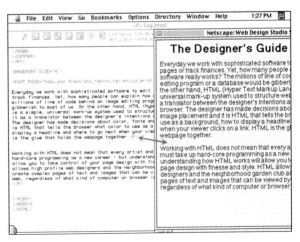

4.24

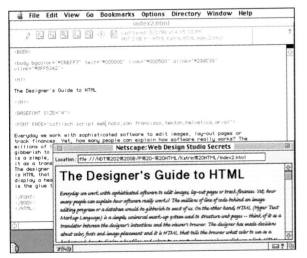

4.22

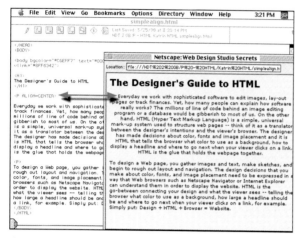

4.25

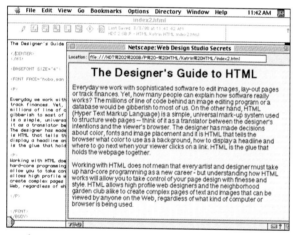

4.26

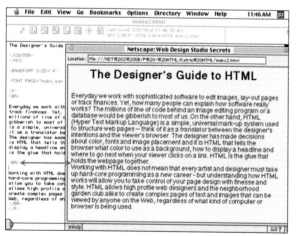

4.27

\<P ALIGN\>

ALIGN is an attribute of the \<P\> tag, so you can specify the position of a paragraph of text by typing \<P ALIGN=RIGHT\>, \<P ALIGN=LEFT\>, and \<P ALIGN=CENTER\> (4.25). You can also control centering of objects (not just text) by enclosing them within \<CENTER\> and \</CENTER\> tags. Notice that the second paragraph does not have the alignment attribute and the paragraph is aligned left automatically.

\<BR\>

The \<P\> tag is inconsistently spaced in different browsers and for many designers the space is visually too large (4.26). Often designers will use one or two \<BR\> tags in place of one \<P\>. Use the line break tag of \<BR\> to create a single carriage return between paragraphs (4.27).

\<NOBR\>

By default, resizing a Web browser window causes the text to rewrap to fit in the new size. If you want to make sure a line doesn't wrap when the window size is adjusted, use the \<NOBR\> tag. (We cover other methods for controlling text-wrapping when we talk about tables later in this chapter.) There are times when you do not want a headline or a sentence to be broken up (4.28). Using the no line break tag forces

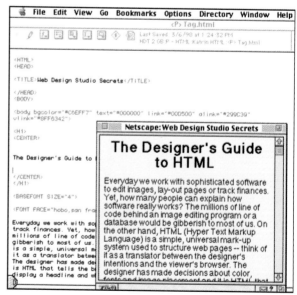

4.28

the browser to keep the text together. Notice in the illustration that although the browser window is very narrow, the headline does not break (4.29).

<SPACER>

Once again, browsers do not recognize spaces and tabs in HTML documents, but you can add a horizontal spacer to create an indent (4.30). Spacers can also come in horizontal and block forms, and you can control their height, width, and alignment: <SPACER TYPE="horizontal" SIZE="48">.

LISTS

Working with lists is an easy way to organize text on the page. You can create plain, numbered, and bulleted lists through ordered or unordered lists. Unordered lists allow you to indent blocks of text without using table elements or invisible GIFs (4.31). Be warned, unordered lists add fairly ugly bullets unless you leave off the <LI> tag before each item. Paragraph spacing is likely going to be less than ideal. Using the <BR> tag helps keep things together.

Start the unordered list with the <UL> tag, paste in the item to be listed and end the section with the </UL> tag. Add the paragraph tag <P> or line break

tag <BR> after every list item to control the space between the lines. Different browsers and browser versions handle spacing differently, so you may have to experiment.

Ordered lists (<OL>) differentiate themselves from unordered lists in that you can assign a counting system to them: numbers, Roman numerals, or alphabetic notation order (both lower- and uppercase). To define the type of list, use <OL TYPE=X>, where X can be 1 for numbers, I for capital Roman numerals, i for lowercase Roman numerals, A for capital letters, and a for lowercase letters.

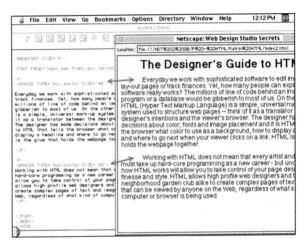

4.30

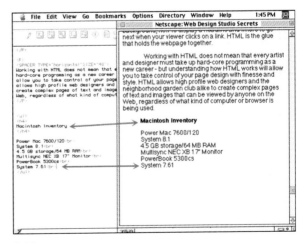

4.31

4.29

HTML TEXT VERSUS GIF TEXT

All of the font, alignment, and list tags discussed to this point are used to format HTML text. As you have probably noticed, HTML text is not a typographer's or designer's dream, but it has one redeeming feature — speed. Browsers can display it very quickly, and the page's file size remains very small. Use HTML text when you require speed and don't require a specific, nonstandard typeface for body text, navigation links, and text-only pages. The glaring disadvantage to HTML text is its lack of aesthetic control — without using Cascading Style Sheets (see Chapter 7), you cannot directly control kerning, leading, tracking, or word spacing.

4.32

So what's a designer to do? Design type in Illustrator or FreeHand and Photoshop to be a GIF when you want stylized text and typographic effects such as drop shadows, glows, kerning, leading, letter spacing, and so on. As Jeff illustrates, "On the ZAP site, the long quotes from reviews are ideal as HTML text, while the quotes from the book needed a specific typeface that fit into an area of fixed dimensions. GIF images were the best choice (4.32)."

To learn more about the ins and outs of GIF text, refer to Chapter 3.

LINK ME UP

Using a word or image as a link to another Web page, frame, file, or e-mail is what makes the Web so interesting. All link tags begin with `<A HREF="xxxxx">`, where the `xxxxx` can be a local file, Internet URL, e-mail address, and so on.

A link to a fictitious e-mail address would look like this: "For more information, please e-mail me at `<A HREF="mailto:myhouse@mytown.com">myhouse@mytown.com</A>` (4.33)." When the viewer clicks the link, the e-mail interface appears and they can write you e-mail (4.34).

To create a link to another part of the Web site, start with `<A HREF="http://www.NAME OF WEBSITE.com">Text to be Displayed</A>` and the text to be clicked. "The literary index of eSCENE links to short stories and the author biographies. To create the link for Lucy Harrison's story 'Just

4.33

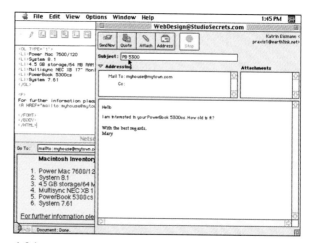

4.34

Another Night and Day,' I started with `<a href= "nightandday.html">`, which is the actual Web page containing the story (4.35). Then I typed in what the viewer sees, JUST ANOTHER NIGHT AND DAY, to signify the text to be clicked (4.36). Finally, I wanted to link the author's name with her biography, so I typed `<a href="authors. html#harrison">Lucy Harrison</a>`. In this case, the browser loads the author's page, then jumps to the tag named `harrison` (4.37)."

ABSOLUTE VERSUS RELATIVE URLS

URLs can be either absolute or relative. Absolute URLs reflect the entire file path, and relative URLs show where the file is in relationship to the file location. "My opinion is that relative URLs are better because you can set up a test site on your own computer and have the links work. A link will look for 'file.html' instead of wanting to go to a whole server on the Web someplace. The syntax for writing relative URLs is as follows: If the linked file or image is in the same folder as the current HTML file you're working on, the filename is just referenced straightforwardly.

```
<a href="bob.html">
```

If the file exists in a subfolder of the folder your active file is in, you list the folder name, and then the filename:

```
<a href="images/bob.html">
```

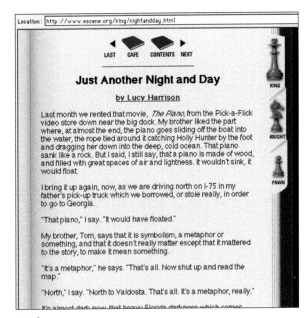

4·36

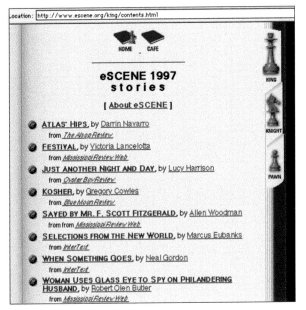

4·35

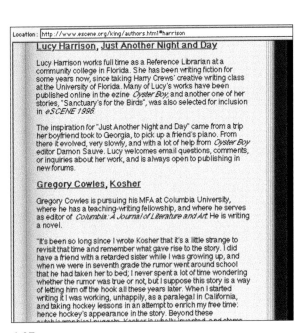

4·37

If you have more than one directory, you can dig down through the hierarchy with slashes, such as shown here:

```
<a href="family/events/picnic/
images/bob.html">
```

If you need to go up a level in the hierarchy, you use two dots and a dash. Given the preceding URL, suppose you're in the images directory and want to get a file in events:

```
<a href="../../hiking_trip.html">
```

WORKING WITH IMAGES AND HTML

For an artist, designer, or photographer, the greatest appeal of having a Web site is to display images. Images can be as simple as a company logo or a family portrait, or they can serve to set the entire tone of the site. To insert an image requires that you define the image source, placement, and alignment. The tag is `<IMG SRC="file/location of file">`. Using BBEdit to insert images is the easiest method because it automatically writes the image path plus the width and height attribute tags (4.38), and gives you an opportunity to add an image `alt` tag right away. (Note that you need to install HTML Extensions to add this functionality to BBEdit Lite.)

When an image comes into an HTML document, the image and text do not interact. Doesn't look very good does it (4.39)? To wrap text around an image, use `<IMG SRC="file/location of file" ALIGN=left or ALIGN=right>`. As you'd expect, setting the alignment to the left or right positions the image to the left or right of the text (4.40).

To make an image be a link or hotspot, start with `<A HREF="url.address">`. The URL is the actual address that the user will go to when they click the image. After the `<A HREF>` tag you need to insert the image with `<IMG SRC="imagefile. location">`. "In the eSCENE site, the home page and the Cafe can be reached by clicking the red and blue books, or a viewer can go to the less graphics-intensive versions by clicking the knight or pawn icons on the right (4.41). This allowed me to create attractive links that are more than just boring colored text."

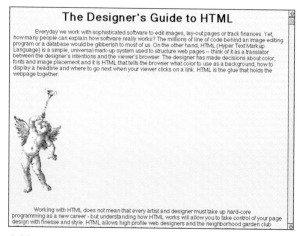

4.39

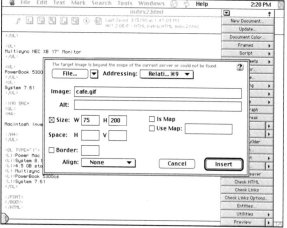

4.38

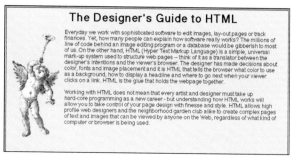

4.40

To create a link to eSCENE's home page, Jeff used the following HTML:

```
<a href="../default.htm">
<IMG SRC="images/home_nav.gif"
ALT="Home" WIDTH="46" HEIGHT="36"
BORDER="0"></a>
```

Unless you want a 2-pixel blue line (read ugly) surrounding your linked image, make sure to specify a zero border in the image tag, like so: `<IMG SRC="name of file" border="0">`.

PLEASE LEAVE THE LIGHTS ON!

Imagine walking into a dark and unfamiliar room. You orient yourself by feeling your way around to "see" how big the room is and what is in it. At the same time you try to avoid stumbling into the furniture. Now imagine walking into that same unfamiliar room with the lights on. It is a completely different experience as you quickly orient yourself, seeing exactly how large the room is and where the furniture is. Web browsers do the same thing! When the lights are off (in other words, when you do not include width and height tags for images), the browser must load all the images before it knows where to place them. Using width and height attributes in the `<IMG SRC>` tag is like leaving the lights on. The browser can read the size and dimensions of the image and block out the appropriate amount of space without actually loading the image. This way, the browser can display the page more quickly, then go back and grab the images.

Using the width and height attributes also maintains the integrity of the page in case the viewer is surfing with graphics turned off. If the ZAP site did not have any image attribute tags and a viewer came to the site with graphics off, they would see a jumble of image icons (4.42). With the image tag attributes, at least the browser will know how large a certain image is supposed to be, and it will display a properly sized box (4.43).

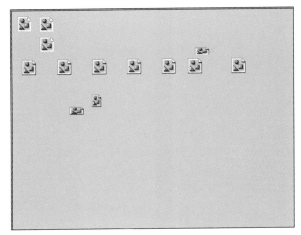

4.42

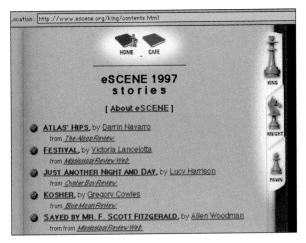

4.41

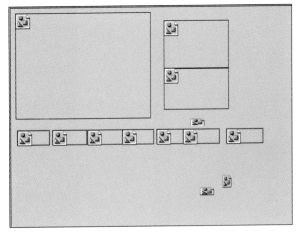

4.43

Using the image `Alt` tag is just like taking your vitamins or eating a lot of fruit—just do it! The `Alt` tag is text that is displayed when the viewer is surfing without graphics or using a slow modem connection. Rather than seeing an empty box, the viewer can read a description of the image (4.44), and when they want to actually see the file they can click on it and the image will load. The image attribute tags are as follows:

```
<IMG SRC="name_of_image.gif"
WIDTH="200" HEIGHT="100" ALT="Text you
want the viewer to read goes here!">
```

Give the viewer that browses without graphics as much information as possible by using `Alt` tags so that they read what the image represents. This is especially important when an image is a link. Rather than seeing the generic image icon, the viewer could see the word "Order" or "Info". If the viewer is intrigued by what the `Alt` tag says and they want to see the image, they can click it and the image will load (4.45), or the viewer can load all images at once (4.46, 4.47). "On the ZAP site the image is so large that I could type in the entire quote from the GIF file. On the links, the image `alt` tag really makes a difference, since the viewer can see what the button would do even when graphics are turned off."

WORKING WITH NOTHING TO DESIGN THE PAGE

Massaging a page with the use of tags and attributes only works to a point. Using invisible images to create space of any size and dimensions—also referred to as the "single-pixel GIF trick"—allows you to position images and text wherever needed. "Some designers scoff at using the single pixel GIF technique, referring to it as a design kludge, but the fact remains that it works and it's simple to use. In Photoshop, create a one pixel by one pixel file, index it, and export via the GIF 89 Export command. Specify the one color as transparent, and save the file in your images folder as something like spacer.gif."

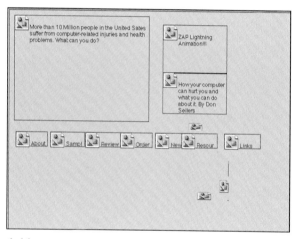

4·44

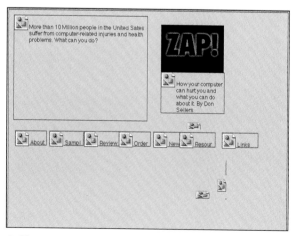

4·45

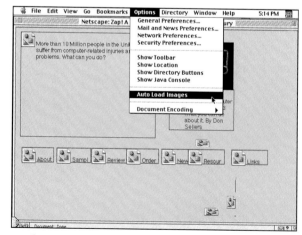

4·46

Combining this file with an image tag that specifies the size of the empty space allows you to create empty boxes that serve as blank placeholders to position images and text. Start by defining the image source with `IMG SRC` and then by defining the width and height of the space you need. In this case, by aligning the text left, the text aligns flush left to the spacer.gif file: `<IMG SRC="spacer.gif" WIDTH="50" HEIGHT="200"ALIGN=left>` (4.48). If no alignment is defined, then the spacer.gif will serve to create vertical space between blocks of text or images.

"On the ZAP site, I wanted the links and my logo to be 'pushed' down a bit. Instead of trying to experiment with `<P>` or `<BR>` tags, I added the spacer file with the image attribute tag of a 1 pixel width and a 50 pixel height:" `<img src="images/spacer .gif" width=1 height=50 border=0>` (4.49, 4.50).

USING THE LOWSRC TAG

The `LOWSRC` (low source) image tag is good for large images when you need the viewer to get an impression of an image quickly. "You're actually loading two images on top of one another, but one is usually created as a low resolution version—perhaps a sketch or black-and-white version (4.51)—that gives an impression of the final image (4.52). Using low source actually increases the load time because an extra image is being fetched, but the perceptual effect

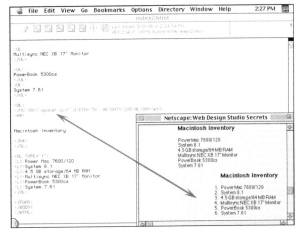

4.48

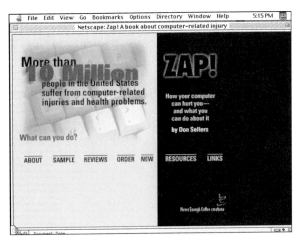

4.49

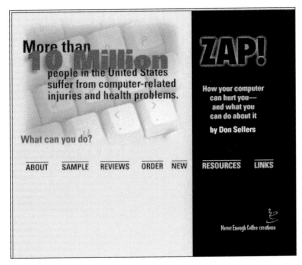

4·47

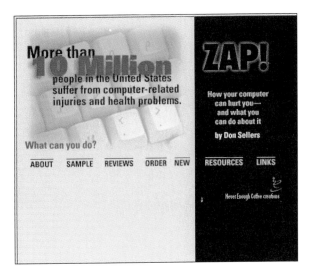

4.50

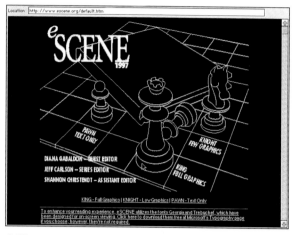

4.51

is that the viewer sees an image quickly. Low source is especially good for image maps, where you want the visitor to see the navigational options immediately."

The low source tag resides in the `<IMG>` tag. `SRC` defines the main full-resolution file, whereas `LOWSRC` points to the low-resolution file. The `LOWSRC` image loads first when the tag is present: `<IMG SRC="images/title_chess.1.jpg" lowsrc="images/title_outline.3.gif">`. Make sure your `LOWSRC` image is the same size as your main image; otherwise, the height and width tags that describe the image will be applied to the low source image as well: `<IMG SRC="images/title_ chess.1.jpg" lowsrc="images/title_ outline.3.gif" alt="eSCENE 1997" width="470" height="368" border="0">`.

4.52

IMAGE MAPS

Links are what make the Web the Web! It's like going into a good bookstore to buy a travel book for your next vacation and within a few minutes you are flipping though a book about the history of Super Heroes. One thing leads to another just as one link leads to another. As discussed previously, text and individual images can be links to another page or to a completely different Web site.

Image maps offer an intriguing method to create links that don't shout "click me" because they are a part of a larger image — subtle, yet active. Building image maps begins by mapping out where you want clickable parts of the image to be, noting the coordinates, and using these coordinates in the HTML document to define where the active part of the image is. The three shapes that image maps recognize are rectangles, circles, and polygons for irregularly shaped areas.

Most Web-editing software, even Web graphics software, now generates all you need to create and post image maps. However, if your software doesn't have these capabilities, there are a number of tools to help you determine coordinates. For example, MapTool (4.53, 4.54) and ImageMapper generate all the required coordinate information for you (4.55 – 4.58).

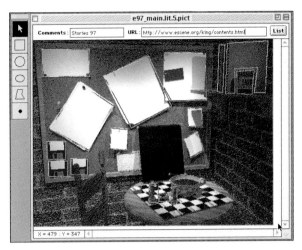

4.54

4.55

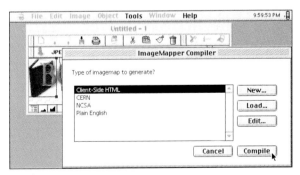

4.56

4.53

4.57

4.58

Of course, working with the Info palette in Photoshop does the trick, too! In Photoshop, set the Info palette to read out in pixels. Use the marquee tool to select the area that is to be mapped (4.59) and note the upper-left and lower-right coordinates of the marquee selection (4.60).

After noting the coordinates of the area to be mapped out, type in the image map tag of `<MAP NAME="XXX">`; the XXX reflects the name of the file that is being mapped, in this case "cupid". Following this tag comes the area shape tag: `<AREA SHAPE="xxxx"COORDS="xx,xx,xx,xx" HREF="name of link or url that opens when the viewer clicks">`. The area shape equals either rectangles abbreviated as "rect", circles abbreviated as "circle", or polygons abbreviated as "poly". Then come the coordinates. For a rectangle, use the upper-left XY coordinates and the lower-right XY coordinates, separated with commas and no spaces. For a circle, the coordinates are X,Y,R where X and Y are the center of the circle and R equals the radius. Polygons require all coordinate points X1,Y1,X2,Y2,X3,Y3,X4,Y4 that identify all points of the polygon. Here's an example:

```
<MAP NAME="cupid">
<AREA SHAPE="rect"COORDS="29,106,
64,130" HREF="http://www.escene.org">
</MAP>
```

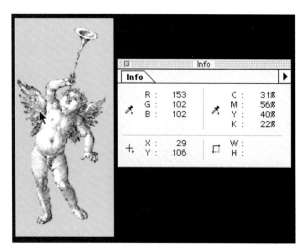

4.59

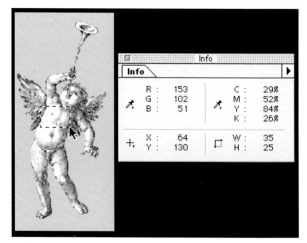

4.60

```
<IMG SRC="cupid2.gif" ALT="Angel
Blowing Horn" ALIGN=left WIDTH="116"
HEIGHT="248" BORDER="0"
USEMAP="#cupid">
```

After the coordinates have been placed in as attributes and the `HREF` tag has been inserted, close the map tag with `</MAP>`. Identify the image source, in this case cupid2.gif, and include the alternative tag and image attribute information (4.61). Finally, type in `USEMAP="XXX">` where the map used refers to the map name, in this case "cupid". Clicking the cupid now opens up the link to the eSCENE Web site (4.62).

SETTING THE TABLE

You may find it frustrating that text and images get repositioned whenever the viewer resizes the browser window. What is a designer to do? Tables to the rescue. A table is a grid with rows and columns in which you place text and images that always stay in relationship to one another. Using tables creatively allows you to design sites that offer sophistication without complex coding. Each table cell is an opportunity to be creative with file formats and the roles that each table cell can play.

The Meany Theater of Washington University Web site (*www.meany.org*) has a beautiful opening page that implements a table very well (4.63). The image

has been cut up into five pieces: the navigation bar on the left (4.64), three smaller files with a GIF animation in the middle (4.65 – 4.67), and then one large file to the right (4.68). By cutting up the image in Photoshop and placing the separate elements into a table, the site designer has the opportunity to treat each element differently. In this case, the important elements include the navigation bar with a seven hotspot image map and the GIF animation that radiates a ripple pattern out from Seattle.

Start a table with the `<TABLE>` tag and then define the basic table parameters. Consider if you need table borders around each frame, how much padding or space the contents of the cell should have from the cell wall, and how much space there is between cells. These attributes are usually zero when stitching images back together. In the case of the Meany Theater site, the designer also specified the width of 673 pixels that the browser was to reserve for the table.

Now, before we start building tables, we need to cover how tables are structured. Otherwise, you'll find yourself building tables without knowing where to put the legs. Although the HTML code for tables looks daunting, it's really quite simple if you remember the following rules. Build across, then down. Once you've set up your table with the `<TABLE>` tag, the next step is to create a row using the tag `<TR>`. Rows seldom need any additional attributes, so leaving it like this is fine.

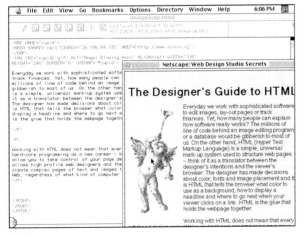

4.61

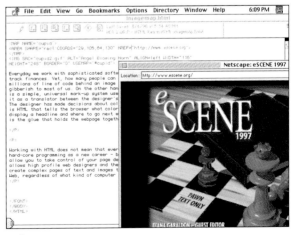

4.62

4.63

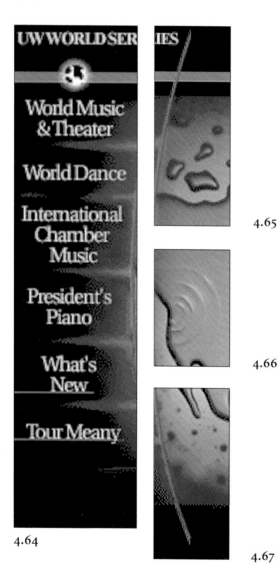

4.64

Once your row is specified, you then start filling it with table cells, which get specified moving across the table from left to right. Table cells are created with the tag `<TD>` and can contain attributes such as width, alignment (which affects the alignment of elements within the cell), and vertical alignment. After you've placed your content in the cell, close it by using the `</TD>` tag. If there are more cells in that row, repeat the cell-creation process; if not, close the row with `</TR>` and move down to the next row. At the end, close the table with `</TABLE>`. The following code generates a very basic table with one row and two cells, and illustrates the "build across, then down" concept:

```
<TABLE WIDTH=100 BORDER=2>
   <TR>
      <TD WIDTH=50>
      First Table Cell<p>
      </TD>
      <TD WIDTH=50>
      Second Table Cell<p>
      </TD>
   </TR>
</TABLE>
```

One of the most powerful features of tables is the ability to set the width of the table cells. Similar to the `<NOBR>` (no break) tag mentioned earlier, you can include text in a table cell whose width has been fixed. Changing the browser window's size won't affect text wrapping. Widths can also be specified in

4.65

4.66

4.68

4.67

percentages, so that the table will shift in size according to the window's dimensions. This comes in handy when designing a site that needs to be readable on small screens as well as larger ones.

You can also stretch cells across other cells if you want. Obviously, you won't always want an even grid of cells, so the designers of the HTML table specs added the `<ROWSPAN>` and `<COLSPAN>` tags. `<ROWSPAN>` will literally cause a cell to "span" across a certain number of rows. `<COLSPAN>` spans cells across columns. The following table is a slightly more advanced version of the preceding table, incorporating cell spanning and dynamic widths:

```
<TABLE WIDTH=100% BORDER=2>
   <TR>
       <TD WIDTH=50%>
       First Table Cell in First
Row.<p>
       </TD>
       <TD WIDTH=50%>
       Second Table Cell in First
Row.<p>
       </TD>
   </TR>
   <TR>
       <TD WIDTH=100% COLSPAN=2>
       Spanned Cell in Second Row.<p>
       </TD>
   </TR>
</TABLE>
```

FRAMES

Frames have been around since version 2 of Netscape Navigator. Essentially, frames make it possible to display two or more individual HTML files in one Web page.

The "shell" of a page is called the *frameset*. Within the frameset, you specify the size of each frame and include links to the files that appear in the frames. You describe frames from left to right and top to bottom. The HTML for a page with a 50-pixel-high frameset in the top frame and a variably sized bottom frame would look like this:

```
<frameset rows="50,*>
```

```
<frame src="top.html" name="top">
<frame src="main.html" name="main">
</frameset>
```

Note that the `<frameset>` tag replaces the usual `<body>` tag, and the frameset is defined using rows (horizontal units). You can also define a frameset in terms of columns, or vertical units.

Carlson says that frames are useful because they ensure that an important page element, such as navigation or a logo, appears on the screen at all times, no matter how far you scroll down a page or what content loads in other frames.

Despite this advantage, Carlson is not a fan. "When they're not used well," he says, "frames border on evil." Those are strong words for what amounts to a few lines of code, but Carlson is supported by the facts, past and present.

Early implementations of frames were infested with browser-crashing bugs. Although most of these have been squashed, a few remain. Frames also come with several gotchas for the unwary information architect. For example, many Web surfers have problems bookmarking a framed file. Carlson says the difficulty arises because "you're not looking at one page — you're looking at a shell that then loads different pages. When you bookmark, you probably get just the shell, and you have to click through to find the content frame you're really interested in."

Furthermore, search engines may incorrectly or incompletely index framed sites. "Some search engines look only at the HTML that specifies the frameset, and that's usually very minimal. The search bot may miss all the content and metatags in the linked framesets."

Finally, some users and search engines may link directly to a page in a frame, which means that the structure of the frameset shell is lost. However, you can add a JavaScript redirect to each framed page so visitors will be taken to the shell.

Still, Carlson places most of the blame for frame problems squarely on designers. "Sometimes designers use frames just because they can. Eighty percent of pages with frames could have been done just as easily without them. Usually things like navigation or a logo don't have to be in a frameset; they work just fine at the top or bottom of your page, and you avoid the overhead and complexity of frames."

Carlson explored the pros and cons of frames while writing a book on Web-editing software. He created a demonstration site, *www.jeffcarlson.com/hugemoon*, for a fictitious adventure travel company, Huge Moon Expeditions (4.69). The frameset code follows:

```
<frameset rows="159,*"
framespacing="0" border="0"
frameborder="NO">
<frame src="logohead.html" name=
"heading" scrolling="NO" noresize>
<frameset cols="97,*" framespacing="0"
border="0" frameborder="NO">
<frame src="moonnav2.html" name=
"moonnav" scrolling="NO" noresize>
<frame src="highlights.html"
name="main" noresize>
</frameset>
</frameset>
```

Were you surprised by the repetition of the `<frameset>` tag? It's no mistake: You can nest framesets for more complex layouts.

Because Carlson specified `frameborder="NO"`, the frames are invisible. "Unless you use frames creatively, there's no reason to see them." The illustration (4.70) shows the page with blue lines drawn to indicate the invisible frame borders.

Although Carlson set scrolling to "NO," he says that you should take practical and visual issues into consideration before you set scrolling. "The good thing about scrolling is that no matter what kind of monitor and resolution people have, they'll be able to see all the information in a frame. The downside is that scroll bars are ugly, and the more you have, especially in the middle of a screen, the uglier they are."

Although frames are far from glamorous, Carlson sees parallels to Hollywood. "In action movies, there's always some secret weapon that's fine in the right hands, but deadly dangerous in the wrong hands. Frames can be the same way. When you use them well, they work." If you use frames when more basic HTML would fit the bill, you've just added unnecessary complexity and created the potential for user headaches and confused search engines. And that's a sure recipe for a flop.

COMMENTING ABOUT <!-- COMMENT TAGS -->

Working HTML to bend to your design wishes requires experimentation, patience, and a good dose of caffeine. Before you upload your Web site to the server, there are a few modifications you can make to the HTML document that will make the site easier to maintain. Think of the comment tag like flags or notes, inserted into the HTML document for you to

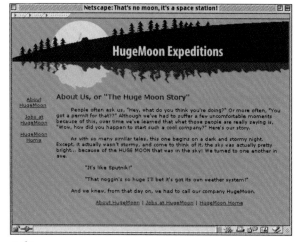

4.69

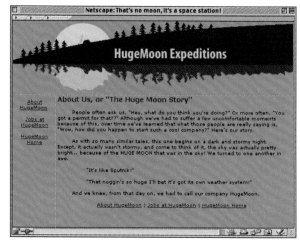

4.70

reference when working in the HTML. Because comment tags are invisible to the browser, they won't be displayed.

"Many clients want to be able to add or change site content themselves once the design is finished. Comment tags are invaluable for pointing out elements in the HTML such as `<!-- BODY TEXT BEGINS HERE -->`. This makes it easy for them to navigate the HTML, and goes a long way to preserving the HTML as I created it, without chunks of important code being mangled or deleted." The secret is in the comment tags `<!--` and `-->`. Whatever is inside the bracket/exclamation point/double-dash, and double-dash/close bracket will not be displayed by the browser." On the Movie Maven site, the client maintains the site by updating it with weekly reviews. Rather than teaching the client all the HTML required, Jeff used comment tags to point out to the client where the new movie titles and reviews would go (4.71).

In the following example, Carlson used the comment tag and all caps to help his client find the right spot to insert the movie title into the HTML (4.72).

```
<!-- FIRST MOVIE'S TITLE -->
<td width=200 valign=top>
<tt>
<b>101 Dalmatians</b> with Glenn
Close, Jeff Daniels; directed by
```

```
Stephen Herek
</tt>
</td></tr>
```

One additional use of the comment tag is that "you can store frequently used strips of code in one HTML file. The Movie Maven home page includes the code for each variation of rating star animation (4.73). The client just has to copy and paste the correct rating for the week's review in the appropriate place. The increase in file size in this case was minimal."

4.72

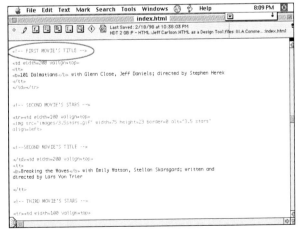

4.71

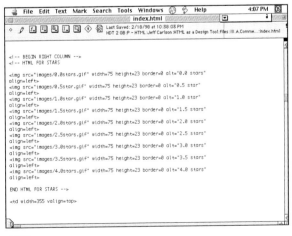

4.73

METATAGS

Once you've built a site, how will viewers ever find you? Designers are finding themselves taking on the roles of marketers, as clients not only want great design, but hits and traffic too. When search engines index Web sites, they look for keyword metatags to store in their databases. If you created a site for a museum, for example, the metatag description keywords could include the name of the museum, the city that the museum is located in, art, names of artists in the collection, culture, painting, sculpture — anything that is associated with the specific museum.

Please do not type in the same word over and over again so that your site is the first thirty matches for a search. Using the word "sex" to get hits is pretty low, too. Interestingly enough, debates are raging whether you can include the name of a competitor in your metatag. For example, if you make Coca-Cola, should you be able to use the word Pepsi in your metatag?

The description metatag is the sentence that comes up when the browser displays the search results (4.74). The eSCENE metatag is a clear example that uses both description and keywords to aid the search engines in finding the site for viewers that are interested in short fiction.

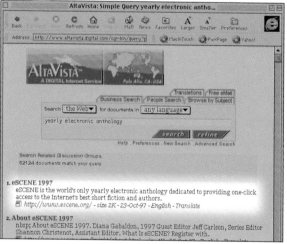

4.74

```
<HTML>
<HEAD>
<TITLE>eSCENE 1997</TITLE>
<META name="description"
content="eSCENE is the world's only
yearly electronic anthology dedicated
to providing one-click access to the
Internet's best short fiction and
authors.">
<META name="keywords" content=
"fiction,ezine,short stories,world's
best fiction,best american short
stories,story,stories,best short
stories,best fiction,anthology,
writing,fiction writing,story
writing,internet fiction,web
fiction,internet stories,web
stories,jeff carlson,robert olen
butler,diana gabaldon,frederick
barthelme">
</HEAD>
```

<THE END>

Finally, you need to tell the browser that the body of the page is complete, and that the HTML document is done by typing the following:

```
</BODY>
</HTML>
```

AND IN THE END . . .

The site is done! A very important step before uploading the site for the entire world to see is to have as many people as possible test the site on different computers and with various connection rates. The people that test your site should be looking for links that don't work, interface that is not clear, and image files that are missing. Once you are happy that the site is ready, you can upload it to your Web server. If you have direct access (usually requiring a password) to your server directory, you can use a program such as Fetch or Anarchie to copy the files directly. Some hosting companies prefer that they do the uploading, in which case you can send the files off to them by e-mail or on disk.

The best and worst thing about Web design and Web publishing is that you are never done and can always improve a site. If you like to tweak and experiment, then page layout with HTML is right for you. As the Web tools get better, and WYSIWYG becomes more than an odd term, the need to write your own HTML will decrease, but knowing how it all works and what is and isn't possible will make your Web pages more exciting and unique.

< typospace > 2.5

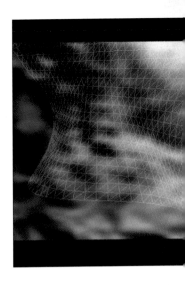

CHAPTER 5
DYNAMIC HTML AS A DESIGN TOOL

D ynamic HTML is a slippery concept. It can encompass everything from text that changes color when you mouse over it, to animations flying on and off screen, to sites that act like operating systems. To make matters more difficult, DHTML isn't one technology, but the interaction of HTML, Cascading Style Sheets (CSS), and JavaScript. Essentially, a page's HTML and CSS are the elements that can change, and JavaScript is the tool with which you change them.

Because of incomplete browser support and its intimidating complexity, DHTML practitioners are a rare breed. Designers who are equally comfortable with the aesthetic opportunities and the underlying code are even rarer. Thomas Noller's level of expertise is practically unique.

Noller was born and raised in Germany, where he studied graphic design and photography. After graduating, he came to the United States on a Fullbright Scholarship and studied at New York's Pratt Institute. Since then he's worked at several heavyweight design firms in both countries, including MetaDesign in Berlin and Method in San Francisco.

Noller first explored the possibilities of DHTML in a student site (*http://pratt.edu/~tnoller*) (5.1), then in typospace (*www.typospace.com*), a multifaceted tour of dynamic computer media (5.2). He's also worked on DHTML sites for Audi and Adobe Systems. You couldn't ask for a better guide through the maze that is DHTML.

The best DHTML designers I know have one common characteristic: They keep saying, 'I think this should be possible.' And then they go to great lengths to make it happen...

THOMAS NOLLER

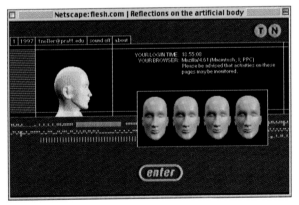

5.1

THE GOOD NEWS

DHTML boasts several advantages that make it appealing. Noller explains that "DHTML introduces the concept of depth, which means you can stack HTML elements over each other and handle them independently, much like you stack transparent layers of film onto each other to create a composite." Furthermore, designers can place elements on a page precisely without spacer GIFs or headache-inducing nested tables. We examine these abilities in detail a bit later.

Noller is most attracted by the capabilities that put the *D* in *DHTML*: Web page elements that change after the page loads. "Before DHTML, that was possible only in a limited fashion. But with DHTML, you can move, hide, and show almost every HTML object — including images and texts — on demand, in real time, without having to reload the entire page. That opens possibilities that are much closer to the way an application functions. Your site is no longer a collection of static pages that you browse like a book."

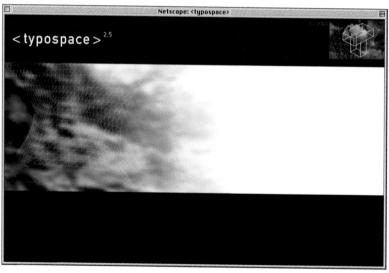

5.2

ARTIST:
Thomas Noller

ORGANIZATION:
Method
512 Second St., Fourth floor
San Francisco, CA 94107
415/764-1440

SYSTEM:
Apple PowerBook G3/333
Mac OS 8.6
4GB storage/256MB RAM

CONNECTIVITY:
T1

PRIMARY APPLICATIONS:
Adobe Photoshop 4.0, BBEdit 5.5, Adobe GoLive 4.0, Adobe ImageReady 2.0

WORK HISTORY:
1993 — Finally finished grad school in sleepy German hometown.
1995 — Moved to the Big Apple. "The most mind-boggling experience."
1996 — Bored by classes on shopping bag design, he turned to HTML. A smart move.
1997 — Forced return to Europe. MetaDesign makes it bearable.

Typospace is an excellent example of how well a Web page can function like an application. "At its core, typospace is a one-page site (5.3). But it has menus and windows, and you can scroll content and move it around just like you're used to in Windows or the Mac OS (5.4). You don't have to rely on the preset elements of the visitor's operating system. You can create your own look and feel—at best, your own immersive environment." For an introduction to the technology that powers this interactivity, see Chapter 8.

Noller's arguments in favor of DHTML are compelling. "Every medium is at its best when you use its particular language to communicate. Film has a different way of telling a story than a book. Likewise, the Web has an underlying language, and that's HTML. DHTML basically sticks to the language of the Web. It offers you all the advantages of HTML: As text, it's very fast to download. You can create dynamic information by linking it to a database. You can copy text and paste it into another program, and you can quickly change information by retyping it. You can use the language and create amazing things with it. You don't need fancy formats like Macromedia Flash or Shockwave."

THE BAD NEWS

Despite DHTML's potency, there are good reasons why it doesn't dominate the Web. "The code is rather difficult to understand," Noller admits. "Also, the more complex the site, the bigger the chunks you have to download at a time. Some sites load the entire set of elements into the browser's cache first. Once you've loaded everything, you can walk through the presentation in real time without any annoying page reloads. It feels more like an entity. But loading everything first means the user has to wait for quite a while."

The old foe, uneven browser support, is another major deterrent. DHTML is viewable only in 4.0 and higher browser versions. And to no one's surprise, Netscape and Microsoft implement DHTML differently. "To understand the differences, you have to understand that there's no such thing as a unique DHTML. It's the combination of specific HTML tags, such as `<div>` or `<span>`, and the underlying

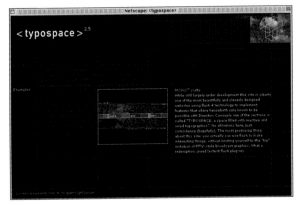

5.3

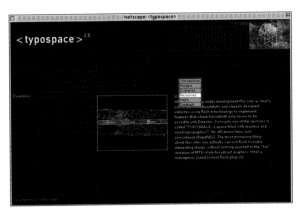

5.4

1999—Back in the United States, this time on the West Coast.

WHAT'S YOUR FAVORITE BREAKFAST FOOD?

"A coffee and a Marlboro Light. The first wakes me up after another late nighter; the second calms me down from the onslaught of ideas and problems that threaten to overwhelm me the instant I wake up."

JavaScript that manipulates these block objects. The difficulty is that Internet Explorer and Netscape Navigator have different Document Object Models (DOMs), which means the HTML tags and JavaScript interact in slightly different ways.

"The DOM organizes the objects on a page into a hierarchy the browser can understand and render. To make a real-world analogy, imagine you wanted to describe a specific chair called 'myChair' in your apartment 2C on 23 Prince Street in New York City. In Navigator you have to tell the browser the whole chain of dependencies, from more general to more specific. If we use New York City as our global entry point, the chain would be

```
object = NYC.23PrinceStreet.
Apt2C.livingRoom.myChair
```

"Internet Explorer addresses the chair by just its name, so it would be something like

```
object = NYC.allChairs.myChair
```

"You want to cater to both major browsers, which means your workload doubles."

Browser difficulties don't stop there. Noller points out that even within one browser, implementation across platforms is inconsistent. "There are a lot of things Internet Explorer for Windows can do that I.E. for the Mac can't."

The DHTML designer is left with two choices: You can develop versions for each browser permutation—if budget and schedule allow—or you can use only code that works in all DHTML-capable browsers. To keep this ever-moving target in site, refer regularly to The Web Standards Project's list of resources (*www.webstandards.org/dhtml.html*).

LOVE YOUR LAYERS

Understanding layers is key to understanding the power of DHTML. You group elements into a layer by enclosing them in the HTML tags division (`<DIV>`) or span (`<SPAN>`). The `<DIV>` tag is most common. You can have many `<DIV>` tags, and thus many layers, in one HTML page.

Noller pictures layers as "sheets of transparent film, stacked over each other. Each film can have its own content, ranging from simple text blocks to images to complex tables and entire independent structures that behave like separate HTML files. As a whole, the stack of layers form an entity, a complete layout. But with JavaScript, you can address each layer individually and manipulate its behavior without affecting the other layers."

Noller and a team from the Method design studio created the Adobe experimental site Defy the Rules (*www.defytherules.com*) to take layers to their limits. Defy the Rules introduces visitors to Adobe software. By clicking on various page elements enclosed in layers, you activate images that float on and off screen and demonstrate the capabilities of After Effects, GoLive, Illustrator, Photoshop, and Premiere (5.5, 5.6, 5.7).

"The whole site consists of only one HTML page," Noller explains, "but this page contains about 100 individual layers. Some are visible, and some are outside the browser window, waiting to enter the stage on command.

"The biggest challenge was to orchestrate all these layers in a seemingly logical fashion. I felt like a playwright with 100-plus cast members to control. Some clicks on the site change the state of more than 20 layers at the same time in all kinds of ways. It really is like a script: When I click here, you over there come to the front, you move from the stage, you move over there, and you just disappear, but only briefly, because I'll need you again in a second. It required a level of abstraction and a feeling for time and rhythm to pull off."

Noller also relied on layers for pages he designed for Audi to promote the Audi TT sports car. The site, *www.audi-tt.com* (5.8), uses a heady mixture of Flash, Real Audio, and DHTML. Because of its complexity, Noller used a different approach. "It would have been impossible to load all elements of this site into the cache first. No user would have the patience to wait so long. Instead, the programmers built empty containers that fill only when a user clicks the appropriate button."

5.5

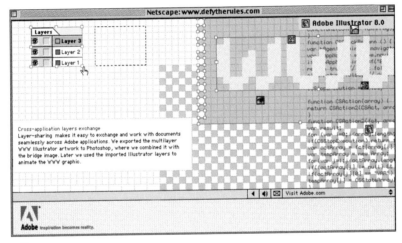

5.6

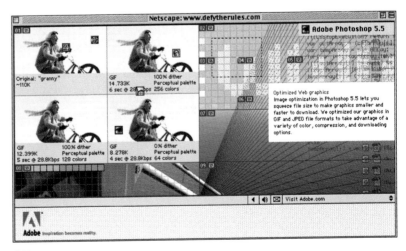

5.7

This approach is particularly useful given the Web's propensity for rapid content changes. "You can build a structure and fill it with any kind of content. When there are major changes, you need only change the content, not rewrite the structure. It's like an apartment building. If after a year one tenant moves out and another moves in, you don't have to rebuild the place from scratch. You just renovate the apartment."

FAKE LAYER TRANSPARENCY

Although Noller uses the metaphor of stacks of transparent film to describe DHTML layers, the layers are in fact not quite so flexible. Layers and their contents are either on or off, visible or hidden. Noller sidesteps this limitation with transparent GIFs.

"When I want underlying content to show through, I create a GIF image consisting of a very rapid succession of two pixel colors, such as white and black, and make one color, for example the black, transparent. The effect in the Web page is that all white pixels are opaque and cover the underlying image, while all black pixels are transparent, showing the underlying structure through. It creates the illusion of semitransparency." For transparent GIF basics, see Chapter 3.

5.8

ABSOLUTE POSITIONING

Absolute positioning, which is part of the Cascading Style Sheets specification, delivers one of the holy grails for Web designers—control over the placement of page elements. (If you're not familiar with CSS, you may want to first check out Chapter 7.)

Noller explains how it's done: "Absolute positioning takes the upper-left corner of your browser window as a zero reference. From there it's very easy to position an object exactly to the pixel anywhere on the page. With pre-DHTML-compatible browsers you had to build cumbersome tables and spacer GIFs to push content to specific *x* and *y* values. Now you just tell a layer to begin at, say, 20 pixels from the top and 10 pixels from the left." It's also wise to specify the layer's width. The positioning code for such a layer would look something like this:

```
position: absolute;
left: 10px;
top: 20px;
width: 200 px
```

Noller says that the biggest problem with absolute positioning is a bug in Netscape Navigator that scrambles layers' content and position when you resize a page. The bug workaround, which follows, repositions the content on resize:

```
var ns = document.layers ? true :
false;

if(ns) {
var thisWidth = window.innerWidth;
var thisHeight = window.innerHeight;
window.onresize = NSreloadFix;
}

function NSreloadFix(){
if(innerWidth!= thisWidth ||
innerHeight != thisHeight){

   document.location.href =
document.location.href
               }

}
```

It's not an ideal solution, however, because it returns the page layout to its initial state; any change the user made after the page was loaded is lost. Keeping the audience's likely screen size in mind when you design is an important part of avoiding the behavior that triggers this bug.

There are many CSS properties in addition to position that you can manipulate in DHTML sites. Not all properties render in the same way across browsers, so if you don't have time to write multiple versions of a page, you may want to limit yourself to the following relatively "browser-safe" list:

- `height` specifies the height of the `DIV` tag.
- `clip` tells the browser how to crop a layer. (See the next section for the `clip` property in action.)
- `visibility` controls whether the layer is visible or hidden.
- `z-index` determines layers' stacking order.

TAKE A CLOSER LOOK

When you're in command of the technical aspects and have an artist's vision, DHTML's possibilities are amazing. One small portion of the Audi TT site (*www.audi-tt.com*) provides ample evidence. Click the word "Coupe" and then the Explore button. Don't be thrown off by the German words on the next screen. Click the word "Technik," then "Sicherheit." Finally, click the image of the car's roof, and you'll see these instructions: "Move the magnifying glass by dragging it with your mouse (5.9)." Powered by DHTML, the magnifying glass effect seems simple. It isn't.

"I started with three basic elements," Noller says. "The original image of the car; another image of the car twice the size of the original, which functions as the projection; and a transparent GIF stretched to the size of an invisible frame. It acted like a loupe.

"To stack these elements, I created a layer for each, with the image of the normal car at the bottom, the magnified image above, and the invisible loupe — the transparent GIF stretched to the exact size of the magnifying frame — on the top (5.10)."

At this point, the magnified image covered up the smaller one. To solve this problem, Noller used DHTML clipping, which makes sections of a layer transparent so that the underlying layer shows through. "There are four values to clip: from the left, top, right, and bottom edge. You can clip one or two of these values, but in this case I needed to clip all four edges of the magnified image so it became a small square with the exact size and position of the invisible loupe frame." Don't confuse clipping with cutting away portions. "The clipped image still exists as a whole," Noller says, "but DHTML makes it possible to see only portions of this image at a time."

The next task was to let the audience move the loupe (5.11). "Much like in real life, I wanted to move the loupe element around. Via JavaScript, you can make virtually every HTML element moveable in the browser window." Noller wrote a script that made the transparent GIF loupe match a user's mouse movements. "The magnified image also had to move with the loupe. I achieved this by tying the amount of the four clipping values to the position of the loupe in JavaScript."

So far, much of the work had been a matter of knowing how to write code. Then Noller's eye, trained in photography and graphic design, told him that the illusion of magnification was incomplete.

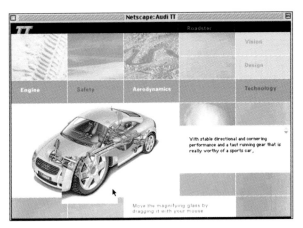

5.9

"To understand what was missing," he says, "I had to closely examine the way an actual loupe behaves. If you move around a loupe on a drawing, you'll notice that not only the loupe moves, but the magnified image of the drawing also seems to move in a direction opposite to the direction of the loupe. And the magnified image seems to move faster than your loupe at a speed that depends on the magnification."

Noller translated his observations into a script that says when a user's mouse moves 50 pixels to the right, the magnified image moves 100 pixels to the left, and vice versa. "The script changes the position of the loupe and its clipping values according to the constantly changing mouse coordinates. The script also shifts the x and y position of the clipped image in the appropriate counterdirection."

WYSIWYG DHTML?

As the previous example shows, using DHTML to its fullest requires a certain aptitude for logic and code. But what about those of us who feel more comfortable with visual design than programming? Although he has used Macromedia Dreamweaver and Adobe GoLive to write DHTML, Noller says such WYSI-WYG editors can limit your creations. "If you're not interested in abstract commands and signs, you won't be able to understand everything that's possible.

"I prefer to code files by hand, even though that's become an increasingly time-consuming and nerve-wracking task. I might use editors for the rather tedious HTML part, and for quickly positioning the layers necessary for my files. But when it comes to the JavaScript, which is in many ways the underlying engine, I never rely entirely on an editor.

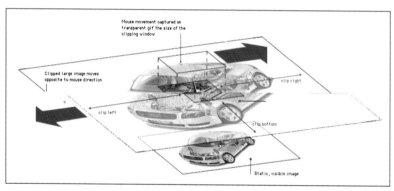

5.10

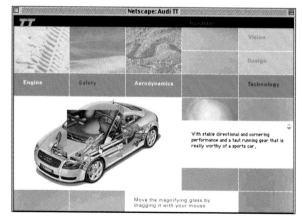

5.11

"To write the code yourself is the only way to have absolute knowledge about what's going on and where. If you encounter a problem — and there will be lots of them — it's always better to look for a solution in your own 'handwriting' rather than in the cryptic, idiosyncratic, propriety code of an editor." You'll also stay on the cutting edge, which is probably your goal if you're using DHTML in the first place. Noller believes that the development cycles of WYSIWYG editors means they're always "behind the edge and targeting the mainstream.

"Some people think these editors allow you to create sites in a snap and give you exact control over how things will look without having to learn about what's going on beneath the surface. But if you don't know what a brush is and what it can do, then an icon of a brush in some painting program won't help you. You'll never be able to produce a painting, be it analog or digital."

ADVICE FOR DHTML ASPIRANTS

For those designers hardy enough to venture into DHTML territory, Noller has some words of advice. "To start with, understand the Document Object Model and how individual elements on a Web page relate to each other. Learn how the browser builds a page and how JavaScript addresses elements. And always ask questions and stay curious. The best DHTML designers I know have one common characteristic: They keep saying, 'I think this should be possible.' And then they go to great lengths to make it happen, only giving up when it really is impossible, which has the benefit of showing you where the limits are.

"There are some great resources online, like Dan Steinman's Dynamic Duo (*www.dansteinman.com/ dynduo*). But you learn most by looking at the source code of other pages. Study what they did and how they did it, and adapt — don't steal! — the best concepts to make your ideas reality."

the D**avis** GROUP

Our firm produces effective and
exciting graphic design solutions for
a diverse group of clients, including
web sites, printed materials, and more...

Portfolio

web design

file exchange

who are we?

CHAPTER 6
CONSTRUCTING PAGES USING TABLES

The term *table* is one of our least favorite words in the dense and ravenous computer lexicon. For us, it conjures up images of tedious spreadsheets sporting column after rigid column, chock full of insider gibberish, and formatted by a middle manager who wouldn't know one font from another if the letters leapt off the page and impaled him with their serifs. Tables hold price lists, comparative data, amortization payments, and a bunch of other bottom-line dreck that make us wish to heck computers had never been invented.

But HTML tables are different. While you certainly *can* use a <TABLE> tag to house something as mundane as an online spreadsheet (though we naturally shudder at the thought), its primary value to designers is something altogether different. Tables bring order to the otherwise unstructured world of the Web. They hold text blocks, permit columns, and align graphics. Simply put, tables in HTML are the equivalent of snap-to guides in electronic page design.

Tables involve remarkably little coding. You frame the table with <TABLE> and </TABLE>. Within that, <TR> denotes a row and <TD> (table data) marks an individual cell. From a designer's perspective, a <TD> cell is equivalent to a column. So you start by breaking up the table into horizontal rows and then dividing the rows into vertical columns. You always have to work in that order, and that's all the control you have.

It's amazing how much you can do with this one tool. If there's a more versatile tag than <TABLE>, *I'd like to know about it.*

BRETT DAVIS

If you want to go any further—by, say, dividing a column into additional rows—you have to start a new table inside the `<TD>` cell. A table inside a table is said to be nested, and while it might sound weird, nesting is a commonplace convention. In fact, a typical Web page design may require you to nest tables four or five levels deep. For example, you might create one table to establish the page margins, another inside that to hold two or three columns of text, another inside that to hold a graphic with a caption, and another inside that to align a row of buttons below the caption.

As you can imagine, nesting requires a stout heart and keen attention to detail. Setting up the proper tags, editing them when things don't go according to plan, and recognizing which tags go with which table is enough to test the resolve and the patience of the most even-tempered Web designer.

BRETT WAXES TABLES

That's why we brought in Brett Davis, a guy who eats tables for breakfast. "I wouldn't go so far as to say tables are bucketloads of fun. The interesting part of designing a Web site is creating and experimenting with the look and feel in Photoshop. Coding the site is pretty boring. The biggest joy of tables is the moment when you see the site in a browser and everything fits together perfectly.

"But just because tables are dull doesn't mean they're hard to use. They're really not. I mean, there are some weird things you have to remember about setting column widths and alignment, but once you get that down, it's simple stuff.

"Here you have this old tag that dates back to the earliest days of the Web. It was designed to be easy to use, so you could throw some data into a spreadsheet without thinking. But then it dawned on designers how much control this simple tag gives you. You can put anything inside a table, you have all kinds of alignment options, you can color cells, you can nest tables inside tables—it's just incredible how many different designs you can create.

"In fact, in my opinion, tables are the number one tool for getting a precise layout on the Web." Really? But what about frames? "Well, frames are fine. They let you scroll different areas inside your pages, which you can't do with tables. But some older browsers don't support frames. Even though they've caught on more lately, there are still a few people with old browsers out there. And if your page includes frames and the browser doesn't support them, you've got a

ARTIST:
Brett Davis

ORGANIZATION:
The Davis Group
14730 NE Eighth
Bellevue, WA 98007
425/641-5758
www.groupdavis.com
brett@groupdavis.com

SYSTEM:
Power Mac G3/300
System 8.0
6GB storage/196MB RAM

CONNECTIVITY:
DSL

PERIPHERALS:
Sony 17-inch 200SF monitor, Epson ES800C scanner

PRIMARY APPLICATIONS:
Optima PageSpinner, Adobe Photoshop, Macromedia FreeHand

WORK HISTORY:
1986 — Experimented with color animation on a Commodore Amiga as high-school sophomore.

big problem. If you want to be universally compatible, tables are the way to go.

"Another advantage to tables is that they don't have to look like tables. A frame is always a frame, but a table can be invisible. You can set up a rigid structure for a page without anyone seeing that it's there. To the user, it looks like a straightforward page design (6.1), but the HTML code may really be a complex network five or six tables deep (6.2)."

Davis uses a WYSIWYG program to set up his basic designs and then edits them in HTML. However, the program he uses—the $25 shareware PageSpinner (*www.algonet.se/~optima*)—boasts a modest feature set. "PageSpinner helps me when I'm picking colors and importing images." But does PageSpinner do tables? "No, when it comes to tables, I type in all the `<TABLE>` tags with the `<TD>`s and `<TR>`s and all that good stuff." Why not use a program that automatically creates tables, such as NetObjects Fusion? "I've tried out a demo of NetObjects. I don't have anything against it, but I'm doing fine without it. And ultimately I feel like I have more control working manually. I don't need to spend $100 or $300 on all these other applications when I'm meeting my clients' needs with PageSpinner."

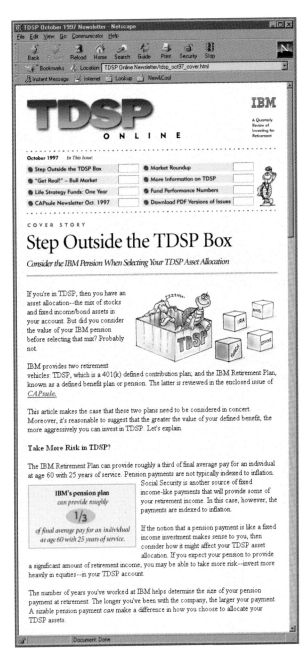

6.1

1992 — Rescued from selling shoes by designer friend who needed temporary substitute; ended up taking over job permanently.

1994 — Hooked up with The Davis Group design firm (no relation to Brett).

1995 — Designed first online project before he had even tried out America Online. Never got paid.

FAVORITE FABRIC SOFTENER:

The Downy Ball ("It's a little ball that pops open in the spin cycle and gives you freshness.")

6.2

So here's a guy who routinely creates nested tables five and six levels deep, he constructs every table by hand, and he thinks it's easy. Either he's completely out of his mind or he's onto something. You'll have ample opportunity to make up your own mind on this and other burning topics in the next few pages.

MAKING GRAPHICS THAT STRETCH

To see a creative use of HTML tables, you have only to follow Davis to work. In constructing the home page for his employer, The Davis Group (*www.group-davis.com*), the unrelated artist Davis wove a tapestry of invisible tables to create an open, uncluttered design that adapts perfectly to the viewer's screen.

"The idea behind The Davis Group page was to establish some structure while keeping the text at the top of the page loose with a lot of white space (6.3). The words look like they're floating in space, but if

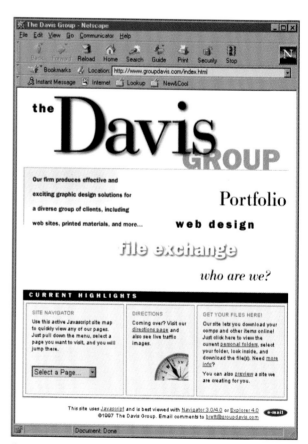

6.3

you size the browser window, the title always stays centered, and the text along the left and right sides of the page stay toward the outside (6.4). The purple line under the word *Group* stretches as well.

"The thing that I see people getting out of this example are a couple of tricks that work reliably and look great. One of them is object alignment and the other is graphic stretching. Tables are perfect for both."

Like so many Web artists, Davis mocks up his basic page design in Photoshop. He uses Photoshop's guides to divide the page design into separate rows and columns (6.5). "The guides show me where to crop the GIF files. This way, I can make sure the heights add up and that all the graphics line up just right."

After cropping and saving the individual GIF images, Davis begins work on his first HTML table, which describes the overall structure of the page. He divides the table into three columns using a trio of <TD> tags (6.6). The two outer columns (highlighted in green) serve as page margins; the middle column (in blue) will hold the contents of the page. Notice that for the present, the middle column is only partially coded. If we were to see every tag for the type and graphics that fit in this area, the code would not only be confusing, it would fill several pages.

"To keep the table invisible — so the page doesn't have a bunch of lines going through it — I set the `cellspacing`, `cellpadding`, and `border` attributes to 0. Then I set the left and right columns to 20 pixels wide using `<TD width=20>`. The cells need to have something in them, so I put transparent GIF spacers in both the outside columns. For the middle column, I entered `<TD width=100%>`.

6.5

6.4

```
<TABLE cellspacing=0 cellpadding=0 border=0>
<TR>

    <TD width=20 valign=top align=left>
        <IMG SRC="gifs/spacer16.gif"
        WIDTH="20" HEIGHT="63"
        HSPACE="0" VSPACE="0">
    </TD>

    <TD width=100% valign=top>

            **************************

    </TD>

    <TD width=20 valign=top align=left>
        <IMG SRC="gifs/spacer16.gif"
        WIDTH="20" HEIGHT="63"
        HSPACE="0" VSPACE="0">
    </TD>

</TR></TABLE>
```

6.6

"Now if you think about it, setting the middle column to 100 percent doesn't make any sense. How can you take 20 pixels on one side and 20 pixels on the other and add it to 100 percent? I mean, 100 percent is everything. But it's not. Anything with a real pixel width takes up the exact amount of room you specify, and the percentage value takes up the rest. So the 100 percent value stands for 100 percent of what's left." The upshot is that the left and right columns never vary from 20 pixels wide. Only the middle column expands and contracts to accommodate the size of the browser window.

```
<CENTER>
 <BR>
    <IMG SRC="gifs/dglogo_big32.gif"
    WIDTH="492" HEIGHT="146"
    HSPACE="0" VSPACE="0" BORDER="0"
    ALT="The Davis Group"><BR>
```

6.7

6.8

```
<TABLE width=100% cellpadding=0
    cellspacing=0 border=0
    bgcolor="#915C8C" height=1>
<TR><TD width=100%>
    <IMG SRC="gifs/purpleline3.gif"
    width=100% height=1
    HSPACE="0" VSPACE="0"
    border="0" align=right>
</TD></TR></TABLE>
```

6.9

THE EXPANDING LINE

"I leave the left and right columns empty so nothing gets too close to the outside of the page. From now on, everything is happening in the middle cell" (in the space marked with green asterisks in 6.6). After opening a `<CENTER>` tag, Davis adds a nonbreaking space (` `) followed by a line break (6.7). This results in a top margin that approximately matches the empty side columns.

Davis then inserts the Davis Group's logo. "The logo graphic is nearly 500 pixels wide (6.8), but the GIF file is less than 10K. Just 32 colors, no dithering. But I still get smooth letters and a soft drop shadow because there are really just two colors, black and purple." And thanks to the `<CENTER>` tag, it always appears centered on the page.

"Now notice the `<BR>` that appears at the end of the `<IMG SRC>` tag (6.7). This ensures that the next item — the purple line — lines up directly beneath the logo graphic without any gap. If I didn't have the `<BR>` tag, the browser would insert a space."

Next, Davis adds a new `<TABLE>` tag to create a nested table below the logo. But this time, the table includes only one row and one column set to 100 percent (6.9). Davis also adds a height attribute set to 1 pixel. So what in the world is the purpose of a one-cell, 1-pixel tall table set to 100 percent of the column in which it's nested? Why, to hold the expanding and contracting purple line, naturally.

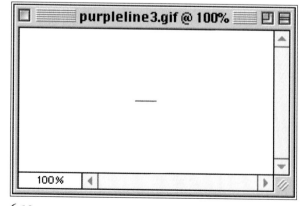

6.10

"If you look at the code, you'll see that I've got an image called Purpleline3.gif in the Gifs folder. This is the line that stretches. In reality, that purple line graphic is just 20 pixels wide (6.10). But because I include `width=100%`, the line stretches to fit the entire table, which stretches to fit the column." But there's one caveat. "You have to say `align=right`. I know, it doesn't make a lot of sense, but if I didn't right-align the graphic, it wouldn't stretch. It would just appear 20 pixels wide. All the way back to Netscape 2, it works this way. Don't ask me why. But if you use `width=100%` with `align=right`, you can stretch graphics.

"I had been using this trick for a while when Netscape 4 came out and, suddenly, it stopped working. But then I found a great way to force the stretching line to display, without losing anything in other browsers. I simply added `background="gifs/ purpleline3.gif"` to the existing `<TABLE>` tag, right before the first `<TR>` tag."

This trick works so well with the purple line because the line is a single color. "If the line had a texture, you could see the graphic stretching. It would look pretty awful. But because I'm using a solid color, you can't tell that it's being stretched out."

ALIGNING THE BUTTONS

Not surprisingly, the next item in The Davis Group home page is another nested table. This time, the table contains a total of four elements—the corporate quote aligned to the left, two buttons aligned right, and a spacer graphic in the middle (6.11). All are GIF images created in Photoshop.

"I start with my standard `<TABLE>` tag, again set to `width=100%`. Like usual, I use just one row. And then there are three columns, set to `width=50%`, `width=4%`, and `width=46%`, which add up to 100 percent (6.12). The middle column is a spacer, just to make sure that the words from the quote never touch the Web Design button." Davis used a single `<TD>` tag to house both the Portfolio and Web Design buttons. A line break `<BR>` divides the two GIF images so they're flush, one directly on top of the other. And the `align=right` attribute assigned to the `<TD>` tag keeps the buttons aligned to the outside of the page. "I guess I could have made a nested table with two rows just to hold the buttons, but I didn't need it, so what's the point? With practice, you learn to recognize when you need a table and when you don't."

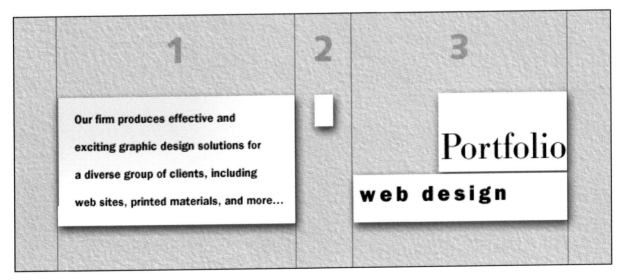

6.11

```
<TABLE width=100% cellpadding=0
 cellspacing=0 border=0>
<TR>
  <TD valign=top width=50% align=left>
  <A href="whoarewe_capabilities.html">
     <IMG SRC="gifs/dg_quote3.gif"
     width="248" height="134"
     hspace="0" vspace="0" border="0"
     </A><BR>
  </TD>

  <TD valign=top width=4% align=left>
     <IMG SRC="gifs/home_spacer19.gif"
     width="19" height="32"
     hspace="0" vspace="0"><BR>
  </TD>

  <TD valign=top align=right width=46%>
  <A href="portfolio_brochures.html"
     onMouseOver = "imgOn('img1')"
     onMouseOut = "imgOff('img1')">
     <IMG SRC="gifs/home_portfolio5_off.gif"
     width="136" height="80"
     hspace="0" vspace="0"
     border="0" name="img1"></A> <BR>

  <A href="webdesign_websites.html"
     onMouseOver = "imgOn('img2')"
     onMouseOut = "imgOff('img2')">
     <IMG SRC="gifs/home_webdesign3_off.gif"
     width="226" height="48"
     hspace="0" vspace="0"
     border="0" name="img2"></A>
  </TD>
</TR></TABLE>
```

6.12

The last two buttons — File Exchange and Who Are We? — are flush right with no elements to the left of them (6.13). This time, Davis codes a simple table with two rows consisting of one column each (6.14). "The table has a width of 100 percent all the way around, and I'm simply aligning everything to the right. One row contains the File Exchange graphic, the other contains 'who are we?'. Couldn't be much easier."

So why use a table at all? "Actually, I'm not sure if I could get these two graphics to line up without a table. As I recall, you can end up with one graphic slipping to the left of the other. It's weird. A table is just more predictable. By giving each button its own row, I know nothing can go wrong."

THE EXPANDING TITLE BAR

The final item on The Davis Group page is a traditional table — albeit colored in a nontraditional shade of lavender — with an expanding title bar along the top (6.15). "The part of the table that looks like a table is pretty predictable. This is one of the few cases that I use borders, just like a spreadsheet-type table. I set the width attributes for the columns to 37 percent, 26 percent, and 37 percent. That adds up to 100 percent, so no surprises there. I also set the cellpadding to 11 pixels, which makes a nice margin around the text inside each column. The cellspacing is 4 pixels and the border is 2."

6.13

Davis uses `bgcolor="#ECE8F9"` to give the cells their color. "The `bgcolor` command doesn't work inside tables in all browsers—including Netscape 2—but who cares? Most people don't use Netscape 2, and if you do, you'll get a white background. But when it does work, I think it looks good. The purple helps the table stand out from the white page. And it echoes the other purple elements on the page."

The unusual part of the table is the header. Like the purple line below The Davis Group logo, the title bar automatically expands and contracts to fit the size of the browser window. Better yet, the stretching is isolated to the black portion of the title bar; the title itself never changes. Davis accomplishes this feat by using two separate GIF files. One contains the Current Highlights title, the other is a random-sized chunk of black that doesn't even match the height of the title (6.16). Then, as is so frequently the case in this chapter, Davis binds the two GIFs together in a table.

"I set the `width` of the table to 100 percent and I set the `height` to 17 pixels (6.17). The next part is just a variation on the purple line trick. The table contains just one row with two columns. I put the Current Highlights graphic in the first column and the black bar in the second. I set the first column to a fixed `width` of 254 pixels, which is the width of the Current Highlights graphic. Then I set the second column to `width=100%`. Again, that's 100 percent of what's left over after the 254 pixels of the first column. Finally, I enter `align=right`, which makes the black spacer stretch out and fill all the remaining room on the page. And though I don't have it here, if I want the graphic to stretch in Netscape 4, I'd also have to add `background="gifs/blacknav_spacer.gif"` right before the first `<TR>` tag."

```
<TABLE width=100% cellpadding=0
 cellspacing=0 border=0>
<TR>
  <TD valign=top align=right width=100%>
  <A href="exchange_yourfiles.html"
    onMouseOver = "imgOn('img3')"
    onMouseOut = "imgOff('img3')">
    <IMG SRC="gifs/home_exchange_off.gif"
      width="344" height="51"
      hspace="0" vspace="0"
      border="0" name="img3"></A><BR>
  </TD>
</TR>

<TR>
  <TD valign=top align=right width=100%>
  <A href="whoarewe_capabilities.html"
    onMouseOver = "imgOn('img4')"
    onMouseOut = "imgOff('img4')">
    <IMG SRC="gifs/home_whoarewe4_off.gif"
      width="177" height="28"
      hspace="0" vspace="0"
      border="0" name="img4"></A><BR>
  </TD>
</TR></TABLE>
```

6.14

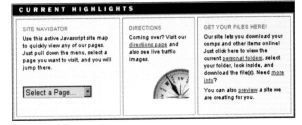

6.15

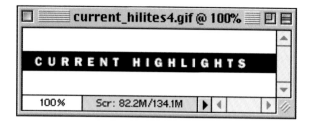

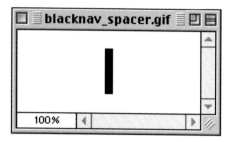

6.16

The black bar stretches and the title does not. And because the black bar is a solid color, it can scale to any size without the slightest trace of stretch marks. This is the kind of basic effect that works all the better because it doesn't attract attention to itself. Visitors to *www.groupdavis.com* haven't the slightest idea that they're looking at a complex network of no fewer than a half dozen tables. All they know is that this is an elegant page design that looks just as sleek and orderly on one screen as it does on the next.

CONSTRUCTING COMPLEX PAGE DESIGNS

Davis also designs and maintains the Web site for Thunder Lizard Productions (*www.thunderlizard. com*), an organization that conducts a series of top-flight conferences on subjects near and dear to the hearts of designers, including Web design, QuarkXPress, and Photoshop. (This same company

```
<TABLE width=100% cellpadding=0
 cellspacing=0 border=0
 bgcolor="#000000" height=17>
<TR>
    <TD valign=top align=left
    width=254 height=17>
        <IMG SRC="gifs/current_hilites4.gif"
        width="254" height="17"
        hspace="0" vspace="0"> <BR>
    </TD>

    <TD width=100% height=17
    valign=top align=right>
        <IMG SRC="gifs/blacknav_spacer.gif"
        width="100%" height="17" hspace="0"
        vspace="0" align=right> <BR>
    </TD>
</TR></TABLE>
```

6.17

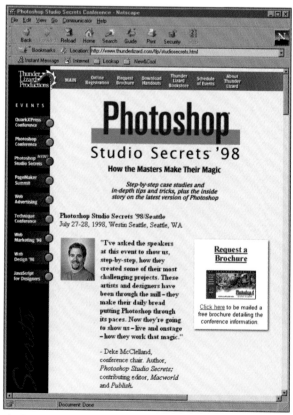

6.18

has generously cooperated in the production of this book—as well as another in this series that will go unnamed (6.18)—a fact which I'm sure you recognize to be a matter of the purest coincidence.)

By comparison to The Davis Group's page, the home page for the Thunder Lizard site is packed to the gills (6.19). Every conference has to be available from page one, a terrific design challenge whether you're working in print or on the Web. But with the help of tables, Davis manages to organize the wealth

of information into tidy visual containers that are always at least partially visible regardless of the size of the browser window (6.20).

"Looking at the home page, we have an expanding width, as always. But we also have a strip of red buttons along the left side of the screen, a green strip of buttons along the top, and a floating gray Schedule of Events. That's a lot of stuff to try and stick in a single massive table. So this time, I work incrementally, one group of elements at a time."

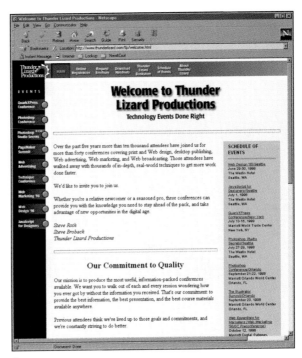

6.20

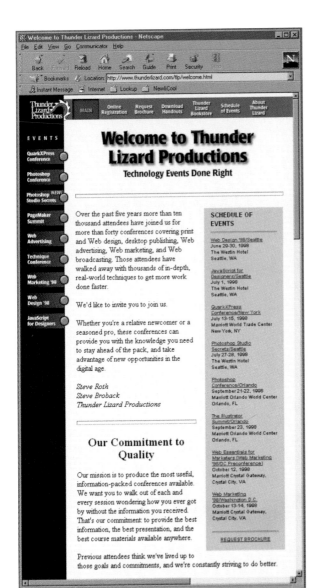

6.19

```
<TABLE width=100% border=0
 cellspacing=0 cellpadding=0>
<TR>
    <TD width=10>
        <IMG SRC="gifs/spacer.gif"
        width="10" height="15" hspace="0"
        vspace="0" border="0">
    </TD>

    <TD width=96 valign=top>
        <A HREF="menu.html">
        <IMG SRC="gifs/logo_tlp2.gif"
        width=96 height=45 hspace=0
        vspace=0 border=0></A>
    </TD>
```

6.21

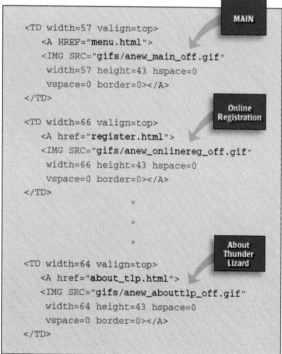

6.22

TABLE 1: THE GREEN BUTTONS

Davis begins by coding a table to hold just the top strip of green buttons. But as he works, he has to bear in mind how the green buttons at top will align with the red buttons along the side. "The first two columns hold an invisible spacer GIF and the Thunder Lizard logo (6.21). The spacer GIF is set to a `width` of 10 pixels; the logo is set to `width=96`. The red buttons below the logo are also 96 pixels wide, but the dinosaur tail sticks out an extra 10 pixels beyond the buttons, so I need the 10-pixel spacer to make everything line up right.

"After that, I code each of the green buttons across the top of the screen using a separate `<TD>` tag. The Main button gets a `width` of 57 pixels, the Online Registration button is `width=66`, all the way along until About Thunder Lizard, which is `width=64` (6.22).

"Now for the last column, which holds a gradient that fades out to the right. So far, I've coded everything in pixels. But I want this gradient to stretch to fit the window. So I set the last column to `width=100%`. Even though there are nine columns before it with specific pixel widths, I still set this last one to 100 percent.

"To keep the gradient aligned with the buttons, I set the column to `align=left`. But as you may remember, the graphic will stretch only if `align=right`. So I put a new table inside the column, put the gradient inside that table, and add `align=right` at the end (6.23). That's all it takes — now the gradient will stretch across the page."

TABLE 2: THE RED BUTTONS AND TEXT

"My next table holds all the rest of the stuff. The table is divided into four columns (6.24). The first column contains the red side buttons, the next column contains a 15-pixel spacer, the third column contains all the body copy, as well as the Schedule of Events, and the fourth contains another 15-pixel spacer."

But Davis has another special concern that complicates the table. "The page is so long that you have to scroll to get to the bottom of it. So to avoid having to scroll up and down to get to the buttons, I decided to repeat the buttons at the bottom of the page. This means adding another row to the table just to house the second set of buttons."

Meanwhile, Davis needed the body text and Schedule of Events sidebar to flow all the way down the page, beyond the point at which the second row of buttons begins. The solution is `rowspan`, which tells the browser to continue a column across a specified number of rows. "I add `rowspan=2` to the third and fourth columns so that they both stretch all way to the bottom of the page (6.24). I also add `valign=bottom` to the `<TD>` tag for the second row of buttons. That way they align to the bottom of the screen, which turns out to be wherever the body copy ends. The background pattern is a 10-pixel-tall, 1,200-pixel-wide image that includes 95 pixels of black on the left side of it. So the black area fills in the region between the top and bottom buttons. The result is a vertical stretching effect, with the black area from the background pattern growing and shrinking according to the length of the page. You can only do that with `rowspan`—I couldn't have gotten the columns to align any other way.

"Otherwise, the code for the red buttons is really simple. I list each of the nine buttons inside the column, divided with a `<BR>` so one button is flush up against the next. Because I created each button to be the exact same size—96 pixels wide—they line up just right."

```
<TD width=100% valign=top align=left>
  <TABLE width=100% cellpadding=0
  cellspacing=0 border=0>
    <TR>
      <TD width=100% valign=top align=left>
        <IMG SRC="gifs/finishband.gif"
          width=100% height=43 hspace=0
          vspace=0 border=0 align=right>
      </TD>
    </TR></TABLE>
</TD>

<TD width=15 valign=top align=left>
  <IMG SRC="gifs/spacer.gif"
    width="15" height="15" hspace="0"
    vspace="0" border="0">
</TD>
</TR></TABLE>
```

6.23

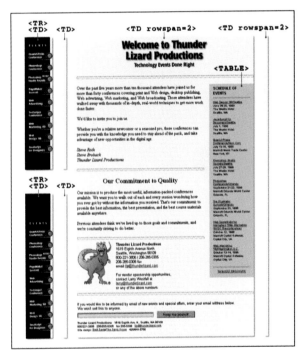

6.24

```
<TD width=100% valign=top rowspan=2>
  <CENTER>
  <IMG SRC="gifs/headline_main2.gif"
   width="367" height="106" hspace="0"
   vspace="17" border="0">
  </CENTER>

  <A name="schedule">
  <HR SIZE="7">
    <BR>
```

Welcome to Thunder Lizard Productions
Technology Events Done Right

6.25

```
<TABLE cellpadding=0 cellspacing=0 border=0
 width=190 align=right>
<TR>
  <TD width=15 valign=top align=left >
      <BR>
  </TD>

  <TD width=170 valign=top align=left>
    <TABLE cellpadding=3 cellspacing=0
     border=0 width=170 align=right
     bgcolor="#C0C0C0">
    <TR>
      <TD valign=top align=left width=5>
        <BR>
      </TD>

      <TD valign=top align=left>
        <IMG SRC="gifs/spacer.gif"
         width="4" height="4"
         hspace="0" vspace="0"><BR>
        <FONT size=-1 face="helvetica">
        <B>SCHEDULE OF EVENTS</B></FONT>
        <HR>
        <FONT size=-2 face="helvetica">
        <B><A href="webdesign.html">
          Web Design '98/Seattle
          </A></B><BR>
          June 29-30, 1998<BR>
          The Westin Hotel<BR>
          Seattle, WA<BR>
           <BR>

            .
            .
            .

      </TD>

      <TD valign=top align=left width=5>
        <BR>
      </TD>
    </TR></TABLE>
  <TD width=5 valign=top align=left>
     <BR>
  </TD>
</TR></TABLE>
```

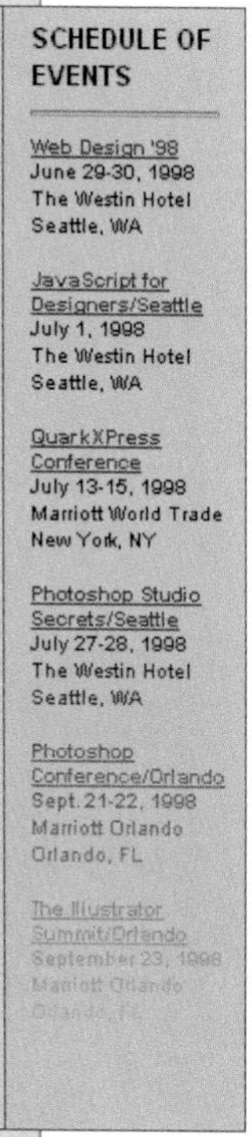

SCHEDULE OF EVENTS

Web Design '98
June 29-30, 1998
The Westin Hotel
Seattle, WA

JavaScript for
Designers/Seattle
July 1, 1998
The Westin Hotel
Seattle, WA

QuarkXPress
Conference
July 13-15, 1998
Marriott World Trade
New York, NY

Photoshop Studio
Secrets/Seattle
July 27-28, 1998
The Westin Hotel
Seattle, WA

Photoshop
Conference/Orlando
Sept. 21-22, 1998
Marriott Orlando
Orlando, FL

The Illustrator
Summit/Orlando
September 23, 1998
Marriott Orlando
Orlando, FL

6.26

THE NESTED, FLOATING TABLES OF THE GRAY SIDEBAR

"The only other item of interest on this page is the Schedule of Events sidebar, which is actually a floating table inside the third column — the same column that contains the body text. At the top of this column, I center the Welcome to Thunder Lizard Productions headline, which is a GIF graphic. Then I enter <HR size=7> for a horizontal rule (6.25).

"Next, I script the sidebar. The code for the sidebar follows the headline, so it will appear below the headline in the browser. That much makes sense. But here's the weird part: Even though the sidebar appears to the right of the copy, I have to put it *before* the copy in the HTML file. Then whatever text comes after the table will wrap around to the left of it."

The sidebar is actually two tables, one embedded inside the other. "I start with a fixed-width table of 190 pixels (6.26), with align=right so it floats along the right side of the page. This first table is actually a container for the sidebar; it determines the amount of standoff between the sidebar and the body copy. That's why the first column and the last one just contain nonbreaking spaces (   ). They're buffers between the sidebar and the body copy to keep the text legible.

"The table nested in the second column (green in 6.26) is the actual sidebar. It has three columns. The outer two columns are margins, the middle column contains the text.

"And that's it. After I closed the sidebar tables, I entered the body copy. The text is aligned left by default, so I don't have to give it any special instructions. It automatically fills the area to the left of the floating table. When the sidebar ends, the text fills the area beneath it. It's like a wraparound graphic, all done with <TABLE> tags."

THINKING IN TABLES

"As a designer, I don't relish the idea of coding tables for hours or days in a row. The real excitement for me is sketching the site in Photoshop. But if I want to get my sketch to work in a browser, I have to use tables. The great thing about them is that they always work, regardless of what kind of screen or browser the page is viewed in.

"If you understand how I put together The Davis Group and Thunder Lizard sites, you know everything I'm doing with tables. It's really just a matter of being able to see a page and deconstruct it with <TR>, <TD>, and a few nested tables. Tables are also a great way to divide buttons inside a graphic. Where one designer might use an image map, I use a table instead."

The graphic treatment Davis did for *www.premedical.com* is a good example. The home page features a series of buttons built into a title graphic with a photo montage (6.27). Davis could have saved the entire graphic as a single GIF file and then painstakingly scripted image map coordinates around each of the buttons in HTML. But instead, he divided the site title, montage, and each of the seven buttons into separate GIFs. Then he constructed a two-level table with the title in the first row, the buttons assembled into a single-column table nested in the second row, and the montage in a second column in the second row (6.28).

"I know designers who say HTML doesn't give you precise enough layout options. I agree with them to an extent, but I also think a lot of them are missing the potential of tables. Here's a tool that provides incredible control, and it's been around since the very beginning of the Web. What other HTML tag lets you build page designs, piece together image maps, or simply pour text into columns? It's amazing how much you can do with this one tool. If there's a more versatile tag than <TABLE>, I'd like to know about it."

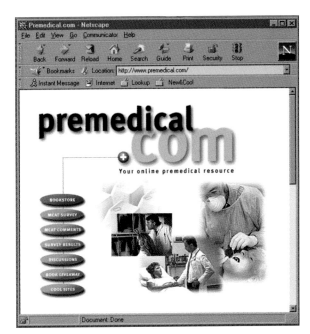

6.27

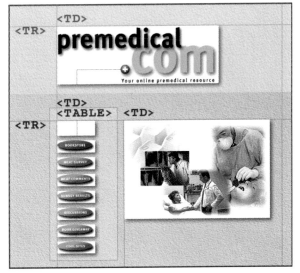

6.28

Empire of the Disconnected

D. Keith Robinson

YOU OWN YOUR SELF

joe clark

CHAPTER 7
DESIGNING TYPE FOR THE WEB

I n the beginning, the Internet carried only words and numbers. Still images, moving images, and sound have since sweetened the deal, but content is still king. Only problem is squinting at 72-dpi, single-spaced, default Times or Helvetica text gets old fast.

The early Web relied on tags like <H1>, <B>, and <I> to differentiate levels of text. If you couldn't live without a particular typeface, you had to make it a bandwidth-snortin' image. That was the creme de la characters until the <FONT FACE> tag came along. Then you could specify any face for HTML text . . . and hope your viewers had it installed.

Always an inventive lot, designers found ways to affect type by forcing short line lengths, mimicking leading, and faking columns. Software companies came out with technology that embedded fonts in a Web page. But none of these tricks and techniques is easy.

The ratification by the World Wide Web Consortium, or W3C, of Cascading Style Sheets (CSS) in late 1996 was the first real ray of hope. CSS lets you specify a pile of variables, including typeface, type size, leading, margins, and even letter and word kerning. All this is packed into a few lines of code that can apply to hundreds of pages. (Other CSS capabilities, such as absolute positioning and layering, are covered in the Chapter 5.)

This being the Web, there are still serious inconsistencies in the ways Microsoft and Netscape browsers display CSS. (For example, letter and word kerning are properly supported in so few versions that they're not worth covering here.) And if your audience doesn't upgrade browsers every year or so, it may not

Style sheets to a large extent separate markup from code. When you need to update a layout, you can edit one page instead of tediously going through hundreds of pages, searching for each and every <FONT FACE> *tag.*

JEFFREY ZELDMAN

7.1

7.2

7.3

have CSS capabilities at all. But the promise is there, and it is being realized, albeit at snail-mail speeds.

Web typography is still in its infancy, but at least Baby is starting to crawl.

Jeffrey Zeldman was smitten by the Web in 1995. Within a week of writing copy for *www.batmanforever.com*, he learned HTML and started making sites of his own. By the end of 1996, *www.zeldman.com* had clocked one million visitors. Zeldman is a founding member of a popular site for Web designers, A List Apart, and of the Web Standards Project, which fights to eradicate the evil of noncompliance with W3C standards. He is now creative director at SenseNet (7.1), a software company that bases its products on Web technology.

WHY CSS?

True to his writing roots, Zeldman says he is "all about content." He was drawn to CSS because he found Web pages hard to read. "If I could add leading and margins," he says, "it would be easier on the reader's eye." He had already rejected turning blocks of text into GIFs as a wholesale solution, calling it "cheating. You can't highlight it, there might be trouble printing, and search engines can't recognize it." However much he eschews the wide-scale use of GIF text, Zeldman's no slouch at creating tasty examples when the occasion calls for them, such as article headers on A List Apart (7.2, 7.3). (For tips on how to make the best GIF text, check out Chapter 3.)

ARTIST:
Jeffrey Zeldman

ORGANIZATIONS:
Creative Director, SenseNet Inc.
New York, NY 10013
Designer/Editor, A List Apart
New York, NY 10016
212/725-0847
www.sensenet.com
www.alistapart.com
jeffrey@zeldman.com

SYSTEMS:
Power Mac G3 and Power Tower Pro
Mac clone
Mac OS 8.6

CONNECTIVITY SPEED:
Office: Shared T1
Home: 33.6 Kbps modem

PRIMARY APPLICATIONS:
Adobe Photoshop, Optima Systems
PageSpinner, Bare Bones BBEdit, Adobe
Illustrator, Furbo Filters

In addition to the lure of legibility, Zeldman sees several advantages in Cascading Style Sheets. "The code is much more efficient, so your page loads faster." A layout that used to require tables within tables now needs a few lines of code. "It's not just that tables' code takes longer to transmit," Zeldman continues. "Browsers won't display the page until they've figured out where everything goes in the table. They start calculating: 'OK, this table is inside this one, but that's 100 percent, divide in five, but it's 100 percent of this column. . . .' It's so convoluted and time-consuming." CSS doesn't require that initial calculation to load a page.

CSS also saves you time. "We all started with `<FONT FACE>` tags," Zeldman reminisces. "The problem was, it got mighty repetitive typing `<FONT FACE= "VERDANA, GENEVA, ARIAL, HELVETICA">` dozens of times on every page. It added hours to the creation of Web pages. It also made updating a nightmare, because code and content were interlocked throughout every level of a document.

"Style sheets to a large extent separate markup from code," he points out. "When you need to update a layout, you can edit one page instead of tediously going through hundreds of pages, searching for each and every `<FONT FACE>` tag. In the Web Standards Project (7.4, 7.5), I used one linked style sheet. Linux readers told me they couldn't read a certain font at a certain size, and in about two minutes I went in and changed it. If I had used font face tags, I'd still be doing it."

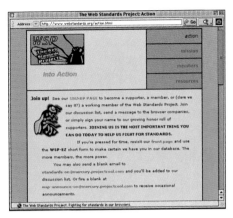

7.4

7.5

WORK HISTORY:

<u>1984</u> — Wrote ad copy while composing and producing music with audio tape, synthesizers, and a cheesy old IBM PC clone.

<u>1990s</u> — Worked as copywriter at good ad agencies in New York City. Started playing with Macs at work — and paying attention to the art director.

<u>1995</u> — Created batmanforever.com for Warner Bros. in collaboration with Alec Pollak (art director), Steve McCarron (art director), and Doug Rice (producer at Interactive8.com). Learned HTML, bought a Mac, and began making own Web sites.

<u>1998</u> — With Brian Platz, created a moderated list for Web designers: A List Apart. Joined the core group that started The Web Standards Project (*www. webstandards.org*), which advocates for complete support of core W3 standards in browsers.

<u>1999</u> — Delivered two keynote speeches in one month for Web design conference and photo exposition.

TYPE OF BAKED GOOD YOU'D CHOOSE TO BE?

"I would be garlic bread. Some people really like garlic bread."

Zeldman also uses CSS with an eye to the near future. "The ⟨FONT FACE⟩ tag isn't a standard, so it will go away eventually. If you use CSS now, you won't have to recode later. And style sheets and JavaScript work together to make DHTML. Assign a style sheet class (substyles within a tag) to any object, and it becomes an object that JavaScript can recognize and act on. ⟨FONT FACE⟩ tags don't work that well with JavaScript." See Chapter 5 for more on how CSS and JavaScript work together.

SPECIFYING TYPEFACES

If you're convinced CSS is the wave to ride, it's time to hit the beach. Like our old friend ⟨FONT FACE⟩, CSS lets you specify fonts. It's a very simple piece of code (called a "declaration" in CSS), but there are some general guidelines to keep in mind.

Always give your audience a choice. "People who don't know what they're doing sometimes declare just one font for a whole site," Zeldman says. "That's OK if you're designing for an intranet, but it doesn't help someone without the font."

Strike a balance between appeal and availability. "Use your dream font first and specify in descending order of nightmare," advises Zeldman. "Matthew Carter's Verdana is round, friendly, and readable at a small size. And every Windows and almost every Mac user has it, so I like to put it first. Then I usually put Geneva before Arial, because if you're on a Mac, you'll have both, but Geneva will be a little easier to read than Arial. When you run out of options, always include a generic — serif, sans serif, monospace — to cover your bases."

If you specify the size of your type (more about that in the next section), consider how size will affect font choice. "On the Mac, Helvetica works really well at 12 points and higher because it's a well-made font," Zeldman explains. "When you go below 12 points, it gets hard to read on the monitor. But Geneva, which is kind of a cruddy little font, was made to display at 72 dpi, so it looks better than Helvetica at sizes below 12 points."

And note that if you specify a font name that's more than one word, like Times New Roman, you should enclose the name in quotation marks so the browser doesn't read it as three names.

If you want to specify a particular style or weight for your type, you're much better off doing so in additional code than by specifying something like Garamond Book, which few readers have on their systems. Instead, use the font-style tag to add italics and the font-weight tag to specify thicknesses ranging from extra-light to extra-bold.

A font-face declaration that follows all of the preceding advice might look like this:

```
font-family: Georgia, "Times New
Roman", serif;
font-style: italic;
font-weight: demi-light
```

Mind you, we're not saying this particular declaration would win any design awards.

SIZING UP THE SITUATION

CSS allows you to specify type size in several ways. According to Zeldman, the most flexible is to "specify a font family and use 'ems' or percentages to shrink fonts and blow them up." An *em* is a relative unit based on the size of the type. When type is set at 12 points, one em equals twelve points, and .5 em equals six points. On the Web, ems are based on the viewer's default size preference. This can make for some surprisingly small and large text if the viewer default is unusual. A sample em declaration follows:

```
BODY {
    font-size: 1em;
    font-family: verdana, arial,
helvetica, sans-serif;
    }

SMALL {
    font-size: .92em;
    }

BIG {
    font-size: 1.17em;
    }
```

This kind of declaration should work on any operating system, including finicky Linux. However, it doesn't allow for much control by the designer, plus at least one version of Internet Explorer renders ems incorrectly. "I'm going for the majority of my users," Zeldman says, "and covering my bases so Linux readers can see the main text. That's why I use a slightly different approach.

"In the past, I always used points, not pixels, to specify type size. Then I did *www.zeldman.com/emzee* (7.6)." The site relies on frames to mimic the look of a business card. You scroll through frames of information by clicking arrows at the bottom of the "card." "Although the site displayed well on a Mac," Zeldman remembers, "in Windows, I could only put in a few words before I exploded the frames that create the illusion it's a solid card with writing in it. I had to find a way to get in a good chunk of text before you had to click to read more."

Pixels were the answer. Controlling type size with pixels neatly addresses one difference that plagues designers creating cross-platform sites. "Ideally, points and pixels would be interchangeable. On the Mac they're the same, whether I say 72-point or 72-pixel. But what looks small on the Mac may look gigantic to Windows users because the resolution is different."

Pixels, on the other hand, are relative to the size of browser windows and images on the page. "I know the size of the other elements on the page," Zeldman points out, "so I can make font sizes relate graphically to those elements. I know about how much text I'm giving you on a line. If I use points, I don't know." For an example of browser differences in action, compare the first graphic (7.7), which was taken on a Mac, to the second (7.8), which is the same page as seen on a Windows system.

When your audience includes people on Linux systems, you've got a special set of demons to contend with. Linux can't render sizes for which it doesn't have the bitmap. Thanks to PostScript and TrueType, "Mac and Windows systems can mimic 11-point type even if they don't have it on the system," says Zeldman. "But Linux can't fake it. Even if your style sheet includes sans serif in the font declaration, which should mean that no matter what fonts you have, the system will display a san serif face, Linux won't display the sans serif."

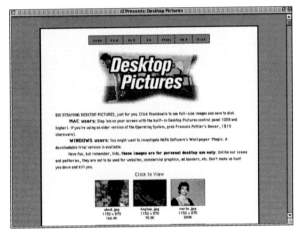

7.7

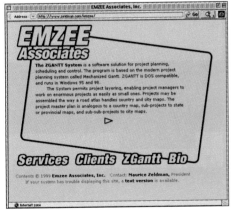

7.6

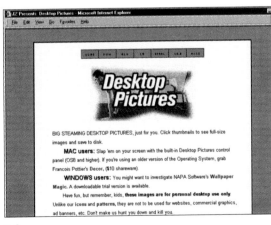

7.8

Some people argue we should never specify type size, reasoning that it prevents site visitors from using the browser to change the size to something more comfortable. This is true in most browsers; however, print readers have faced the same situation for centuries. It's all about audience: If you know the majority of your audience can better read larger sizes, you can choose not to declare a smaller size or any size at all.

LEADING

If you've been a Web designer for long, you've probably tried to control leading with tricks like transparent pixel GIFs and Netscape "spacer" elements. You'll be relieved to know that specifying leading with CSS is, as Zeldman says, "bone simple."

There are two ways to spec leading. You can make it relative, a percentage of the height of the text. For example, {line height: 150%} gives 12-point type a leading of 18 points. You can also use absolute values, such as {10px/14px}, which signifies a line height of 14 pixels.

Zeldman generally chooses absolutes because he prefers the control they offer. However, check out Dr. Web at *www.zeldman.com/askdrweb* (7.9), which is brimming with helpful, funny articles about Web design and development, and "you'll see I specify only font faces and a 180 percent line height because the site needs to be really readable. Where words are a component of a layout and already easy to read, I'll spec absolute type size and leading."

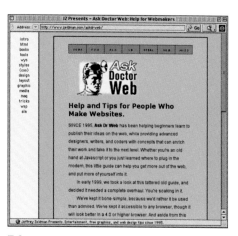

7·9

EMBEDDED VERSUS EXTERNAL STYLE SHEETS

You can place a page's style sheet in two locations: embedded in the page, in which case the styles apply only to that document, or in a page of its own that other pages link to. Zeldman says, "You always want to use a linked or external style sheet. There's less code on the page," which makes for faster downloads. "And once it's cached, it's in the computer's memory and you don't have to download it again and again." Best of all, "it's easy to change one line in an external style sheet and magically change 100 pages at once." A simple external style sheet might look like this:

```
<STYLE TYPE="text/css">
<!--

body {font: 12px/18px verdana, geneva,
arial, helvetica, sans-serif;}
B {font-weight: bold;}
H1 {font: 24px verdana, arial,
helvetica, sans-serif; font-weight:
bold;}
H2 {font: 18px verdana, arial,
helvetica, sans-serif; font-weight:
bold;}
H3 {font: 14px verdana, arial,
helvetica, sans-serif; font-weight:
bold;}

-->
</STYLE>
```

So why would anyone bother with embedded style sheets? "You might be doing something quirky on a particular page," says Zeldman. "Also browser bugs: Netscape 4.0 couldn't support external style sheets at first."

You can also add a single set of styles anywhere on a page to affect only a few words or lines. It's still embedded, but it's called an *inline style sheet*. When you use more than one style sheet for an individual page, the inline style takes precedence. Next, browsers act on any embedded styles; finally, the external style gets its day in the sun. This cascading action is where CSS gets its name.

STRUCTURE OR DISPLAY?

Nobody (except people trying to sell you things) said designing for the Web is easy. You've got to make hard choices. One of those is whether to use a structured layout or a styled one.

The early Web was all structure, such as `<H>` and `<P>` tags. Browsers knew how to display the structure, and search engines relied on the tags to define the most important parts of a page.

Cascading style sheets let you make up your own tag names such as `<divclass+"big deal">` or `<divclass="legal crap">` to describe text. Homemade tag names work because you define their qualities in other parts of the style sheet, whether it be a separate, embedded, or inline style sheet. Zeldman points out a snag to this newfound freedom: "If I use all custom tags, then a search engine can't recognize what's most important on a page. It doesn't have a built-in rule that tells it that this custom tag is important and should be indexed. Instead, the search engine indexes just the first 50 or 100 words, and that could be functional junk like the left-hand navigation bar or copyright information."

However, if your CSS tag-naming conventions mimic those of traditional HTML, such as `<H1>`, you run into another problem. Browsers "tend to impose their own built-in rules on what you're doing," Zeldman says. "For example, if my CSS tells the browser I want 10 pixels above my headline and no pixels of margin below my headline, Navigator 4.0 is going to add a bunch of pixels below the headline anyway because it always does after an H1 tag."

Zeldman avoids browsers' imposed rules by employing the CSS division class — a block element that defines a division of a page. "I often end up saying division class equals headline or division class equals subject. Then the earlier browsers that didn't have a problem in the first place still don't have a problem, but Netscape searches its memory banks, asking, 'What are my built-in rules for division class equals subhead? Hey, I don't have any. OK, I'll look at the style sheet and see what it tells me to do.' "

NO-FAULT CSS

Web designers often use invisible tables to corral text that would otherwise stretch across the entire browser window. Get a little fancier and tables start nesting inside tables. Soon you've got a mess that's hard to edit and long to download. CSS could remedy the situation, but half-baked browser support and the specter of text and images overlapping if the audience hasn't upgraded make some designers stick to their mammoth tables.

Zeldman's solution is what he calls "no-fault CSS." It mixes CSS with older HTML conventions for pages that are at least readable by a wider variety of browsers.

Take some pages on A List Apart. Many pages, including *www.zeldman.com/funhouse.html* (7.10, 7.11) use the division class tag `<DIV>` to control line length. A custom `<DIV>` tag "wrapper" replaces nested tables with cleaner code. Invisible tables still play a role, but they're farther down the page, keeping text links in two tidy columns. Zeldman notes, "I included tables so those items don't overlap for people with older browsers or voice-recognition software."

7.10

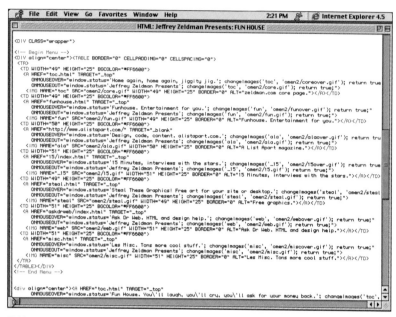

7.11

You probably noticed that funhouse.html has a nifty black border. The border is also courtesy of the wrapper `<DIV>`. "I just made a style sheet rule that said 'This is a wrapper, and the wrapper has a two-pixel solid black outline, this color orange background, and this color text.'"

As with all standards that aren't fully implemented, make sure to test custom tags like "wrapper" before you plunge in. Zeldman has discovered that, even though the code is validated and therefore completely correct according to the W3C, some Windows Netscape 4.0 and later users may "crash like drunks on the highway" when they visit pages with the code.

CSS ON COMPUTER ALTERNATIVES

As if planning for Windows, Mac, and Linux systems isn't enough of a challenge, the pundits say that soon folks will be surfing the Web with "appliances." Automatic icemakers may not download your page next year, but WebTV and handheld systems can do it now.

The smart designer keeps alternative platforms in mind. You can't make every page look great on every system, but you can shoot for pages that degrade gracefully.

Zeldman thinks that no-fault CSS can help. "WebTV ignores pure CSS. The Palm Pilot does for now. But it's not a problem in a way. When you replace everything on your page with style sheets and don't use tables at all, you have a display quality issue. But as long as you use some inner tables and they're readable—as opposed to pretty—then it's just a decision based on your browser statistics.

"When I look at my stats," he continues, "90 percent of the visitors use 4.0 or higher major browsers. The WebTV people may miss the orange square or whatever, but they'll still get all the text and links. That's another definition of no-fault CSS."

WHITHER CSS2?

Cascading Style Sheets 1 was finalized in late 1996, and it's still not fully supported. The W3C has ratified CSS2, but there's no use drooling over its rich pickings. "Until browsers start implementing it," says Zeldman, "CSS2 is theoretical. But there is one CSS2 property that's already implemented in Explorer: HOVER." Mouse over a HOVER declaration and type will alter. "It can change a link's color, or margins, or font-size — it's pretty flexible. Like all of CSS, you can use it for readability and elegance, or to make stupid, obvious, flashy tricks that may impress at first but quickly grow tiresome. I like to subtly change the highlight color." Which is exactly how Zeldman used HOVER in the Ad Store site (*www.the-adstore.com*) (7.12, 7.13).

Here's one way to implement HOVER:

```
A:hover { color: #cc00cc; }
```

7.12

7.13

OLDIES, SOME GOODIES

The code to indent paragraphs in Cascading Style Sheets is simple. Just specify the amount of indent with ems or points (P {text-indent: 2em}, for example) and you're done. You can even create hanging indents. But there's a catch. "Almost all browsers I've tested can't handle this properly," says Zeldman. "They typically indent all paragraphs, even the ones that aren't supposed to be indented. I can't stand to look at it.

"So I do something the framers of HTML would find extremely objectionable. I use invisible, non-breaking spaces to create my text indents." The resulting code looks something like this:

```
<P>This is the lead paragraph. It is
not indented. La, la, la. <BR>
```

```
        This is
the second paragraph that uses a
visual trick to look indented. What a
sad world we live in. </P>
```

Sad, maybe, but the old trick still works (7.14, 7.15). More no-fault CSS.

Zeldman is less fond of other older type technologies, including embedded fonts. According to Zeldman, "about two years ago, Netscape and Bitstream came up with a way to embed fonts in Web pages, adding as little as 32K to each page. Microsoft then came up with a different way to do it. Naturally.

"The technology never caught on, in part because it was one more Netscape-Microsoft incompatibility to deal with, in part because you had to pay for the Bitstream technology to embed fonts. The fee was

7.14

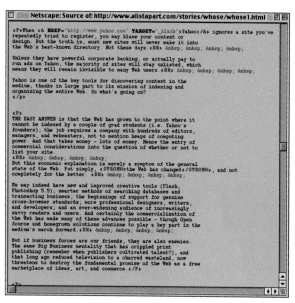

7.15

low, but it was one more fee, and at the time it was only going to reach maybe 20 percent of your audience.

"And the embedded fonts didn't necessarily look all that great," he believes. "The built-in antialiasing made them look fuzzy. So you were basically paying for some technology that wasn't going to reach most of your users, then adding kilobytes to your pages, in order to serve fuzzy type that was going to give some readers eyestrain. It was just easier to make a 5K type GIF when you needed one, and let the reader's operating system provide the bulk of the type."

WHO CARES ABOUT TYPE?

There's much more to CSS than can fit in one chapter. Zeldman's sites, Ask Dr. Web and A List Apart, are great places to learn more, as is the Little Shop of CSS Horrors at *http://haughey.com/csshorrors*. If you want a style sheet instantly validated, go to the W3C's free validation service at *http://validator.w3.org* and type in a URL. Don't be dismayed if your code is rejected.

"The HTML validator is quite strict," Zeldman says. "It barks at the JavaScript "NAME" element. It growls at nonstandard, proprietary workarounds like MAR-GINHEIGHT. It even lifts its leg at meaningless code strings if it doesn't like one of the characters in that string.

"One way to approach this is to write only strict HTML 4.0. But if you do this, your display will be poor in most of today's browsers, so what I do — and this is just for me — is use the workarounds I need to use. When they come up as errors in the validator, I expect that, and I ignore those messages."

It's all a part of the Web's evolution. "We're still totally in the Flintstones era," Zeldman states. "Even if every standard on the Web Standards Project's list of demands was supported by all the browsers, even WebTV, we'd still be in the Stone Age."

But that doesn't mean we should give up the crusade for good type. Zeldman believes that despite being hamstrung by browsers, CSS is not just a Web workhorse, but a thoroughbred. "Most Web designers have an unfortunate blind spot. They think like special effects guys. They're into whiz-bang, 'How the hell did they do that?' kind of effects, interactive effects that call attention to themselves. There are some really fine designers who aren't that way, of course, but a lot of the Web is designed by people who want to 'blow you away,' like their favorite video game blows them away.

"They're interested in whizzy, zippy, interactive technology, and content—which is really the bulk of the Web—is an afterthought. Content gets shoveled through templates by low-level HTML producers. Many Web designers don't give it a second thought. 'Readable typography? Who reads?' So style sheets get overlooked by a lot of otherwise good Web designers."

CHAPTER 8
CREATING ROLLOVERS WITH JAVASCRIPT

HTML is the one necessary evil on the Web. Like it or not, you can't make a Web site without it. As a result, hundreds of thousands of designers have had to resort to entering and editing computer code, a task they never in a million years wanted to perform.

But while HTML is an inescapable part of the online landscape, every other online language is optional. And as a result, these languages are widely regarded as tools for engineers, programmers, and other propeller heads.

Take JavaScript, for example. Just mention the word and a typical artist will make the sign of the cross and reach for the garlic. In many minds, JavaScript is part of the same crowd as CGI, Active X, Perl, and a whole host of other arcane Internet terms. No doubt you've heard of these things, but you haven't the vaguest idea why you'd ever want to integrate them into your Web site. And even if you knew a reason, you're quite certain you'd never be able to pull it off.

If that describes your opinion of JavaScript, then Neil Robertson has news for you. A relatively recent convert to the Web, Robertson regards many elements of JavaScript as every bit as essential to online design as HTML. "Just as HTML lets you get your pages up on the Web, JavaScript lets you make your pages dynamic. JavaScript is what distinguishes Web pages from traditional printed documents — it makes your site interactive."

> *JavaScript is what distinguishes Web pages from traditional printed documents — it makes your site interactive.*
>
> NEIL ROBERTSON

NEIL WELCOMES YOU TO ROLLOVERS

Let's start at the beginning. What exactly is Java-Script? "Well, for starters, JavaScript has absolutely nothing to do with the Web language Java. It's purely a licensing ploy from Netscape. Java was getting really hot and some guys at Netscape thought, 'Oh, we've got this little thing called LiveScript that we're going to incorporate into our browser. Let's license the name Java from Sun and call it JavaScript and that way we'll ride Java's coattails.'

"So, okay, the licensing thing is dumb, but Java-Script is actually great. It's a way to make online pages more intelligent and dynamic and interactive without having to rely on a lot of server-based CGIs and stuff. For example, let's say you have a form and you

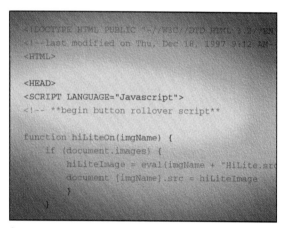

8.1

want the user to be able to type in his e-mail address. Before, you would have to make a CGI script to confirm the e-mail address, and the CGI would send back a separate page saying, 'No, that's not an e-mail address,' or, 'Swell, got it, thank you for answering.' With JavaScript, you can create an intelligent form that prequalifies the address and other data before anything gets sent to the server. And best of all, you don't have to create a separate document. You just enter the commands directly into your HTML file. You start the code with a single line `<script language="JavaScript">` and you're set to go (8.1)."

Sounds great. But let's say you don't know squat about servers or forms or any of that techie stuff. What can a designer do with JavaScript? "One of the coolest functions of JavaScript started with Netscape 3.0. Version 1.1 of JavaScript was the first to let you swap out one image with another according to the user's mouse actions. So if the user clicks a button or moves the cursor over a link, you can have that image change. This is called a JavaScript rollover. It's actually not excessively hard to do, and you don't need to worry about using a plug-in or a Java applet or any of that weird stuff.

"I like to use rollovers because they make the page more responsive. It gives people a good clue as to what's clickable. I think a lot of Web pages err on the side of making their buttons too obscure. Making a 3-D button is good, but if the button actually

ARTIST:
Neil Robertson

ORGANIZATION:
Phinney/Bischoff Design House
614 Boylston Avenue E.
Seattle, WA 98102
206/322-3484
www.pbdh.com
neilr@pbdh.com

SYSTEM:
Power Mac G3/350
Mac OS 8.6
8.5GB storage/256MB RAM

CONNECTIVITY:
DSL

PERIPHERALS:
Apple 17-inch monitor, Sony 15-inch second monitor, Wacom ArtPad II, UMAX S12 scanner, and Fuji DS-7 digital camera

PRIMARY APPLICATIONS:
Adobe GoLive, Adobe Photoshop, BB Edit, Macromedia Fireworks, Macromedia FreeHand, Connectix VirtualPC, Allaire ColdFusion Studio, and Microsoft Personal Web Server

highlights, it calls attention to itself and invites the user to interact with it (8.2). The button is saying, 'Hi, I'm an active element. Click me!'

"You can also preview links to lead the user through your site. When the mouse moves over the link, you can supply information about that link in the status bar (8.3). Instead of simply listing the URL for the page where the link is going to go, which is the way it works by default, you can tell the user, 'Check out the latest news from So-&-So Design,' or whatever. You can spell out the destination in plain English with JavaScript."

Naturally, like any relatively recent advancement, rollovers are not compatible with all browsers. "What I'm doing with rollovers is applicable to Netscape 3.0 and later, as well as Internet Explorer 4.0 and later. Earlier browsers are spotty. Internet Explorer 3.2 for Windows doesn't support rollovers, but Internet Explorer 3.1 for the Mac (which came out later) does. The good news is that JavaScript is officially standardized and all the new browsers support rollovers and all the rest."

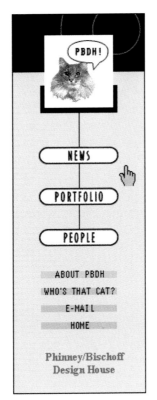 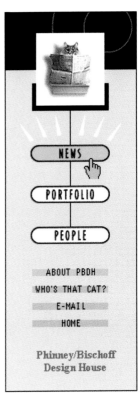

8.2

MOUSE OVER AND OUT

A basic example of rollovers at work is Robertson's home page for Teledesic, a company involved in laying the groundwork for high-bandwidth, satellite-based Internet access (8.4). Most of the page is static, run-of-the-mill HTML. But stretching along the

WORK HISTORY:

1986 — Interned at large Portland ad agency pasting up comps "with real typeset type, no computers," for ads.

1989 — Forced by a hated boss to use his first Mac.

1991 — Forced by beloved boss to create multimedia project in Macromedia Director.

1995 — Moved to Seattle and started work for Phinney/Bischoff Design House.

1996 — Plunged into Web design by creating 1,000-page site for large Texas law firm.

1997 — Began teaching introductory JavaScript night class at Ivey Seright in Seattle.

FAVORITE TELETUBBY CHARACTER:

Tinky-Winkey ("Love the purse.")

bottom is a row of interactive buttons, each of which highlights — from dull blue to bright green — when you hover your cursor over it (8.5). The button changes back to blue when the cursor moves away.

Because this page is so simple, it serves as an excellent introduction to both rollovers specifically and JavaScript in general. So I asked Robertson to bare all, starting with the basic structure of the page and working up to the way he makes the buttons highlight.

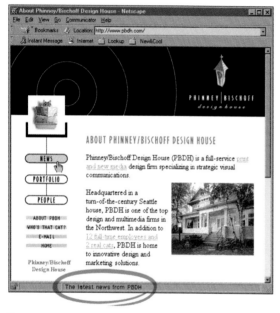

8.3

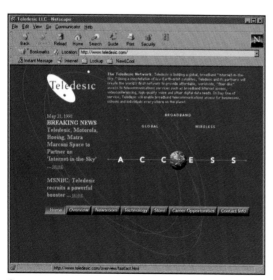

8.4

GIVING JAVASCRIPT THE GAS

"I start with the `<SCRIPT LANGUAGE>` tag. Everything after that is identified by the browser as JavaScript code. Immediately after that line, there's an HTML comment `<!--` (8.6). This tag hides all the JavaScript code from a browser that doesn't understand JavaScript at all. If I didn't have that comment tag in there, all that script would be displayed as text on the page in an old browser.

"The bit after the comment tag `**begin button rollover script**` doesn't really matter; that's just a note to me so I remember what I'm doing. But the comment tag `<!--` is important — HTML thinks everything after the tag is a comment; JavaScript just ignores it and interprets the code as always.

"At the end of the JavaScript code, I have to close the HTML comment tag with the standard `-->`. Now, JavaScript ignores the opening HTML comment tag, but it gets confused by this closing tag. So I have to add JavaScript's comment tag `//` before the HTML closer. As a result, I end up with `//-->` (8.7)."

PRELOADING THE IMAGES

"Before you script your rollovers, you want to preload all the images for the buttons so that they're all in cache, ready to go, when requested by the browser. If the images aren't preloaded, the user would have to wait for a new image to download every time the cursor moves over a button. And by the time the image finally downloads, the user may have moved the cursor elsewhere. There would be a string of lags and it would get pretty ugly.

"With JavaScript, you can preload any graphic as an image object. Do you see `overviewOn = new Image` (8.8)? That creates a new image object called `overviewOn`, which represents the highlighted Overview button. Of course, I don't have to call it `overviewOn`, I'm making up a variable, so I can call it anything I like. The next line, `overviewOn.src`, puts the actual GIF button in the image object. So now whenever I ask for `overviewOn`, I get that specific GIF file."

8.5

```
<HEAD>
<SCRIPT LANGUAGE="Javascript">
<!-- **begin button rollover script**

function hiLiteOn(imgName)
    if (document.images)
        hiLiteImage = eval(imgName + "On.src")
```

8.6

```
    contactOff = new Image()
    contactOff.src = "gifs/2contact.gif"


    }

//-->
</SCRIPT>
```

8.7

```
if(document.images)

    overviewOn = new Image()
    overviewOn.src = "gifs/2overOn2.gif"
    overviewOff = new Image()
    overviewOff.src = "gifs/2over.gif"

    newsroomOn = new Image()
    newsroomOn.src = "gifs/2newsOn2.gif"
    newsroomOff = new Image()
    newsroomOff.src = "gifs/2news.gif"
```

8.8

ENSURING BROWSER COMPATIBILITY

Memorizing which browsers support JavaScript and which specific versions of JavaScript they support is a nearly impossible task. Luckily, you don't have to. "I set up my code so it automatically sorts out whether the browser can handle rollovers or not. And the line of code that's doing this is `if (document. images)` (8.9). This tests if the browser can handle image objects, in which case it can do the rollovers. If it can't, then `if (document.images)` returns a 'no,' and the browser skips the function."

```
function hiLiteOn(imgName) {
    if (document.images) {
        hiLiteImage = eval(imgName+"On.src")
        document [imgName].src = hiLiteImage
        }
    }

function hiLiteOff(imgName) {
    if (document.images) {
        originalImage = eval(imgName+"Off.src")
        document [imgName].src = originalImage
        }
    }

if(document.images) {

    overviewOn = new Image()
    overviewOn.src = "gifs/2overOn2.gif"
    overviewOff = new Image()
    overviewOff.src = "gifs/2over.gif"
```

8.9

"(If you want, you can insert an ~~else~~ script that points people to a different page that says something like, 'To see all the functionality of this page, download a new version of the browser.' But I'd rather just make it seamless. When I'm surfing the Web, I don't want to have to download new browsers and plug-ins. Show me the page or shut up.)"

"You have to run this test each time you define a new function and when you preload the images. That way, you aren't wasting time preloading when the browser's not going to see the images anyway. With `if (document.images)`, nobody will notice that they're missing anything if they use a browser that doe n't support rollovers."

"Next comes `overviewOff`, which is the blue Overview button as it looks when it's not highlighted. Here I repeat the process—I make a new image object and put a GIF image inside it.

"Each time I create a new image object, I'm actually accomplishing two things. I'm defining my variables, so I can call them up later in my script. And I'm telling the browser to store the image in cache. The caching occurs automatically whenever I define a new image object."

CREATING THE ROLLOVERS

After you assign the image objects and cache all the buttons, it's time to script the rollovers. "The row of buttons on the Teledesic page are essentially just a series of `<A HREF>` and `<IMG SRC>` tags. The first image is the Home button, so it doesn't even have an `<A HREF>` link. It's a dead button that's there to show that we're already on the home page (8.10).

"So far, this is all the same kind of stuff you'd do if there weren't any rollovers. The only difference is that I've added the JavaScript commands `onmouseover` and `onmouseout`. These are called *event handlers*. JavaScript is driven by events, whether it's a timed event or an action initiated by the user. If the user moves the cursor over a button, that gets picked up by `onmouseover`. When the cursor moves away from the button, that gets picked up by `onmouseout`. Both of these commands are associated with links, so they have to be inside an `<A HREF>` tag."

```
<CENTER><PRE>
<IMG SRC="gifs/2dhome2.gif"    Home
 width="58" height="23"
 align="bottom" alt="home"
 border="0" name="home">


<A HREF="../finalSite/overview.html"
  onmouseover="hiLiteOn('overview')"
  onmouseout="hiLiteOff('overview')">
  <IMG SRC="gifs/2over.gif"    Overview
   width="70" height="23"
   align="bottom" alt="overview"
   border="0" name="overview"></A>
```

8.10

"To let the browser know what to do when the cursor moves over an image, I say `onmouseover= "hiLiteOn('overview')"`. This is where it gets kind of tricky: `hiLiteOn` isn't a JavaScript command—it's a function that I made up at the beginning of the script in the initial JavaScript section. And `hiLiteOn('overview')` sends `overview` to the function `hiLiteOn`, then the browser looks back to my earlier definition to figure out what it needs to do (8.11).

"Let's go back to the top. At the outset of my script, I have a `function` command. This lets me define my own function, in this case `hiLiteOn`. I also introduce a variable `imgName` which gets replaced by whatever I put in parentheses. So when I call `hiLiteOn('overview')`, the browser places overview into the variable `imgName`. Wherever you see `imgName` in this definition, the browser is thinking `overview`.

"The next line in the definition—`if (document. images)`—just checks to see if the browser understands the image object. If it does, it goes to the line after that. Starting on the right-hand side, I have `(imgName + "On.src")`. In this case, the browser adds `On.src` to `overview` and gets `overviewOn.src`. This is that same image object that I discussed earlier, the one that contains the green Overview button (8.8). So the browser puts `overviewOn.src`—the green button—into `hiLiteImage`, which is the variable on the left."

At this point, Robertson has called up the green button. But he still needs to tell the browser to replace the "off" blue button with the "on" green one. And this is exactly what `document [imgName]. src = hiLiteImage` does. "With JavaScript, every object gets an address. `document` is the address of the document that's open in the current window—in this case, the Teledesic page. The `<IMG SRC>` tag for the Overview button includes the line `name="overview"` (8.10), which tells the browser that the name of the button is `overview`. So the address of the button is `document overview .src`. The line `document [imgName].src = hiLiteImage` just tells the browser to replace the source of the object called `document overview. src` with `hiLiteImage`, which is the green

Overview button." This is one of the strengths of this technique. Both the images and the address for that image share the same name and, thus, you need pass only one variable to the `hiLiteOn` function.

The `onmouseout` line does the opposite, switching out the green button for the blue one when the cursor moves away from the button. This command relies on another function defined by Robertson, this time called `hiLiteOff` (8.12). "As you can see, `hiLiteOff` is more or less identical to `hiLiteOn`. The only difference is that it puts `overview Off.src`—the blue button—into a variable called `originalImage`. But the basic workings are the same."

THE POWER OF FUNCTIONS

Could Robertson have pulled off his rollovers without defining the custom functions at the beginning of his script? "Well, yes and no. You can put some of that function code directly inside the `<A HREF>` tag, but not all of it. For instance, it's a pain in the neck to run an `if` statement inside an `<A HREF>`, so it would have been harder for me to test browser compatibility.

```
<A HREF="../finalSite/overview.html"
  onmouseover="hiLiteOn('overview')"
  onmouseout="hiLiteOff('overview')">
  <IMG SRC="gifs/2over.gif"
    width="70" height="23"
    align="bottom" alt="overview"
    border="0" name="overview"></A>

function hiLiteOn(imgName) {
  if (document.images) {
    hiLiteImage = eval(imgName + "On.src")
    document [imgName].src = hiLiteImage
  }
}

function hiLiteOff(imgName) {
  if (document.images) {
    originalImage = eval(imgName + "Off.src")
    document [imgName].src = originalImage
  }
}
```

8.11

```
<A HREF="../finalSite/overview.html"
   onmouseover="hiLiteOn('overview')"
   onmouseout="hiLiteOff('overview')">
   <IMG SRC="gifs/2over.gif"
   width="70" height="23"
   align="bottom" alt="overview"
   border="0" name="overview"></A>

function hiLiteOn(imgName) {
   if (document.images) {
      hiLiteImage = eval(imgName + "On.src")
      document [imgName].src = hiLiteImage
      }
   }

function hiLiteOff(imgName) {
   if (document.images) {
      originalImage = eval(imgName + "Off.src")
      document [imgName].src = originalImage
      }
   }
```

8.12

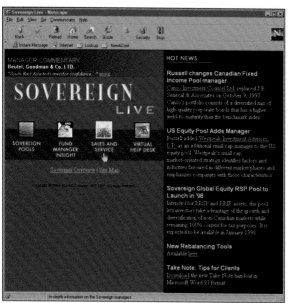

8.13

"But even if I could, I wouldn't have done it. It would have involved a lot more work. What makes the functions useful is that they work regardless of how many images you have highlighting on the page. For each highlight, I can call up a single function instead of entering several lines of code again and again and again. If I want to add another highlighted button, I just add the image names to the preload list, and then call the functions inside the `<A HREF>` tag."

ROLLING IMAGE MAPS

Robertson's next project is a private site he created for Frank Russell Company, an investment consulting firm. The opening page to the site, dubbed Sovereign Live, features an animated GIF title and a group of four rollover buttons (8.13). The border of each rollover button highlights when you move your mouse over it.

But for a more interesting rollover element, you have to surf to the Sales and Service page (8.14). This page features a large image map boasting five rollover buttons (8.15). "The tricky part when working with an image map is that you have to swap out the entire

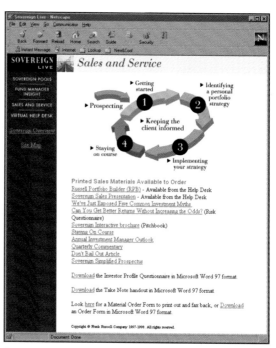

8.14

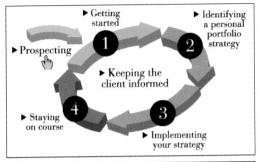

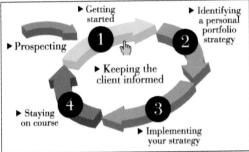

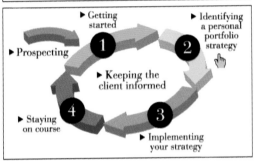

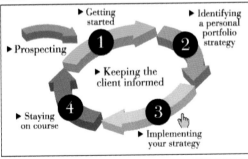

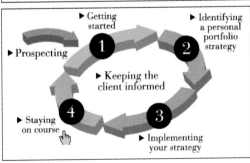

8.15

image. You can't snip out little parts of the image, you have to load the whole thing. That means I have to create a different image for each of the highlighted buttons — five in all — plus a sixth that shows all buttons off."

That's a lot of data. Is any browser smart enough to know which pixels it has cached so it can load only the new ones? "Nope, it has to load each and every pixel. That's why it's a good idea to keep your graphics as small as possible. In the case of the Sovereign Live graphic, I was careful to fill the buttons with flat colors. So while the image map takes up a lot of space on the page, each variation is only about 8K on disk."

THE ROLLOVER FUNCTIONS

"I start my HTML code with a `<SCRIPT>` tag just as before. Then come the functions, `hiLiteOn` and `hiLiteOff`, similar to before (8.16). The main difference is that in the `hiLiteOn` definition, I use a new variable which I call `areaName`. The way I use this variable tells the browser to evaluate the specific area of the image map that the user has moved the cursor over and then display the proper graphic. Also, I add "`.src`" to the end of the image object name instead of "`On.src`".

```
<HTML>

<HEAD>
<SCRIPT LANGUAGE="Javascript">
<!-- **begin button rollover script**

function hiLiteOn(areaName) {
   if (document.images) {
      hiLiteImage = eval(areaName + ".src");
      document.arrows.src=hiLiteImage
      }
   }

function hiLiteOff() {
   if (document.images) {
      document.arrows.src=Base.src
      }
   }
```

8.16

"Then in the function `hiLiteOff`, I switch everything back to the same image. I don't have to build the name, I don't have to send a parameter — whenever the user moves the cursor outside of a hot spot, the image changes to `Base.src`, which is the graphic where no button is highlighted."

Next, Robertson defines and preloads his image objects (8.17). "You can see `Base.src`, which points to the graphic with all buttons off. Then it's `one.src`, `two.src`, and so on for each of the five highlighted buttons. The browser loads all six GIF files into RAM so they're ready to go."

SCRIPTING THE IMAGE MAP

"The image map starts off with the standard HTML `<MAP>` tag (8.18). The first button — the one that starts out `<AREA shape="rect">` — surrounds the central area of the graphic that reads 'Keeping the client informed.' This is the only button that's not a rollover.

"The other buttons start out `<AREA shape="polygon">`, then I name each area `five`, `four`, `three`, `two`, `one`. These names don't go with the numbers in the graphic, they're just the names I assigned the image objects that contain the highlighted buttons (8.19).

```
if(document.images) {

    Base = new Image(407,241);
    Base.src = "serviceGifs/arrowsBase.gif"

    one = new Image(407,241);
    one.src = "serviceGifs/arrows1.gif"

    two = new Image(407,241);
    two.src = "serviceGifs/arrows2.gif"

    three = new Image(407,241);
    three.src = "serviceGifs/arrows3.gif"

    four = new Image(407,241);
    four.src = "serviceGifs/arrows4.gif"

    five = new Image(407,241);
    five.src = "serviceGifs/arrows5.gif"

    }

//-->
</SCRIPT>
```

8.17

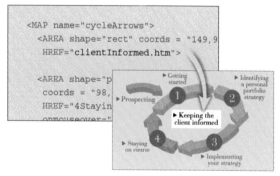

8.18

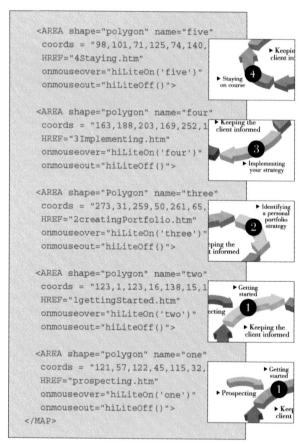

8.19

"At the end of each of button, there's an `onmouseover` and an `onmouseout` command. Here's where I call up the `hiLiteOn` and `hiLiteOff` functions. Notice that I have to put a name in the `hiLiteOn` function so it loads the right image object. But I don't need a name for `hiLiteOff`, because there's just one `Base.src` image."

ADVANCED ROLLOVERS

Like many electronic design firms, Robertson's employer—Phinney/Bischoff Design House—shows off its best scripting techniques at its own Web site (*www.pbdh.com*, 8.20). The site features scads of highlighting buttons (8.21), as well as a couple of extra ingredients.

"When you move your cursor over one of the three main buttons—News, Portfolio, or People—the browser swaps out two images at the same time. One image is the button itself, which changes from white to yellow. The other is an icon that has no connection to the buttons—namely, that picture of the cat (8.22). The changing cat doesn't really serve any purpose, but it's fun and it adds a little extra visual interest to the page."

The browser also displays a special message in the status bar at the bottom of the window. For example, when you hover the cursor over the Portfolio button, the status bar reads, "Browse through our work." Robertson pulls off this little trick with JavaScript as well.

THE DOUBLE-SWAP FUNCTION

"At the outset of the script are the same `hiLiteOn` and `hiLiteOff`—no big deal. After that, there's a new function called `switchIcon` (8.23). It's basically similar to the others, but notice that the `document` line is a little different. In the case of the buttons, the document line includes an `[imgName]` parameter because I can't be sure exactly which button on the page will change out. It could be the first one, it could be the third one. But in the case of

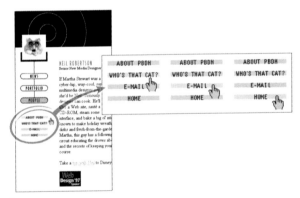

8.21

8.20

8.22

```
<HTML>

<HEAD>
<SCRIPT LANGUAGE="Javascript">
<!-- **begin button rollover script**

function hiLiteOn(imgName) {
  if (document.images) {
    hiLiteImage=eval(imgName+"HiLite.src")
    document [imgName].src=hiLiteImage
    }
  }

function hiLiteOff(imgName) {
  if (document.images) {
    originalImage=eval(imgName+"White.src")
    document [imgName].src=originalImage
    }
  }

function switchIcon(imgName) {
  if (document.images) {
    iconImage=eval(imgName + "Icon.src")
    document.Icon.src = iconImage
    }
  }
```

8.23

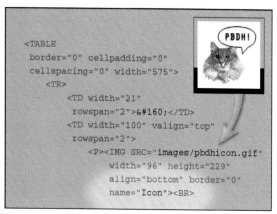

8.24

switch Icon, I'm always swapping out the cat icon. So instead of inventing a special parameter, I refer to it by the fixed address `document.Icon.src`, which refers to the image called `Icon` on the page."

And refresh our memory: How does the browser know that Icon is the cat? "Because later in the HTML file, when I first place the cat icon on the page, I say `name="Icon"` (8.24). This tells JavaScript that this image is called Icon so it can replace it using the `switchIcon` function."

THE DOUBLE-IMAGE SWAP

You may have noticed that the cat icon is part of a table (8.24). Directly following the cat, in that same column, is the News button. "Because it's a link, I script the news button using an `<A HREF>` tag, which includes our old friends `onmouseover` and `onmouseout` (8.25). The `onmouseover` command calls `hiLiteOn`, just like always. I also call the `switchIcon` function, which replaces the cat with the News icon, which shows the cat reading a newspaper in a litter box.

"In that same `onmouseover`, I'm also changing the message in the status bar. JavaScript thinks of the status bar as the `status` object of the window, so the script is `window.status= 'The latest news from PBDH'`. Notice that the text is surrounded by single quotes. That's one thing about JavaScript—nested quotes have to follow a double/

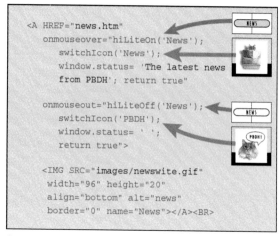

8.25

single/double/single pattern. The whole `onmouse over` script is in double quotes, so anything that needs to be in quotes inside of that goes in single quotes.

"After that is a semicolon and `return true`. This is necessary for the `window.status` line to work." Why is that? "Don't ask me why. It just has to be there. I think JavaScript needs to send back `true` because you're calling . . . you know, I really don't know why. It just does." But it works. "Yes, it does work, and it won't work without it." Well, then, we know all we need to know.

"On the `onmouseout`, I again call multiple functions. I call `hiLiteOff` to reset the button to the plain white version. I call `switchIcon` and change the cat back to the PBDH version. Then I say `window.status=' '` to set the status bar back to empty.

"Incidentally, JavaScript lets you change a lot of different window objects. By saying `window.location=` and then entering a URL, you can tell the browser to go to a different page. For example, you might check with the user to find out what operating system they're using. If they're using Windows, you can switch to one page; if it's a Mac, you can go to another."

MAKING ANIMATED ROLLOVERS

"By the way, since you can use any GIF or JPEG image in a rollover, you can animate a button by calling up an animated GIF (8.26). For example, you can make a button jump up and down when the cursor moves over it and then make it stop when the cursor moves away.

"One caveat, though: Any time you're doing a rollover — whether it's animated or not — the images that you're swapping out have to have the exact same dimension. If they're not the same dimension, the browser will make them the same dimension. So if you try to swap a 50 × 50-pixel button with one that's 100 ×100, the browser will squeeze the second button down to 50 × 50. This means if you want the effect of a button growing and shrinking, you'll want to make sure you build that effect into your original images."

RANDOM ROLLOVER NOTES

With so many scripting languages available to Web designers, why did Robertson take up JavaScript? "I was looking for something beyond flat HTML text on a page. I considered taking up CGI scripting, but CGI is very definitely server-specific. A lot of the Web sites for our clients are hosted on NT boxes or UNIX boxes, and we just don't have those here for me to play around with. I needed a language that I could work on locally, using a typical desktop computer. JavaScript was something manageable that I could pick up and learn on my own and start integrating into my pages right away."

Are rollovers one of the easier elements you can create with JavaScript? "Not really — at least, not the way I do it. There are easier ways to make rollovers, but the way I do it makes them easier to maintain and adapt to different kinds of uses. My way also makes the rollovers easier to test, so the user isn't met with an annoying error message when an image object doesn't work."

How does Robertson code his pages? "I use Adobe GoLive to set up the basic layout of the page, but I

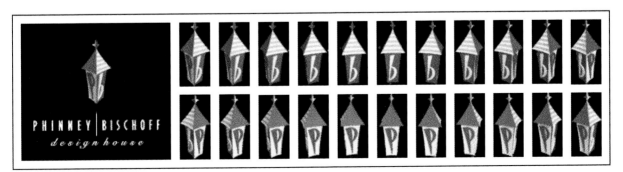

8.26

hand-code all the JavaScript. The great thing about GoLive is that not only doesn't it mess up my JavaScript code when I put it in, but it even has a nice little script editing environment and tools built right in, unlike some versions of PageMill or FrontPage, which might actually break the code.

"There are programs out there like Macromedia Dreamweaver that do JavaScript for you. But it's just like any HTML editor — it's really a good idea if you know what's going on under the hood so you can look at it and say, 'Okay, this is right,' or, 'Gee, I need to fix this.' I've used Dreamweaver a little bit, and while it seems pretty good — it's actually amazing what it does — like all the visual editors, it generates a lot of unnecessary code. So there's always a trade-off."

MI CODA ES SU CODA

I suspect our last question is the one that will most interest readers of this chapter: Is your code sufficiently adaptable that other designers can lift it and integrate it into their own pages. "Oh sure, feel free to copy my functions verbatim and use them any way you want to. For what it's worth, I didn't write this code from scratch. I've looked at the various ways that other people have done rollovers, tested out a few different refinements, and boiled down the code to get it as tight as I could. But like everyone else out there, I'm standing on a lot of other people's shoulders. If you want to jump on board, that's fine by me."

PART II
SPECIFIC
APPLICATIONS

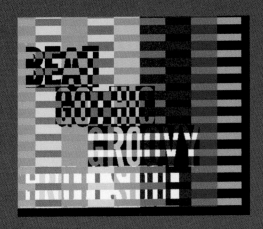

CHAPTER 9
SITE MANAGEMENT AND WORKFLOW TECHNIQUES

W elcome to the second half of the book. We thought we were going to lose a couple of you during the intermission, but here you are. Hope you managed to snag one of the free cocktails that were making the rounds. Participants in our focus groups tell us they enjoyed the book much more when they were looped.

Now that we've examined some of the more fundamental principles of electronic design, we thought we'd kick off Part II with a chapter that divides the amateurs from the pros. In the following pages, we learn the answers to two important questions: What does it mean to "produce" a site, and why should you care? This chapter tells how one producer brings together diverse talents to create great on-line content, while making sure the client falls madly in love with the results. Or as this chapter's artist puts it, "I make sure everyone's on the same page at the same time."

The producer in question is Kelly Goto. A graduate of UCLA's earliest multimedia program, Goto has produced and designed some of the most ambitious multimedia projects published to either CD-ROM or the Internet. Her clients range from the usual media titans (9.1) to button-down corporate interests in the banking and healthcare industries (9.2). She routinely handles big budgets and manages large teams of designers and programmers.

It's all about effective communication. You have to develop ways to communicate with all the different players in the process.

KELLY GOTO

9.1

9.2

ARTIST:
Kelly Goto

ORGANIZATION:
Gotomedia
San Francisco: 415/957-7701
Los Angeles: 310/915-3141
www.gotomedia.com
kgoto@aol.com
kelly@gotomedia.com

SYSTEM:
PowerBook G3/400
Mac OS 9.0
6GB storage/128MB RAM

CONNECTIVITY:
Shared T1, DSL

PERIPHERALS:
Viewsonic 21-inch monitor
Epson ES-1200C scanner

PRIMARY APPLICATIONS:
Microsoft Word, Excel, Inspiration, Visio,
Adobe Photoshop, GoLive, Illustrator,
Macromedia Flash

WORK HISTORY:
1988 — Participated in first multimedia
program at UCLA; created first project in
Macromedia Director.

On first blush, the art of Web site production may strike some as a wee bit esoteric. But if you're looking to attract higher-profile clients or simply to work more efficiently with the clients and coworkers you have, then this information should be right up your alley.

So again, welcome to the second half of the book, where general design techniques run headlong into the real world.

WHAT IT MEANS TO PRODUCE

The producer is the person who supervises the artists, manages the costs, meets the deadlines, and keeps the client happy. According to Goto, "The first job of a good producer is to find out what the client needs from a site. Clients often have unrealistic expectations of what you can do. They know they want all the bells and whistles, but they don't know what it takes or how much it costs. It's my job to educate the client and tell them how much technology they need to meet their goals. After a careful survey of the client's needs, I help them figure out what they want to do, how much it will cost, and how their decisions will impact their users."

If Goto could sum up what she does in one word, it would start with a capital *C*. "It's all about effective communication. You have to develop ways to communicate with all the different players in the process. In this day and age, we communicate with groups of people, not just individuals. So I think the most important thing is to establish methods of communication that work with the different groups. Some of these people are left-brainers, some are right-brainers. We have artists talking to designers and designers talking to programmers. Then we have the client who doesn't understand any of them.

"I have to talk to everyone. If I can communicate the key issues — urgency, priorities, and all the specifics of when the project needs to be completed and how it needs to look — to all parties, then I've done my job. That's the secret. You can put together schedules and programs and budgets. But it's when you convey the necessity of meeting the schedule — when someone looks up and says, 'Oh, my god, this is due next week! I've got to jam!' — that's when you know that you've got everybody's attention and they're on track."

1990 — Hired at Marina Del Ray–based design firm; art directed photography and layout for entertainment clients and Infinity Car collateral.

1994 — Started own business, Goto Design/Media, with clients Gramercy Pictures, Paramount Domestic Television, and Warner Bros.

1995 — Became Senior Producer at Warner Brothers Online; launched sites for Babylon 5 and Rosie O'Donnell.

1997 — Began freelancing in the Bay Area, producing sites for National Geographic and Wells Fargo Online.

1999 — Is a Web consultant and lecturer with a focus on workflow, usability, and information design. Clients include Petstore.com, Webvan, and Food.com.

FAVORITE X-MEN CHARACTER

Kitty Pride, a.k.a., Shadow Cat ("She can move through walls, but her real strengths are her intelligence and problem-solving abilities.")

What kind of background does it take to be a good producer? "You have to be able to put yourself in other people's shoes, so you know the way they think and you know what they need. In the past, I did jobs without a separate producer. I just did the whole thing myself, starting from scratch from concept to design and final production. So I've worn the hats of the designer and the artist. And though I'm not a technical expert, I know enough so that I can go in and fix somebody else's code. I've also hired people to create elements for me, so I know what it's like to be the client. You want to know what's going on — good or bad, you just want to know.

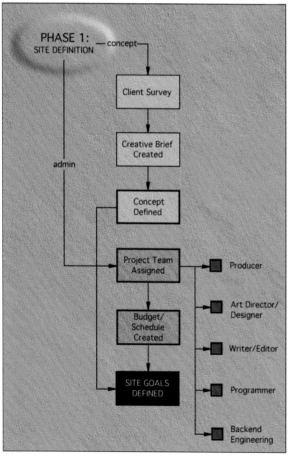

9.3

"Anyone with skills in a variety of different areas can be an effective producer. You just have to find ways to communicate with people who are thinking in different ways than you are. Clients, programmers, designers, CGI and JavaScript guys, the ISP — everyone has needs that have to be met. And you're the one who has to meet them, every step of the way."

THE FIVE PHASES OF WEB DESIGN WORKFLOW

Short of hiring Goto and having her take care of your site for you, what steps can you take to produce an effective site that meets your client's realistic expectations? And more important, how do you do it on budget and on time?

"Although every Web project is going to differ in content, size, and functionality, there's a basic structure that I always follow. From large to small sites, you can work through them in this same way. First you develop the site, then you define the structure, then you create the interface, then you get the technical specifics in order, and finally you publish it online. I call these the 'Five Phases.' Follow these steps, make sure that you keep a running dialog with your team and your client, and you'll get through the experience in one piece."

PHASE 1: SITE DEFINITION

The first step is to define the site. Goto's flow chart of the process shows two tracks, one conceptual and one administrative (9.3). "The conceptualization of the site begins with the client. Once a project has been assigned, you need to sit down with the client and define the goals. What is the overall concept? What is the purpose — what kind of message do they want to convey? What kind of content do they want to include? How do they want to see it organized? What kind of visual style are they looking for? What are their technical needs? You also need to work out the budget, the timeline, when they want what, and the schedule.

"At this same time, you're assembling your project team. You need to decide what people you need, what kind of programmer, a writer, an editor, what kind of back-end engineering you're going to have, the artists, and designers." But Goto cautions that you shouldn't feel compelled to pigeonhole each member of your team in a specific slot. "Collaboration is the secret to a great Web site. Because of the changing nature of roles as we know them, many individuals wear multiple hats when working on projects. You may find it very helpful to allow and even encourage roles to overlap. You need to make your people feel creative and engaged, so they're all partners in the outcome.

"Phase 1 is the preplanning stage, where you get everything together. A lot of people don't take the time to do this because they don't think they have the time. But you've got to build the initial planning into the process. Otherwise, you're going to suffer in the end, when you can least afford it. Proper planning and organization from the outset is the most important part of creating an effective site."

FRASIER'S CRANIUM

Goto thoughtfully provided us with several examples of her trade. While no one project absolutely sums up her style or the way in which she works — after all, every project is different — many of the examples help to demonstrate the various phases in action. To start with, we'll look at a promotional CD-ROM for the television show *Frasier* that Goto produced for Paramount Pictures.

"The *Frasier's Cranium* CD was designed to promote the rerelease of *Frasier* into syndicated television. It went out to all advertisers and affiliates around the country. The CD is really just a collection of promotional photographs and audio clips, which you access by clicking on different parts of Frasier's forehead (9.4). It's a fun, fully interactive piece. There are random audio clips from the show and theme music and graphics that help to create the environment. We created the interface in MTropolis. Even though this is a CD project — it was never intended for the Web — the basic approach is the same.

9.4

© *1997 Paramount Pictures. All Rights Reserved.*
Design Firm: Lawrence Co, www.lawrenceco.com
Art Director/Programmer: Scott Tobin

"Normally, I like to get involved in the creative end of things. But some projects take so much time and require so many people that you have to step back and work strictly as a producer. That's what I did with Frasier. This means that I'm working directly with the client, putting together which information needs to go where, what buttons need to be active, what kind of action has to take place, what sound bites they need, and so on. I'm also in charge of putting together schedules and budgets that work, and then getting everyone — both the client and my team — to stick to them.

"A project like this starts with a simple interface, but putting it all together is a complicated task. The first thing is to create the site map to show everything that the client wants to show. I have to map it all out so an artist can take it and know what needs to appear on each screen. There are a lot of pieces involved — and, of course, the content is the one thing that always lags. It doesn't matter what the project is, getting content from the client takes forever. They're often creating the content at the same time you're building your project, so you have to figure that into the schedule."

FROM SURVEY TO SIGN OFF

"**W**hen you begin putting together a site for a client, it's a good idea to make up a survey to find out what kind of site the client wants. It doesn't say, 'What do you want your Web site to look like?' It asks who their target audience is, what kind of visual sense does the company already have, what message do they want to convey? This gives you a sense of their expectations and what kind of audience they're trying to reach.

"From all these questions, you put together a 'Creative Brief.' Take what you perceive to be the client's expectations and put it in your own words. Then have the client sign off on it. When I talk to the client, I frequently use print media terms. A lot of people come from a print background, so they can relate. When I have clients sign off on each phase, I say things like, 'This is the comp, this is the blueline, this is the finished piece.' Most clients already understand that once they sign off on the blueline, it becomes their responsibility. They can't blow off the blueline; they have to take a close look at it.

"After they've signed off, we have change orders. I try to keep people in line and not let them ask for impossible things. If you set the standard right at the beginning — this is when you signed off, this is what was sent to you, this is what you accepted — then they understand they have to accept responsibility for further changes."

NW FEDERAL CREDIT UNION

Few of us can attract clients with quite as much profile as Paramount Pictures. So in the interests of providing some balance and transitioning our attentions to the Web, Goto also walked us through a site she created for a local banking firm, NW Federal Credit Union (*www.nwfcu.com*) (9.5).

"This is a great site. It's not high profile and it's not glamorous. It's a medium-sized project with a small budget. It really demonstrates how you can be a Web producer on a modest, local scale. Most producers are working in small to medium-sized companies. They have limited means to add multimedia elements, CGI scripts, and that kind of thing, so they have to choose wisely. And they have to get the site done in a certain time frame. The NW Federal Credit Union site came in on time and on budget, and the client was really happy with it.

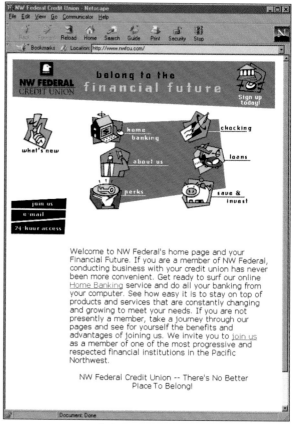

9.5   *Design Firm: Phinney Bischoff Design House, www.pbdh.com*
                                                                Designer: Dean Hart

"The client's goal for this site was to create something that was completely antitechnical. The credit union wanted to encourage their current members to get in the habit of doing their home banking on-line. So we had to come up with something that was fun, friendly, and easy to interact with."

But as with most companies who are itching to make a splash on the Web, NW Federal Credit Union required some education. "The credit union was not at all technically savvy. They had seen all these new fancy things on the Web and they wanted to do everything. It was up to me to explain what was possible and what was simply beyond their means."

From a programming perspective, the most complicated aspect of the credit union site was the CGI scripting, which was required to process the electronic bank forms (9.6). "There was a lot of back-and-forth work with the CGI. We ended up using the CGI programmers that were available at the hosting site. When working with CGI scripters, it's almost always better if you hire folks that work at the ISP. That way, they have direct access to the servers. It makes it easier to test out the scripts and make sure there are no problems. Plus, a lot of times the CGI stuff you're doing is common enough that the ISP guys can repurpose stuff they've already done. You pay less money because they don't have to write the whole thing from scratch."

PHASE 2: DEVELOPING SITE STRUCTURE

"During the second phase, you meet with your team to map out how the site is going to work and what it's going to look like (9.7). The first step is to develop a 'site map,' which is basically a big flow chart that shows how the content will be organized. I use a program called Inspiration. You can get a demo at *www.inspiration.com.* Inspiration is fantastic — you can whip site maps out fast and it's really easy to use.

"Your site map should show every key page in the site and how it relates to the others. Technical notes and main links should appear here as well. It's important to have the client sign off on the site map and note any changes — like taking away or adding pages — that might have an impact on the budget.

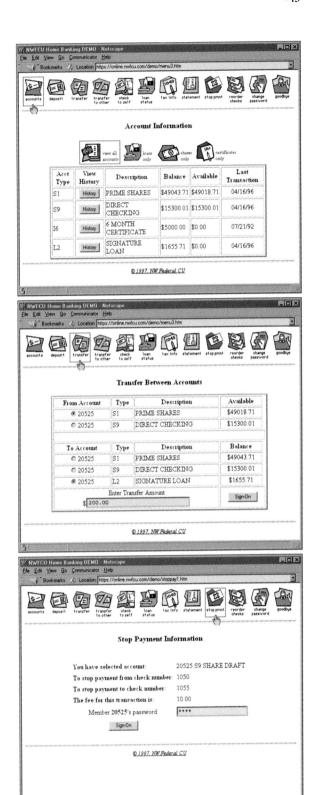

9.6

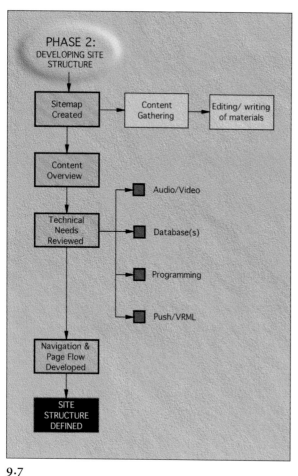

9.7

9.8

"If the client is providing all the content, you need to schedule the transfer of materials. This always takes longer than you think. There are usually several people who you have to get the content from, even in a small company. If you're responsible for some of the content, you need to meet with your writers and editors and get them on a tight schedule as well. This is also the time to discuss the site's technical needs with your artists and programmers.

"Next, you want to decide how the navigation is going to work. How will the user flow through the site? Which pages are accessible from where? You also need to decide what kind of naming conventions you're going to use. What is the folder structure for the files? The naming convention is the secret code that gets used by programmers and artists alike. You don't want each member of the team naming files and sticking them in folders without any direction. It'll turn into a mess fast and you'll have to rename everything at the end. The navigation and naming conventions make up the backbone that the rest of the project builds from."

THE ROSIE O'DONNELL SHOW

An example of a project that required special attention to structure is *The Rosie O'Donnell Show* on America Online (keyword: Rosie) (9.8). "Rosie O'Donnell was a good challenge for me. I took it from start to finish. I designed and produced the site and put together the content. All the while, I was relying heavily on a remote staff. We had about 30 remote staffers in all."

Goto's biggest challenge was developing a site where a community of home workers, children, and other computer novices could take root and flourish. "I had to organize a community for the AOL site that ran parallel to the TV show. In reality, communities create themselves, but controlling them is difficult. AOL is more limited in the ways you can kick disruptive people out of a chat room. And that was a problem, because everyone's a Rosie fan. We had to think about both kids and adults coming to this site," most of whom are used to the relative structure and safety of network TV.

"But if you create the proper guidelines up front and you assemble a staff who knows what they're doing, then you can accomplish anything. Create a chain of command and it runs a lot smoother. We started off with six chat hosts and ended up with 30, most of whom were voluntary. Every host was an adult who was trained in how to control a room.

"We developed software to say hello to every person entering the room. We had different themes — a Saturday morning cartoons chat, sing-alongs, even a virtual-reality room. One room had bean bag chairs on one side, vending machines on the other, and you could interact with it, like a real rec room. People who are very, very used to chats are familiar with these things, but newbies aren't at all. They don't know how to interact or talk. But with proper supervision, the site just grew and grew. It turned into one of the biggest successes that AOL has ever had. Her AOL Live chats were incredibly popular, with thousands and thousands of people."

GO WEST WITH LEWIS AND CLARK

To communicate how she wants the individual pages in a site to look, Goto creates what she calls a "content bible." The bible contains placeholders for text and graphics so that the artists and programmers have a sense of the finished appearance of the site. "When I was creating the Lewis and Clark site for National Geographic (*www.nationalgeographic.com/features/97/west*, 9.9), I created a content bible to show everyone what they were working toward (9.10). Obviously, it was just for internal purposes, something that I handed out to members of my team. The bible showed the pixel dimensions of each element on the page, from the frames down to the National Geographic Kids logo. I also included naming conventions."

"The site came out at the same time as the Ken Burns PBS documentary. The illustrations come from a book by Rosalyn Schanzer. Kids explore with Lewis and Clark and make decisions on each page. The map on the right builds itself as you go on your journey, so you can scroll through it and look where you've been. Because Lewis and Clark didn't have any maps, the map gets made as you go along — you can't

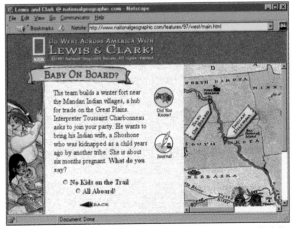

9.9

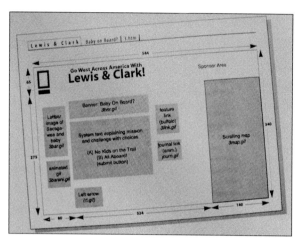

9.10

see any further than you've been. The map is actually a bunch of GIF images arranged in vertical strips. I hired out CGI and JavaScripters to piece them together. Because the map gets filled out incrementally, kids can go through at their own pace, make choices, and see the consequences, just like Lewis and Clark did."

PHASE 3: INTERFACE DESIGN AND PRODUCTION

"The next step is to define the basic interface of your site (9.11). A lot of designers start at this point, but then you run the risk of making your content fit the interface. It's better to work the other way around. After you've finished Phases 1 and 2, you know everything you need to know to do the interface right. You know the goals of the site, you know the navigation, and you know the content. Now you're ready to put together the graphic 'look and feel.'

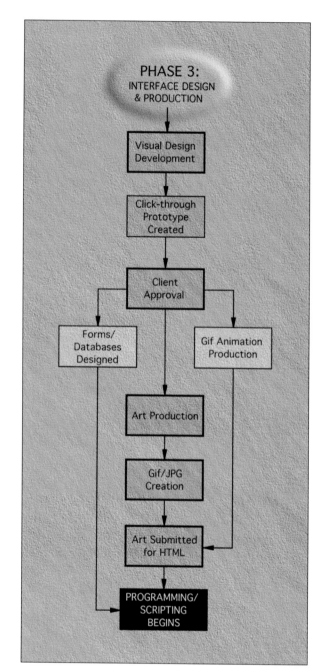

9.11

"Teamwork becomes very important at this point. You have to work closely with your artists and programmers to come up with design elements that work within Web standards. You have to work as a unit to keep file sizes down, come up with efficient uses of color, and establish a clear and consistent visual direction. It's tempting to go nuts with the graphics, but you have to reign it in. A good rule of thumb is to figure that 1K of data takes about a second to download. So a 30K image takes 30 seconds to draw on the user's screen. That's about as much patience as anyone has on the Web. So a single page — the whole thing, including graphics, everything — should be less than 30K.

"I think it's also a good idea to create a 'click-through prototype,' which is a working HTML mock-up of the site that you can test in different browsers and show to the client. Make sure the client takes time to experiment with the prototype. Get them to sign off on it. It's very important that they understand that the prototype represents the actual interface for the site."

EXPEDITION '95

A project that resonates with purposeful interface and strong visual design is a CD-ROM that Goto produced for Paramount Domestic Television. The project, called Expedition '95 (9.12), was a multimedia mock-up of ad campaign ideas and identity treatments for Paramount's budding television station, which eventually became UPN.

© 1995 Toolbox Productions. Design Firm: Gotomedia. Digital Artist: TcChang

9.12

9.13

"We created Expedition '95 to show that the company I was working for could do the naming, advertising, and on-air promotions. This was before there was a UPN. The executives at Paramount Television were still trying to decide if they wanted to get involved with a new television network. For the presentation, we bound the printed notes in a metal book that I had cast, bound, and fired. All the advertising and sales materials were inside. Then at the back of the book was the CD-ROM. We had to put the whole thing together in two weeks. It was one of the slickest presentations I ever worked on.

"The CD contained a series of suggested logos, ad spots, and marketing timelines. The flagship of the new network was *Star Trek: Voyager*. They hadn't started producing the series yet, so there was no real material to work from. We just had this concept of a woman captain, so we came up with promotional storyboards from that. I decided to animate them, so at the bottom of the Campaign screen there are three icons that turn yellow when you mouse over them (9.13). If you click on a button, it tells a story. I had an illustrator draw a series of sketches on paper. To animate the sketches, I took a video camera and moved

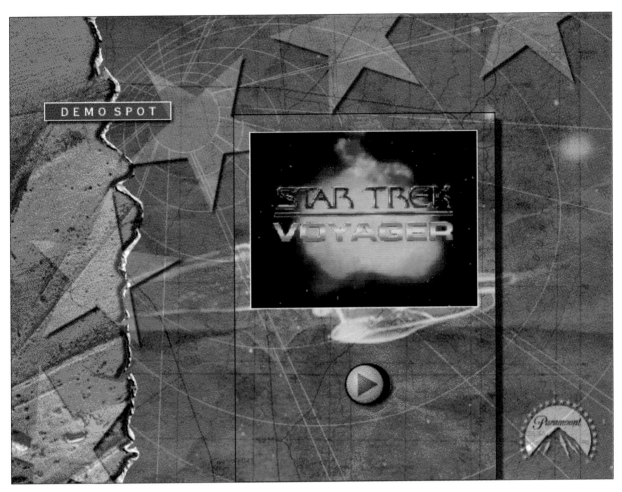

9.14

the paper under the camera. Then I edited the video, added sound, and put together a moving storyboard.

"Another area shows a color demo spot for *Voyager* (9.14). We hired an artist to put it together on an SGI machine. It has lots of explosions and planets flying around. The voice-over is by the same man they later hired for the real on-air commercials.

"I really like to create prototypes for my clients. For Paramount, we could have put together storyboards. And in the old days, we probably would have. But prototypes are better. The client gets a better sense of how the project will look on screen."

UCSC NETTRAIL

Another advantage to putting together a prototype is that it permits you to perform quick-and-dirty usability studies. A prototype can even come in handy when trying to demonstrate how something shouldn't be done. Consider the case of one somewhat recalcitrant client, the University of California at Santa Cruz.

"The UCSC NetTrail was a four-part modular training system for freshmen coming into the University of California system (9.15). It's a secured, intranet site that teaches students how to use e-mail, how to use their browsers, how to search, and how to use the library research resources. It is a big on-line tutorial so every freshman can become fluent in UCSC's computer system.

"The idea was to come up with a basic template that they could then use for each branch of the university. Then all of the UC schools will have their own proprietary on-line education system for students."

But conflicts arose. "I had a few problems with the content. The professors wrote the material and they didn't think that they needed any designers messing around with it. They didn't even like the idea of a graphical interface. The professors wanted to write the content and have it be from their school and that was it. It turned into an us-versus-them thing.

"But after we put together a prototype and they tested the site on a few students, they realized that they needed to make some changes. The students couldn't get through it; they would get to certain parts and stall out. And the content was confusing. The content was not action-oriented. It didn't explain what the student was supposed to do in simple terms—what you were supposed to do next. When the whole thing was put together, they realized that the style of content and the interface really did matter after all.

"The compromise was that we weren't allowed to cut any content, but we did put in markers and graphics to help students know where they were. That's why we came up with the metaphor of the trail (9.16). When the students go through the site, they understand that they're on a trail and here's where they go next.

"What I've found is, people don't have a lot of patience on-line. A lot of people think you can just

9.15

© 1997 Electravision, LLC
Design Firm: Electravision, LLC
Art Director: Lisa Lopuck

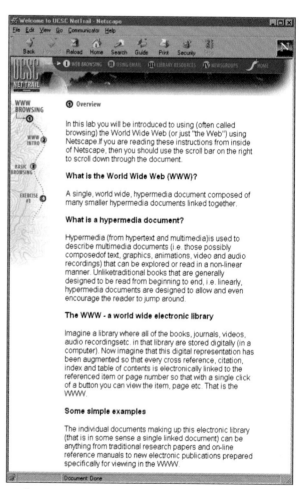

9.16

transfer a brochure directly to the Web, but it's not true. When you're on-line, you expect immediate results. You want to get on and off, not meander through one page after another. There's not a lot of time to explain technicalities or go into philosophy. The Web is not a reading experience. You move through it, you get what you need, and you get off."

PHASE 4: TECHNICAL ENGINEERING

"After you get the design and layout the way you want it, you can start work on the site engineering (9.17). By engineering, I mean all the technical aspects of the site—the real HTML scripting, tables and frames, CGI forms, databases, and all the other programming."

Phase 4 also includes the testing and proofing of the site. "It's critical for everyone involved in the creation of the site—including the client—to be involved in the testing and proofing stage. The more people you get, the more problems you'll catch. I try to make it really clear that problems are going to be found across the board and that no one should start pointing fingers. You want to foster an atmosphere where everyone feels like they're helping each other out.

"The proofing stage is also a great way to get your client involved so that they feel like they're a part of the team. But make sure you give the client some guidelines, preferably a form to fill out. I usually print the entire site out, page by page, and hand the document to each person responsible for proofing. This seems to be the easiest way to take notes and make changes.

"You need to test every browser you can get your hands on. There are some weird ones out there that people don't think of. For instance, Internet Explorer 2 comes preconfigured with a lot of Windows NT machines. You also need to test different platforms, multiple screen sizes, and different modem speeds.

"When testing the site, you can host it from your own computer using a program like Microsoft Personal Web Server, which is available with Internet Explorer 3. You can even password-protect the site to make sure it stays private until the site goes live."

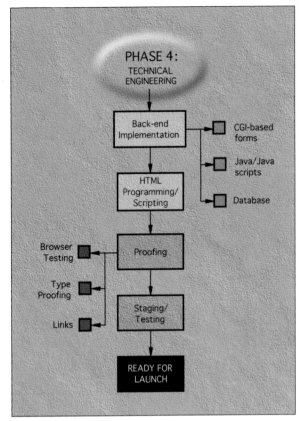

9.17

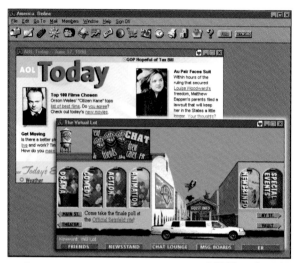

9.18   © *1996 Warner Bros. Online*

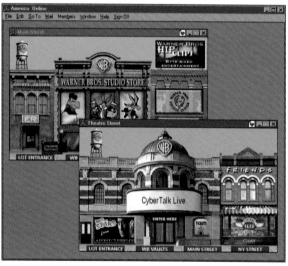

9.19

THE VIRTUAL LOT

An example of a project where an interface problem became apparent in the final testing phase is The Virtual Lot (9.18). "The Virtual Lot is an AOL site for Warner Brothers. The idea is that you're on a movie lot where you can check out information about Warner Brothers' TV shows such as *Friends* and *Murphy Brown*.

"The executives in charge of the project wanted an environmental interface, so you felt like you were at a place. You can go down different streets, enter a subway, and visit a theater (9.19). Not only was it friendlier, they felt, but it was an excellent way to go after a new advertising model. They called it 'environmental advertising.' For instance, you're walking down a street and you pass by a store, that store just happens to be 1-800-FLOWERS. It's more clever than a banner ad and it's not just sitting there flashing in your face.

"This premise worked great as an advertising model. They had a lot of high-end advertisers, but it wasn't a completely satisfying user experience because the pages took so long to download. I had a real problem with that. I wanted to develop interfaces that were user friendly, that were easy to interact with, and that downloaded quickly and lent themselves to continuous updating. We're still learning on every project how to better satisfy both users and advertisers on the Web."

PHASE 5: PUBLISHING AND MARKETING

By now, Goto has devoted a couple of months of her life to the site. "With a team of two to five artists and programmers, a big project typically takes about eight weeks. I've turned a few around as quickly as six weeks, but that's awfully tight." After the site is complete, Phase 5 kicks in. This is when you publish the site, promote it, and begin planning the updates (9.20).

The marketing process is so important that we analyze it in detail in Chapter 14. But Goto is equally concerned with what happens to the site after she leaves it. "Once the site is up on the Web, it's important to have a maintenance schedule in place for at least six months out. Always make sure that there is a way that the client can perform the updates. You may want to help them put together a maintenance schedule. Make sure they know that it's their responsibility, but try to make it as straightforward as you can. You don't want to leave them with a mess that they can't handle — that generates bad will.

"I also like to include little randomizing elements, so that the site looks a little different every time someone visits it, even if it hasn't been updated. You can create scripts that tell the time and date. You can also make randomized graphics and animations. Most JavaScript programmers can put this stuff together really easily. I know it's somewhat of a gimmick, but it helps keep the site fresh.

"You want your site to continue to look good long after you leave it. You want it to remain something you're proud of. Obviously, you can't make the client keep up the site exactly the way you would. But you can put schedules and conventions in place so that everyone has what they need to do it right."

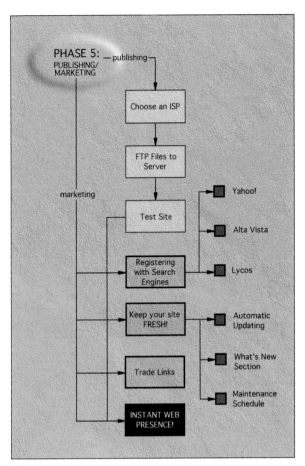

9.20

CHAPTER 10
CREATING DATABASE-DRIVEN SITES

I n Web language, *brochureware* is a dirty word. It refers to sites that are collections of static pages, often little more than recreations of print promotional materials. These sites don't take advantage of the medium's strengths, such as interactivity, personalization, and dynamic content. They're time-consuming to update, and they're difficult to expand if a company's online presence grows. Static sites are still appropriate in a small fraction of cases, but the majority of designers—and their clients—want more. They need active, database-driven sites.

Databases are core components of the modern Web. They're essential to e-commerce sites, the cash cow for many design firms today. You could call including an online form with a credit-card field e-commerce, but for client- and customer-pleasing actions like tracking buying habits and account history, searching for products, and manipulating information in a secure, password-protected environment, only database-driven sites deliver the goods.

"Everything's becoming dynamic, transactional, modular," says Michel Milano. "It's the standard now." Milano is a senior interaction designer/developer at Metrius, formerly Studio Verso, a Web design firm in San Francisco.

Everything's becoming dynamic, transactional, modular.

MICHEL MILANO

Milano is well suited to creating database-driven sites. He began his undergraduate studies in engineering before earning a degree in graphic design. His comfort with computer programming (he regularly out-programmed his high-school teachers) led him to Macromedia Director projects in college and in professional positions after graduation. "I solved visual design problems and communication issues while crafting coding and addressing technology requirements of Director and CD-ROMs. Single- and double-speed CD-ROMs introduced bandwidth issues. It was like a microcosm of the Web."

Milano believes Web designers should be strong technically as well as artistically, though he recognizes the challenges. "It's obviously a more complicated medium these days. You need to understand limitations and advantages and compromises of HTML, browsers, and Internet connection speeds. Then there's a site's technical infrastructure: the Web server, the application server, and the database system. Coordinating all these elements and constructing a site that manages to be beautiful visually and performs well technically is not easy. But designers have to understand and work in these worlds. You must be able to communicate with the technology team."

WHAT IS A DATABASE?

Milano defines *database* loosely. "Databases are passive collections and organizations of information. They can be small or large. On the Web, they're managed by a variety of software, from downloadable shareware like My SQL to multimillion dollar Oracle application systems."

He describes how database-driven sites work: "At one end is a database. At the other are users and the data. In between is active coding that interfaces with the data. It's like a warehouse. No matter what the size, you need standard doorways into the warehouse, and trucks to move the boxes from this shelf to that shelf, and a conveyor belt to bring a box to the front when you purchase it." The boxes are chunks of data, and code such as server-side Java and CGI scripts are the trucks and conveyor belts.

Databases come in so many colors, flavors, and sizes, and the technology changes so quickly, that it's pointless to describe them in detail. "Getting a holistic understanding of the complexity of database-driven sites is more relevant to designers," Milano believes. "You do need to know technical issues, but at some point you just work collaboratively with your technical team to evaluate what's doable."

ARTIST:
Michel Milano

ORGANIZATION:
Metrius
512 Second St., Suite 100
San Francisco, CA 94107
415/278-9900
www.metrius.com
mmilano@metrius.com

SYSTEM:
Apple Macintosh G3/300
Mac OS 8.6
9GB storage/128MB RAM

CONNECTIVITY:
Work: T1
Home: 56K modem

PRIMARY APPLICATIONS:
Bare Bones Software BBEdit 5, Adobe Photoshop 5.5, Adobe Acrobat 4, Macromedia FreeHand 8, Equilibrium DeBabelizer 3, flowcharting software (various)

WORK HISTORY:
<u>1980s</u> — Discovered programming on a Tandy TRS-80 with state-of-the-art storage drive (cassette). Messed around with

WORKFLOW

Although database-driven sites range in size, larger sites tend to be more challenging. There may be many people working on the site, and schedules often dictate that the design and development team members create simultaneously.

Milano is accustomed to working under these conditions. One thing he relies on is a workflow process developed by his company. The process has three phases:

"The initial phase revolves around the discovery approach. We research the market, look into the company's business process, ask their requirements for the Web site, and so on. One of the products of this research are the infrastructure needs." The team, which at this point involves mainly an information architect, project manager, business strategist, lead designer, and technology lead, come up with a vision for the site.

In phase 2, the site's visual design comes into focus. "We set up the visual language and the interface, and we come up with increasingly tangible objects by working through prototypes, revisions, and comps. Both the technical and visual teams use the functional prototype, which began in phase 1." In phase 2, the lead designer and technology lead are the principal figures.

the big Macintosh assembler on an Apple II. Particularly fascinated by self-modifying code.

<u>1994</u> — Designed and built first Web site. Took down site the next day due to personal dissatisfaction.

<u>1997</u> — Played with Java. Pente game first compiled.

<u>1999</u> — Was team lead on designing 14th commercial Web site.

MOST NEFARIOUS THING YOU'VE DONE WITH COMPUTERS:

"In high school, we crashed the high-school server repeatedly. The teachers couldn't figure out how we could do such a thing, much less pin it on us, although they knew in their hearts that we did it. It seems a little mean now, but at the time it was good fun."

Milano calls phase 3 the technical or implementation phase. The technology lead is the primary player. Once design and technical components are finalized, the technology team writes the HTML, builds the database, and weaves all the elements together. Finally, team members from the designer to the engineer test the site in alpha and beta.

Although the process works well for Milano, he says that it can be a "double-edged sword. It's a great framework from which to approach projects. Especially as sites increase in complexity, the process can put them into understandable categories. But it can become dogma. It's a tool set, not the end result."

Another key to successful workflow is the recognition that each member of the process—and the team—is necessary. "No one piece is more important than the other overall. But at any particular point in the project, certain components have greater primacy than others. Designers need to communicate and work closely with the entire team."

10.1

Designers working on the visual aspects of large sites may have to relinquish the traditional pride of ownership. "So many changes are made during a site's evolution," Milano points out. "Sometimes you see the end result and you wonder, 'Is this the same site?' "

DOCUMENTS ARE KEY TO SUCCESS

Databases bring a complexity that necessitates careful planning and record-keeping during the design and development process. Milano's toolbox includes several kinds of documentation: site maps, user flows, functional prototypes, design style guides, and structural experience views. He says they share one purpose: "to facilitate communication among team members so that everybody can have the same source of information and reference points."

Although his roles on site teams vary, Milano's current title is senior interaction designer/developer. When he works on a site's interactive aspects, two fruits of his labor are a site map and a user flow. These core documents "transcend particular visual solutions" to describe a site's building blocks (the site map) and how a user might progress through them (the user flow). They're "focal points for team members and for the client," Milano says. "Clients can step through them conceptually," and they help team members build a common vision.

Also important is the functional prototype, which Milano terms an HTML-based translation of the site map and user flow. "It's a bare-bones interface that you can click through. Because it's tangible, everyone can start wrapping their hands and heads around the ideas it represents. It also shows you how the design does and doesn't work. You can mock up situations that may prove to be critical or difficult, like those where the design's flexibility would be severely tested."

Milano worked on a site for the Family Education Network (*www.familyeducation.com*). The user profile page of the FEN functional prototype (10.1) is typical of its rather sterile breed. There's little indication that it would evolve into the still-straightforward but user-friendly form it became (10.2).

The functional prototype does evolve as you go through site phases, growing closer to the look and feel of the final site. "After I build the first functional prototype, I'll distribute it and elicit feedback." The engineers start building database relationships and greater functionality into the prototype. Visual designers refer to the same mock-up to determine what elements to incorporate in pages. It may go through several rounds of back-and-forth between information architects, engineers, visual designers, clients, and users, becoming more refined with each iteration.

Databases supply discrete chunks of information that may be combined on the fly. Designers build database-driven pages out of those chunks, rather than designing each page individually as a coherent unit. One document that Milano relies on to bring consistency to this approach is the design style guide.

The style guide documents the visual language that the designers develop as the site is built. It defines both the structure of the pages and their elements. For example, page category A has one headline, zero to two subheadlines, and one table. The style guide also specifies the appearance of the structures: The page category A headline is flush left, sans serif, and bold; the subhead is flush left and serif; the table has a light blue background; and so on. Like many other project documents, the style guide continues to grow until the site is complete. Style guides are not only a great help during the initial design, but for long after. "If a month or year later the client changes something," Milano points out, "they'll maintain the design system by using the style guide."

Milano was part of the team that created a large database-driven e-commerce site for Office Depot (*www.officedepot.com*) (10.3). You can see the style guide in action as you click through the site: The basic structure of logo at the top/navigation at the left/variable information in the middle-right is repeated throughout. The colors are also consistent, appearing in every section (10.4).

10.2

10.3

10.4

10.5

You may be asked to redesign an existing site. In that case, a site analysis is invaluable. Hearst Publications asked Milano's company to revamp the home page for *www.homearts.com* (10.5). "It's an online presence for Hearst publications, such as *Cosmopolitan*, *Elle*, and *Good Housekeeping*. Each magazine has a separate online equivalent, but homearts.com is a central place from which you can access little pieces of content from the individual magazines, as well as go to the separate home pages."

Milano's team built a visual map of the site's structure and analyzed the usage patterns. After the analysis, Milano created a structural experience view of the site (10.6). This diagram revealed that the site's architecture required several clicks before visitors could get at some popular information. "I organized the diagram in a layered approach to demonstrate that users had been rightfully complaining that the site organization was hard to understand, annoying, and time-consuming." The design team learned from the structural experience view to design a single home page that was much more accessible and better organized.

TEMPLATES

Database-driven sites deliver dynamic interactivity and demand flexible designs. Key to those concepts are *templates*. In the broadest sense, a template is a Web page or part of a page (also called a page fragment or component) that is designed to be used in conjunction with other data, or with other fragments. Templates are not the final page, but a model for the page.

Milano says that "templates enforce strictness, which can be a good thing for consistency and ease of manageability. They allow for greater design efficiency. Each element in a template must coordinate with other elements on the site. The pieces aren't islands unto themselves, visually or conceptually."

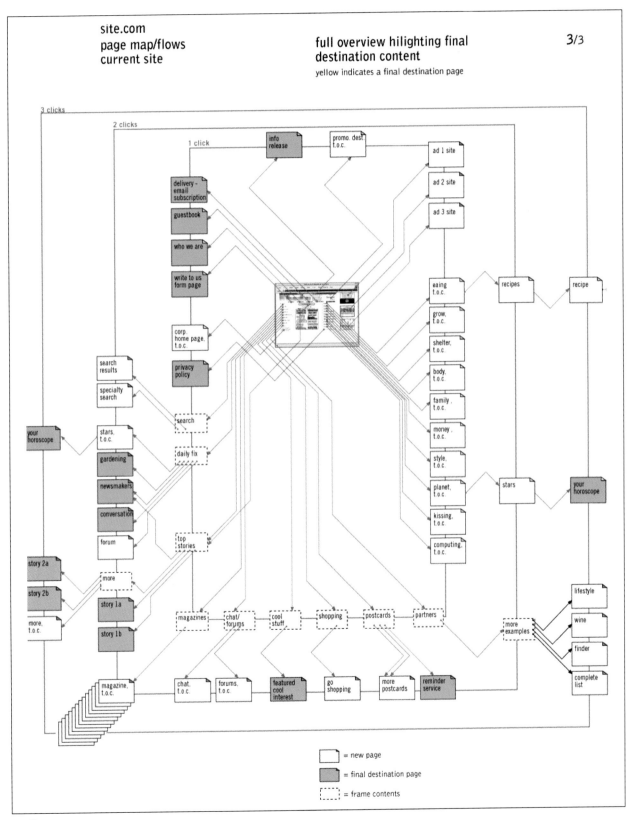

site.com
page map/flows
current site

full overview hilighting final
destination content
yellow indicates a final destination page

3/3

10.6

10.7

TRANSACTIONS: NOT JUST FOR E-COMMERCE ANYMORE

When Milano uses the term *transaction*, he's referring more to a mindset than to money. "From a user's point of view, *transaction* does tend to refer to e-commerce. But from a Web designer's point of view, it's synonymous with sites that have active components — sites where the users can do something. Instead of a bunch of static pages, there's dynamic activity and active processing. A lot of that is commerce, but not nearly all of it. In a very literal sense, *transactional* simply means information is exchanged between the Web server and the database."

For examples, he turns to a business-to-business site for Ingram Micro, a computer products distributor (10.7). (Most of the site, *www.ingrammicro.com*, is inaccessible without an Ingram Micro account.) Take the user profile pages (10.8). "A user profile has the customer's name, address, and shipping addresses." Companies with several branches have more than one shipping address. Therefore, Milano says the user profile template has fields for name and address plus a "flexible area for addresses." The template is designed such that it still functions when one area, such as addresses, is much larger or smaller than normal.

Many Ingram Micro pages are created on the fly by pulling text and graphic elements from the powerful underlying databases. "The header piece with the graphic navigation elements (10.9) is a single template designed and produced independently of the body pieces. The body pieces are templates, but in a slightly different sense. When users open orders or query for their account history, they get a customized page that doesn't appear anywhere else. The components were designed using the site's style guidelines, so it looks consistent when they work together."

Templates are crucial to creating large sites. "When you're dealing with sites that don't work in pages so much as transactions and flows, you may have 300 or 400 pages," Milano says. "Designing those in increasingly small time frames is practically impossible. But you can design a template once and have it apply to many situations. With templates as models, you can solve general design problems, even those you hadn't foreseen when you started designing. And the technology and design and content site work can happen in parallel, at least to some extent."

Milano remembers how templates made it possible to meet the Ingram Micro site schedule. "There were two site revisions. The first basically overhauled the site — introduced a new design, a better look, some new ideas. The second phase built on that initial infrastructure and introduced new features and functionality.

"We did the first site from scratch. We had to create the design language, the page look and feel, and the style in a really short time. My mind has blocked most of that."

The second site revision was another whirlwind affair. "We had to understand the functionality that was desired and figure out how to implement it, and we had to come up with the user flows. Visual design and production time was very demanding and short. We couldn't have done it on schedule from scratch. But because we had established templates and style and design language in the first site design, I could create quick mock-ups of the pages on paper. I assembled collages of photocopies and printouts of pages from the first site revision, with annotations and additions in pen and pencil. It was reminiscent of production layouts from the days of print design.

"I was able to give these pieces of paper, covered in scotch tape and pen and pencil, to the technical manager and the people writing the HTML. The technical manager adapted similar templates from the first design, just changing wording or adding or reducing columns or whatever as necessary. There were multiple people working in parallel, maintaining the consistency, getting the site done faster. If we had been forced to create all the pages from scratch, it would have been impossible to maintain the distributed production."

Templates are also a maintenance boon. "It's a huge problem to manage large sites," Milano says. "When a company's name changes, are you going to manually change all three hundred pages? If you separate the content from the presentation, you can change all the pages at once."

Templates bring their own challenges, however. "There may be a struggle to balance aesthetic and functional needs," Milano believes. "Sometimes coming up with a site that's traditionally beautiful to, say, the marketing people, is at odds with coming up with a fast, flexible, modular site that addresses the technology needs and user experiences."

He cites navigation as a common point of contention. "You need to make navigation clear and accessible. To address user needs, it should be consistent from page to page. That way it's a reference that allows the user to build an understanding of the site structure. But dynamic, database-driven sites may require the navigation to flex. The words in the navigation could change, they could be longer or shorter, there could be three words or ten. . . . You have to build in room for all these permutations.

10.8

10.9

10.10

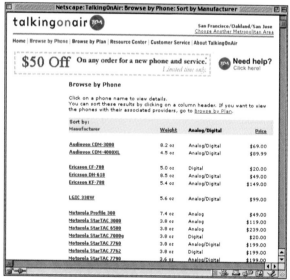

10.11

"Aside from the challenge of satisfying all of the requirements—the users', the clients', the technology's—the biggest problem may be that you don't work with known assets when you begin to design," he concludes. "You have to work from worst- and best-case situations, not the actual situations. You may never see the actual content until the day before the site goes live."

USER NEEDS

For Milano, the heart of designing any site, including database-driven e-commerce destinations, is not the technology, but the audience. "My focus is the user's experience and expectations. The database becomes a tool to carry out the site's purpose. It's not about the underlying technology or the specific products the site will sell, but about how the user will interact with the site."

His creation process begins with research. "There's research of internal client workings and needs, which lead to functional and technical requirements. But the most important voice in the chorus is the user's. Different users have different requirements, and knowledge of those needs must drive the site design."

Say you're designing a site that sells pet supplies. Pet owners can go to local shops. Even when they do shop online, they could be using one of several versions of Netscape Navigator or Microsoft Internet Explorer or the AOL browser. Their connection could be a 28.8Kbps modem or a T1 line. They might be veteran Web surfers, or this could be their first experience. "You have to account for all of those variables in the design," Milano declares. "You need to come up with a consistent design and technical underpinnings that are flexible enough to accommodate all those visitors and to address their needs."

Design decisions for your pet shop can "range from deciding how many tasks are on each page to using understandable metaphors like buttons," Milano says. "User needs affect the end design on all sorts of levels, from how big the font on the button is, to how much they look like buttons. The buttons may be brightly colored to draw attention to them and specific tasks. When people want to view their order history, you may offer a limited breakdown that clearly delineates tasks."

To better understand how these issues play out in reality, Milano describes how user needs shaped the design of two sites, one consumer, one business-to-business.

TALKING ON AIR

If you've ever shopped for a cell phone, you know how confusing the plethora of plans and models can be. Talking on Air (*www.talkingonair.com*) helps people choose and buy cell phones based on user-defined criteria (10.10). Milano says the site's aim is to "remove the hassle of going into the store, dealing with the salespeople, and trying on the spot to understand what phones work with what plans."

In order to make a potentially intimidating task more accessible, the design team strove for a user-friendly approach. Milano cites the "bright, friendly color" as one solution. "Also, we brought the tasks the user wants to the front: browse by plan, browse by phone. You can search by phone and find plans associated with it (10.11), or search by plan and find the phones associated with that (10.12)."

"A third innovation is a wizard-like set of questions (10.13)," he continues. "Depending on the user's answers to a series of scripted questions, they'll see a list of phones that meet those criteria. Clicking on the phone brings up links of what plans work with the phone. When you get the configuration you want, you can purchase it." Milano modestly declines credit for the site's success, explaining that he was not a major player on its design and development team.

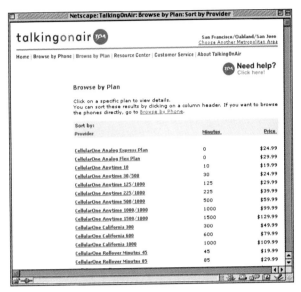

10.12

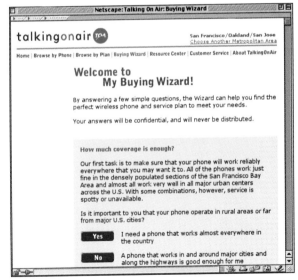

10.13

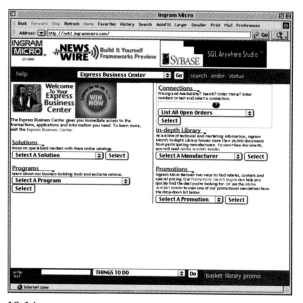

10.14

INGRAM MICRO

The Ingram Micro site redesign was also driven by user needs. "Customers perceived that the original site was difficult to use. And on a purely visual level, it was difficult to read, and it looked like it hadn't been overhauled in the past few years (10.14). Our redesign addressed all those issues."

"We implemented a new collection of home pages: personalized pages for the specific audience segments of manufacturer and reseller, as well as a new corporate home page for the general public. We restructured the functionality and information on those pages by removing the clutter and bringing specific tasks and other previously buried elements to the forefront for quicker, easier access. It became a control center that gave the user tools and more immediate access to what they needed (10.15).

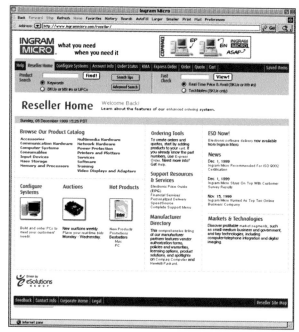

10.15

"In subsequent pages, we cleaned up the user interface." So a customer could conduct business more quickly, the team "clarified which elements on a page are tasks and which are static information."

The team also addressed visual design factors that discomforted some users. "The previous site used color somewhat indiscriminately. There was a visual sharpness that made it difficult to look at for long. There was also a legibility problem; sometimes red text was on top of a red background field.

"We increased contrast to improve legibility while trying to make a more restful, coherent page. Now the page is more unified, even while there's increased contrast or separation between the navigation and the main body. And the colors are a little more subdued—they became ingredients or factors rather than the only voice." For examples of all of the above, compare the new user profile page (10.8) with the old page (10.16).

"We reorganized a lot of the tools and made what was needlessly complicated more simple. Since the new site went up, volume and daily sales have doubled."

KEEP IT SIMPLE, NOT STUPID

Delivering complex information simply is Milano's forte. It's a worthwhile goal for every designer of database-driven sites. Don't let the technology overwhelm you—instead, harness its power to create sites that stretch the limits of the Web. Combine that with a focus on the users' needs, and the results will satisfy them, you, and the client.

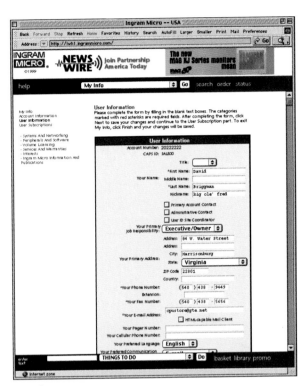

10.16

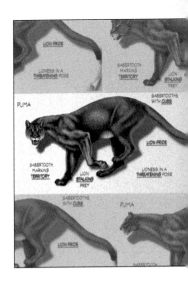

CHAPTER 11
GIF ANIMATION

A nimated GIFs function much like old-fashioned paper flip books. Instead of pages, the animations are composed of frames. As the frames cycle through on your screen, they create an illusion of movement. Adding an animated GIF to a Web page is a piece of cake: The tag is a simple `<IMG SRC="filename.gif">`.

Of course, there are other animation options. Dynamic HTML and Macromedia Flash both have their strengths, which you can read about in Chapters 5 and 12, respectively. These options appeal not the least because animated GIFs share the weaknesses of static GIFs, such as jagged bitmaps, limited transparency, no interactivity, and no sound. But animated GIFs have been around for years, long enough that virtually every browser that displays images can display animated GIFs—no plug-in required. That ubiquity keeps animated GIFs part of a Web designer's repertoire.

Lisa Lopuck is no newcomer to media that moves. In the 1980s, she cut her teeth on HyperCard stacks, and if you don't know what those are, you've got some history to brush up on. In the '90s, big names like Voyager Company, the Apple Multimedia Lab, and George Lucas hired her to design educational, media-rich CD-ROMs.

Lucky for Lopuck, as the CD-ROM market faded into the wings, the Web took center stage. "It was a natural extension to multimedia and interaction design," she says. "In 1995, one of my CD-ROM clients asked if I wanted to take a crack at their Web site. I agreed, even though it felt like a huge step

> *If you're going to call out an image with movement, do it in a concentrated area where it's really important. If you have too many animations, they compete.*
>
> LISA LOPUCK

backward. CD-ROMs had movies and sound, and the Web at the time was little more than limited control over text and graphics."

The Web's still an understudy when it comes to CD-ROM's rich media capabilities, but Lopuck has come to terms with the limitations of bandwidth and browser support. One way she adds depth to Web sites is with animated GIFs.

Lopuck explains how even a simple GIF animation can add value to a site. "For example, when you're trying to sell a product, animation can draw attention to it. You can also squeeze a lot of information in a small space. Each frame can show a different feature or a price or a 'Buy now!' message."

Just make sure you use them wisely. "If animation is gratuitous, why bother?" Lopuck asks. "It only adds to the download time." And like many of life's pleasures, too much of a good thing is a bad idea. "If you're going to call out an image with movement, do it in a concentrated area where it's really important. If you have too many animations, they compete." Lopuck notes that choosing only one aspect to highlight with motion "forces you to prioritize the message of your site, which is important anyway."

EVALUATE POTENTIAL

Before you animate a GIF, you should first understand what makes a good static GIF. "More complex images, such as most photographs, are better off as JPEGs." However, there is no animated JPEG format. You can save complex images as GIFs, "but that could mean huge file sizes," notes Lopuck. "Try to use graphics that are most appropriate for the GIF format, as opposed to forcing images that should be JPEGs." Basically, that means images with relatively few colors and blends. For all the facts on squeezing the most out of a few pixels, see Chapter 3.

TIP

Although it may seem counterintuitive to limit your choices with an already-limited format, don't activate the interlacing option when you save your file. Interlacing, which first displays a low-resolution GIF before downloading the high-res version, only slows down an animation.

ARTIST:
Lisa Lopuck

ORGANIZATION:
Lopuck Media Design
650/728-3280
www.lopuck.com
lisa@lopuck.com

SYSTEM:
Power Macintosh G3/400
Mac OS 8.5.1
9GB storage/128MB RAM

CONNECTIVITY:
Internal 56K modem

PRIMARY APPLICATIONS:
Adobe Illustrator 7 and Photoshop 5.5, Macromedia Flash 4.0, Macromedia Fireworks 3, Macromedia Dreamweaver 3, Bare Bones Software BBEdit 5

WORK HISTORY:
1988 — Robert Abel's SuperCard Stack, "Guernica," inspired her to specialize in interactive media design.

As she creates individual images to make up an animated GIF, Lopuck also considers how they'll work together. "An animation uses a global palette that supplies colors for all the frames. Each frame can have a different color set, but you still have only a limited number of colors for all frames. If one frame is wildly different, your overall quality will be less. You're better off when all frames use the same color palette."

SIMPLE IS BETTER

When you create a site, you consider how individual pages fit together to make the whole. Likewise, you should understand how separate frames combine to form an animation.

Lopuck always keeps the number of frames to a minimum. "The more frames you have, the more things you have to pay attention to: optimizing each frame, movement, transitions. Fewer frames let you compress the file more, as well."

It's tough to project smooth moves in a few frames, but there are ways to give the illusion of fluidity. For example, you can apply a motion blur to an object in an image editor and use the blurred object in transitional frames. Lopuck notes that some applications, such as the shareware program GIFBuilder, add dissolves between frames. "But that slows down the animation because the dissolve takes time. If you had a

---

TRANSPARENCY

Obviously, cropping your animation as tightly as possible cuts down on file size. Transparency also trims the fat. Like static GIFs, you can make individual pixels of animated GIFs transparent. More than just an aesthetic choice, transparency can speed downloads. "If one frame is your background," Lopuck says, "and every frame on top of it uses transparency, with only the action showing, you get some file-size savings."

---

bouncing ball and you tried to dissolve between frames, you'd have to move the ball in one frame, dissolve on the next, then move the ball one step further, and so on."

The better solution is to suit the animation to the format. "I don't animate something like a ball bouncing across the screen that's going to need a lot of frames to look reasonably smooth. If you're going to do that, use Flash, where it can be beautifully smooth, yet the file size stays small. I plan a GIF animation that looks good even though it's jerky." Think *South Park*, not *Toy Story*. "I also decide on the number of frames before I design it," adds Lopuck. "The motion will be choppy anyway, so instead of doing it in 10 frames, try it in 8 or 7."

FAVORITE STAR TREK CHARACTER: KIRK OR SPOCK?
"Definitely Kirk, a man after my own heart. A cavalier, charismatic leader — and William Shatner rides horses, too!"

11.1

11.2

11.3

11.4

TWEEN IDOL

Even with a small number of frames, you may tire of changing an object's position manually. Versions 2.0 and above of industry standards Adobe ImageReady and Macromedia Fireworks take away the tedium with a feature called *tweening,* short for "in between." Tweening calculates the differences between consecutive frames and adds new frames in which the objects are placed between their positions in the original two frames. Although the results are similar in both applications, the tweening process is not.

To help you decide which method works best for you, Lopuck walks through the creation of two ad banner animations, one in ImageReady 2.0, the other in Fireworks 3.0.

The first banner is for a television program on the fictional AnimalChannel (11.1). Lopuck assembled its components — the frog, the foliage, the text, and the black bar — on separate layers in Photoshop. She made the rainforest text a clipping group and applied live layer effects. Now it's time to open the file in ImageReady and take the following steps:

1. Choose Window ➤ Animation to open the Animation palette. One frame already exists; to create another, click the icon at the bottom of the palette that looks like a page (11.2). Click the second frame to select it.

2. In the Layers palette, select the foliage layer and then move it about 100 pixels to the left. Hold the Shift key to constrain the motion to a straight line.

3. Select the Rainforest text layer (11.3). Select one of the Layer effects and change the angle of the bevel in the Options palette (11.4).

4. Back in the Animation palette, click the first frame.

5. Select the Coming This Fall . . . text layer in the Layers palette and adjust its opacity to 1 percent.

6. Shift-select both frames and choose Tween from the Animation palette's pull-down menu (11.5). In the window that appears, leave the default settings but choose five additional frames (11.6). The program automatically adds the new frames and fills in the steps between the first and last frame.

Lopuck animated a similar banner in Fireworks (11.7). Although the parrot is a bitmap imported from Photoshop, the other parts of the illustration are vectors — Fireworks handles both formats. The application also retains Photoshop layers and live layer effects.

1. Select the Rainforest text and convert it to a symbol by choosing Insert ➤ Convert to Symbol (11.8). Name the symbol "Rainforest" and leave the Graphic option selected. The text now becomes a symbol stored in the Library palette. An *instance*, or copy, remains in your document.

2. With the instance selected, go to the Effect palette and assign a drop shadow to the text. Cast the drop shadow far to the left (11.9).

3. Copy the Rainforest instance and paste. It pastes directly on top of the original. In the Effect palette, change the drop shadow angle of the copy so that the shadow is cast to the right (11.10).

4. Now comes the tweening. With the pointer tool, drag-select both instances. Then choose Modify ➤ Symbol ➤ Tween Instances.

5. In the dialog box that appears, enter 5 Steps and select Distribute to Frames (11.11). The new frames appear with the instances distributed automatically.

Lopuck uses both applications, but she believes it's simpler to tween clipping paths in ImageReady. "Let's say you want an animation of a sunset moving behind the word 'sunset.' You've already made a clipping group, and the sunset image is clipped inside the word. In frame 1, you place the sunset in a certain spot. Then you set up a second frame and while it's selected, you change the clipping group's position so it's way over to the right. That then becomes your last frame. You just select the two frames, choose the tween feature, and specify how many frames you want in between the first and last. ImageReady moves the whole graphic in that number of steps. That's really cool."

She thinks that Fireworks' tween feature can be difficult to use. The *symbol* and *instance* concepts take a little getting used to, and there are other drawbacks. Lopuck returns to the hypothetical sunset clipping group example to explain. "In Fireworks, if you make

11.5

11.6

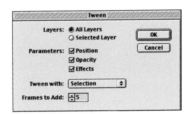

11.7

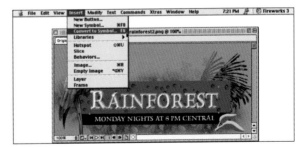

11.8

11.9

11.10

11.11

a clipping group, you have to do a paste inside. So there's a text object—the word 'sunset'—and you have to paste the sunset image inside it. You have to make the whole thing into a symbol, and then make instances of the symbol. If you want to change the position of the sun inside the instance and tween its location, you have to do it by hand."

Nevertheless, Lopuck prefers Fireworks because of its interface. "It's much easier to use overall," she believes. "Even though it's similar to Photoshop, ImageReady is counterintuitive for animation because you manipulate the layers on each of the different frames. When you make a new frame, you have to create a new layer. On each frame you have to make a change in the layers themselves for frame-by-frame animation. You're managing all your frames in all your layers in the same window. There are too many elements to juggle.

"Fireworks has a grid system, and layers cut across all frames. When you're in a frame, you can put items in different layers. On frame 1, for example, you can place the word 'go' in a layer called 'go.' On frame 2, you can delete the word 'go' and replace it with something else. You can delete an item from one frame altogether, but it can still exist in a different frame. It gives you flexibility to spread all kinds of graphics through your frames, as opposed to having this huge layers palette for every frame element."

FILE SIZE AND PLAYBACK SPEEDS

If variety is the spice of life, the Web should be labeled "hot hot hot." Animated GIFs aren't exempt from the guessing game that is cross-platform, cross-browser design.

Besides the gamma and color-palette differences that plague all Web images, GIF animators must account for varying playback speeds. "It's a problem," accedes Lopuck, "but that's the story of the Web. The experience depends on the browser and connection speed."

Lopuck says it's no accident that "ad banners are often around 10K. That small size is difficult to reach, but it's important because then the ads play more consistently. If an animation is under 20K, it should still play relatively consistently. But when you download a huge file, say a 50K animation, you'll get into trouble. Your computer's trying to download it and play it at the same time."

The moral: Small is beautiful.

FRAME RATES AND LOOPING

Once you've created all your frames, you'll want to set their frame rate, or the length of time each frame is on screen. Rates can vary from frame to frame and can be as small as one one-hundredth of a second.

The ideal frame rates depend on the animation, but Lopuck does have a few general guidelines. If the animation is large, she assigns a relatively long delay to the first frame so the entire animation has time to load. "For a National Geographic site on cats, I created a puma that turns its head to look at you (11.12, 11.13, 11.14). Only the head moved, and it was a separate file in a table cell seamlessly butted up to the body. The body was about 22K, and the head was around 17K. The first frame of the head had a significant delay, 3 or 4 seconds, so the body could load before the head started to move."

You may also want an animation to loop — that is, to cycle through its frames two or more times. Looping draws on the image cache, so it extends the animation time without requiring new downloads. That can be an advantage, as long as never-ending loops don't become the Web equivalent of a small dog endlessly yapping for attention. "I may add a delay after the last frame so the animation isn't too annoying," Lopuck says. "And don't forget to think about what's on the rest of your page. You may not want something always going crazy in a corner."

Some animations are clearly unfit for any looping. Lopuck notes that the head-turning puma "couldn't be a loop — you don't want the head spinning around like in the *The Exorcist*."

IMAGE SLICING

Many animated GIFs benefit from image slicing — that is, dividing one image into smaller parts that are reassembled on a page within HTML tables. (Just remember to set table borders to zero.) The National Geographic puma demonstrates one benefit of image slicing: By animating only one section of the image, Lopuck kept down file size.

Image slicing also lets you customize the slices' frame rates, number of frames, and color palettes. "Plus," adds Lopuck, "with more complicated images, parts of them may be better off as JPEGs. If you slice the image, you can save parts in different formats for significant quality and file-size savings." The parrot of the Rainforest ad banner is a good example. When saved as a JPEG set at 70 percent quality (100 being the best), the file was 5K (11.15). To match the JPEG's quality, the GIF had to contain 256 colors; its file size was 9K, almost double the JPEG's (11.16).

"However," Lopuck warns, "image slicing can get out of hand if you chop up a page into an ungodly number of little pieces. They can take a long time to load, even if they're only 1K or 2K each."

11.12

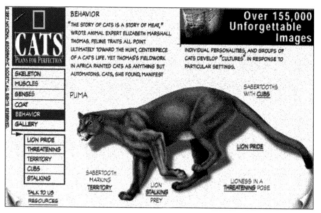

11.13

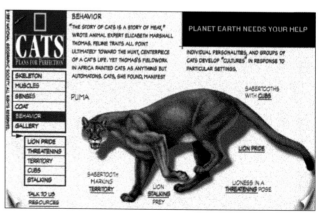

11.14

FROM GIF TO .SWF

Let's say you're designing a site for a client, whom we'll call Edgar, who specified that all animations must be GIFs. A few days before the site goes live, Edgar falls in love with Flash and wants to use it instead. Back in the day, you would have grumbled a few choice invectives, and then started from scratch. But if you've got version 3.0 or higher of Fireworks, you can chirp out a "Right away, Edgar!" and export the GIF animations as Flash .swf files. It's a dead-simple operation: Choose File ➤ Export Special ➤ Flash SWF ➤ Save.

However, there are a few potential potholes. "When you export a .swf file from Fireworks," notes Lopuck, "the background will always be white — even if your Fireworks document was set to a custom background color.

"And don't use vector graphics with fancy fill and stroke patterns." If you go wild with Fireworks' strokes, fills, and live effects and try to retain their look when exporting to .swf, the vectors will convert to bitmaps. The resulting kilobyte bulk defeats one big benefit of Flash — small file sizes. That's why Lopuck advises that your vector graphics have only "a simple pencil stroke, if any, and a solid fill color."

You should also be aware that each frame in a GIF animation becomes a key frame in Flash. Lopuck says that "such frame-by-frame animation is inefficient because most of the movement can be better rendered from Flash's motion tween. That's why it's best to import just a few Fireworks frames if you plan on editing your movie in Flash." Once you open the exported file in Flash, you can manipulate it as you would any .swf file. But don't count on using any symbols and instances you created in Fireworks. They're not recognized in Flash.

Using an animation for a fictitious company, Snow Interactive (11.17), Lopuck demonstrates how she creates source files in Fireworks that she intends to export as Flash movies:

1. Select the snowflake logo (a vector) and convert it to a symbol by choosing Insert ➤ Convert to Symbol.

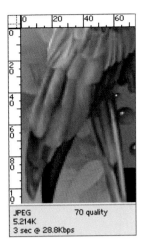

JPEG   70 quality
5.214K
3 sec @ 28.8Kbps

11.15

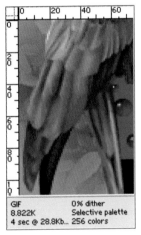

GIF   0% dither
8.822K   Selective palette
4 sec @ 28.8Kb... 256 colors

11.16

11.17

11.18

11.19

2. Copy and paste the symbol to create another instance. Move the copy to the upper-left corner, enlarge and rotate it with the Free Transform tool (11.18), and adjust its opacity to 20 percent using the Object palette.

3. Create a second copy and place it in the lower-right corner, again changing the size, rotation, and opacity.

4. The next task is to tween the instances. Select both and choose Modify ➢ Symbol ➢ Tween Instances. Enter 18 frames and check the Distribute to Frames option.

5. Because the text layer is set to Share Across Frames, the text is present throughout the animation. The snowflake logo, however, appears only on Frame 1. So select Frame 1 in the Frame pulldown menu of the Layers palette, and then go to the main window and select the snowflake logo. In the Layers palette, move the blue dot representing the object to the text layer (11.19).

6. In the main window, select Snow Interactive and bring it to the foreground by choosing Modify ➢ Arrange ➢ Bring to Front.

7. By default, Fireworks sets each frame's timing to 20/100 of a second, which is well-suited for GIF animation, but a little slow for Flash movies. To adjust all frames' timing simultaneously, go to the Frames palette and shift-select each frame. Choose Properties from the palette's pull-down menu and enter a value of 5 in the Frame Delay window (11.20).

8. Finally, choose File ➢ Export Special ➢ Flash SWF ➢ Save.

11.20

THE GIF ANIMATION WORKHORSE

You don't need us to tell you that the Web changes constantly. Sometimes it feels like every week, even every day, brings a hot new technology and an accompanying cloud of buzzwords. But despite this manic movement, animated GIFs remain. They appear on all graphical browsers, regardless of platform or plug-in. They're the bread and butter of ad banners. For these reasons alone, it's worth your time to learn to make them well. And when the creation tools help you transform your sweat into another format, you can't go wrong.

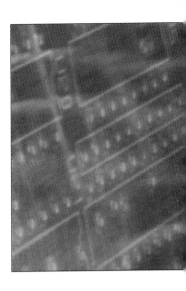

CHAPTER 12
FLASH ANIMATION AND INTERACTIVITY

It's been years since plain-vanilla HTML and still images have caused jaws to drop. As the novelty of the early days wore off, designers pushed for more inventive ways to grab eyeballs. GIF animation was the first format to rattle and roll the Web in a big way. A slew of video types, from QuickTime to RealVideo, followed. DHTML, a combo of JavaScript and Cascading Style Sheets, has also promised a dynamic experience. But none of these solutions are motion Nirvana. Some lack interactivity and visual finesse (oh, those jaggies!), others crash certain browsers, and you always have to beware of the Big Daddy of Drawbacks: large file sizes that force viewers to wait . . . and wait . . . and wait.

Enter Flash. Originally developed as FutureSplash by FutureWave, Macromedia acquired the application's technology and unleashed it on the world as Flash in early 1997. Within Flash, you can draw objects from scratch and modify files from other image-creation and editing applications with common tools such as the pencil and paint bucket. However, the main appeal of Flash is its capability to combine and manipulate objects to make animations called *movies* with astonishingly small file sizes. Here vocabulary such as *keyframes* and *timelines* may be a little less familiar, but learning the language is well worth the effort.

Paul Ingram is practically a native speaker. He is founder and interaction director of Ingram Labs (*www.ingramlabs.com*), which produces Flashed sites for a range of clients, from movie distributor Atom Films to internet storage company Atrieva. He first

> **Flash lets me build something and stretch it. . . . It's a putty-like environment.**
>
> PAUL INGRAM

181

12.1

12.2

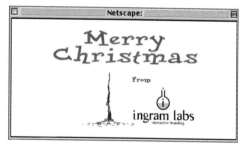

12.3

explored the technology when it was still FutureSplash. Ingram needed a holiday greeting for his company's Web site, so he "slapped together an animation (12.1 – 12.3) and left town for two weeks," he recalls. Pioneering Ingram went on to use Flash for major interface components.

"We did some projects for (modem makers) Rockwell International. The 56K-modem market was in turmoil in early 1998 because of competing standards, and Rockwell wanted to promote their version. So we did a series of animated interfaces to draw people's attention and get unusual interest. We can't take all the credit, but Rockwell wound up dominating the marketplace." Ingram also says the continuing partnership with Rockwell has resulted in a 300 percent rise in visitors to the company's site.

Although it may have helped win that standards battle, Flash itself is not a standard according to the World Wide Web consortium. Visitors must have the Flash plug-in to see the files. Fortunately, millions have downloaded the plug-in, and the newer browsers come with it already installed. Macromedia estimated that about 200 million people on the Web could view Flash content by the end of 1999.

ARTIST:
Paul Ingram

ORGANIZATION:
Ingram Labs
80 South Washington St., Suite 300
Seattle, WA 98104
www.ingramlabs.com
paul@ingramlabs.com

SYSTEM:
Macintosh PowerBook G3/300
Mac OS 8.6
8GB storage/192MB RAM

CONNECTIVITY:
DSL

PRIMARY APPLICATIONS:
Adobe Illustrator and Photoshop, Macromedia Flash 4.0, BIAS Peak, Macromedia Dreamweaver, Apple QuickTime

WORK HISTORY:
1989 – 1991 — Went to art school to be trained as an illustrator.
1993 — Worked as a graphic designer. Introduced to the Internet late in the year.

GOOD THINGS AND SMALL PACKAGES

Ingram believes that whether your project is an entire interface or an isolated animation, Flash has distinct advantages over alternatives like GIF animation and DHTML. First, Flash files are drawn using vectors, not bitmaps. Vectors are more efficient at rendering images than pixels, and that means smaller file sizes and faster downloads.

Vectors also scale up or down without losing quality (or adding to file size). Ingram notes, "I'm a Photoshop guy, it's my tool of choice. But I hate that you can't stretch pixelated images without totally messing them up. Flash lets me build something and stretch it (12.4, bitmap; 12.5, vector). The final product can scale to fit any screen resolution or layout space. I do all my designs in Flash now—even logos. It's a putty-like environment."

Besides Flash's vector base, the key to keeping file sizes trim are symbols. Once you designate something in a Flash movie a symbol, you can use it repeatedly without bulking up the file. Ingram depends on symbols to keep his complex movies manageable.

12.4

12.5

1994 — Started Ingram Labs as an Internet business; couldn't make a living because nobody believed the Internet was worth anything. Became Web designer at an agency.

1995 – 1999 — Left agency for freelance Web design life. Revived Ingram Labs. Acquired big clients but clung to the small-business model.

FAVORITE CHILDHOOD HALLOWEEN COSTUME:

"A Ghostbusters outfit I made out of boxes, an old vacuum cleaner, and two-liter pop bottles. I was one of those 12-year olds who still played with his Star Wars action figures."

Symbols are flexible; you can not only duplicate them (those duplicates are called *instances*), but you can noodle with them in any number of ways—changing color, size, shape, and so on. The original symbol remains the same and appears only once in the symbol repository, the Library. For the Flash-only Ingram Labs site, just about everything is a symbol, including the ViewMaster (12.6), which you click to view client samples, and the Movie-ola (12.7), which tells you about Ingram Labs' services.

Ironically, another advantage was originally a disadvantage. Visitors must have the Flash plug-in, but once they do, they'll see your animation exactly as you intended it, unlike with browser-dependent DHTML displays.

INTERACTIVITY

One of the appeals of Flash is the interactivity it adds. As with JavaScript, when you click or mouse over a trigger, you see an animation. Flash 4 introduced more powerful functionality in the guise of database connectivity and editable form fields.

"Now you can process e-commerce requests and log-in functions," Ingram enthuses. "Before it had this essential database connectivity, we couldn't even consider Flash for a whole site." Like plain HTML forms, Flash files can now work with scripts and databases to get information from viewers and tailor their viewing experience. Because they're created in Flash, the forms don't have to resemble the unimaginative boxes and radio buttons of HTML forms. "For example," Ingram says, "you can set up a site so that after you sign up to be a member, you're welcomed by name, even though the welcome is in Flash. Your whole log-in can be in a Flash interface because of Flash 4's forms feature." Ingram Labs did just that on a site for Atrieva (*www.atrieva.com*), a company that stores files on the Internet (12.8).

The downside: Viewers must have version 4 or higher of the plug-in to enjoy this functionality. But some sites, such as those geared toward entertainment, can get away with requiring upgrades for certain functionality because visitors are more inclined to wait for the big payoff of free games, movies, and so on.

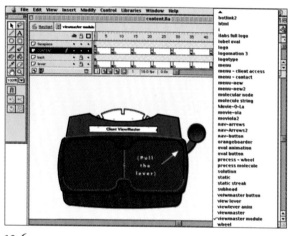

12.6

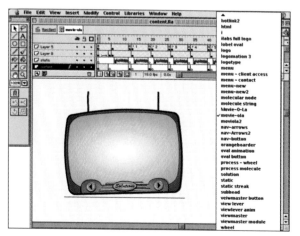

12.7

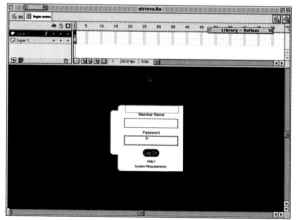

12.8

Ingram's company designed the Web site for Atom Films, which screens movies on its site and distributes them to TV and airline companies. The site makes extensive use of Flash's original and current interactivity. Ingram simplified matters by limiting the amount of information that must be preprogrammed into the Flash files he creates. If you click a button on Atom's site, it loads an Active Server Page with hooks into a database. "We cut out Flash as the content generator," Ingram explains. "We just load pages that create all the commands. It makes Flash more usable in a busy site.

"We can make parts of it easy to update, too," he continues. "There's a window on the home page with a message generated by a text file in Flash. We set it up so the window references that text file, where we set fonts and alignment, the URL link, and so on. Atom doesn't have a Flash person, but they don't need one to update the message in the window—they just update the text file whenever they want (12.9, 12.10)."

WHEN NOT TO USE FLASH

Seems like every Web-design site you surf nowadays is abuzz with talk of Flash. But it wasn't always so popular, especially with clients. "We got tons of resistance from customers, but now people come to us wanting Flash. We have to protect clients from themselves sometimes—Flash isn't always appropriate.

"Many Web sites are more informational than entertaining," Ingram notes. "Not that Flash is only an entertainment tool, but it's difficult to update. If you need a fully database-driven site, then it's more difficult to use Flash. We use it as a major element only when the audience is expecting an extraordinary visual experience. Broadband audiences want something full of sound and motion.

"You have to protect people who come to the site, too," he continues. "What if they don't have Flash? We use browser detection and make non-Flash versions that are automatically delivered to people without the plug-in. For the all-Flash Ingram Labs site (12.11), it wouldn't make sense to try to re-create the same look in HTML, so we route people to our old site (12.12) with browser detection."

Unfortunately, browser detection isn't glitch-free. "We can't tell whether people on the Mac running

Internet Explorer have Flash, so we give them a page that tells them we don't know what they have and gives them options for how to go on. It's okay to offer visitors a quick choice of a Flash or non-Flash version, but you should only ask them once. After that, they can click a 'Download Flash' brick to enhance the experience if they want to. Otherwise, just give them the functionality they're capable of."

And don't forget about the potential for plug-in incompatibility when you use features supported only by the more recent plug-in versions. "For the Atrieva site, we built a detector inside Flash that calls up specific processes to determine which Flash version people have. If they're using Flash 3, they'll see something other than what Flash 4 users will see. They can still view it if they have the Flash 3 plug-in, but they don't get all of the functionality. For example, behind form fields (supported by Flash 4 and higher), there's red text that says 'available with Flash 4 only' (12.13)."

12.9

12.10

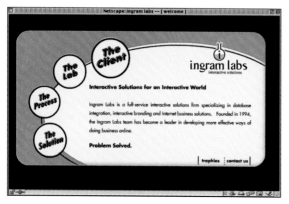

12.11

12.12

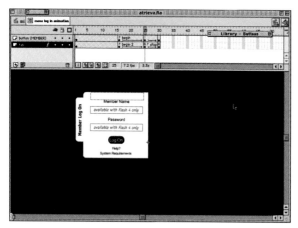

12.13

FLASH AND FRAMES

Ingram believes that Flash is a great vehicle for delivering rich sound and animation, and it's become a successful interactive content engine. Still lacking are the capabilities to load HTML-formatted content and embed stable video. "Many of the projects we work on have a strong need for embedded video and database-driven text content. Macromedia Generator can handle a lot of the database-driven functionality, but we've had to be creative in solving the video problem." One solution is frames. Creating Flash frames is similar to image slicing, where you use an image editor to cut still images into pieces for reconstruction in HTML tables.

"We can make a frame-based design that looks like it's 100 percent Flash but loads HTML pages in a central window with embedded video, which isn't possible in Flash alone," Ingram explains. "Frames are the way to go if you need multiple media types mixed throughout a Flash-based Web site."

Ingram used frames for a project called E-Pass, which debuted on Intel's site as a promotion for the Pentium III processor and then moved to Atom Films (*www.atomfilms.com*). E-Pass is designed to look like a handheld display that shows a map of the world with buttons marking certain countries, from South Korea to Spain, Luxembourg to New Zealand. Click a button and a movie from that area appears inside the display (12.14).

12.14

What looks like one solid display is actually made up of several frames. Each frame contains a Flash movie set to the following Object/Embed code:

```
<object width="100%" height="100%"
classid="clsid:D27CDB6E-AE6D-11cf-
96B8-444553540000"
codebase="http://active.macromedia.
com/flash2/cabs/swflash.cab#version=
3,0,0,0">
<param name="Movie"
value="epass_left.swf">
<param name="Play" value="true">
<param name="Quality" value="high">
<param name="swLiveConnect"
value="false">
<param name="loop" value="true">
<param name=salign value=1m>
<param name=bgcolor value=#000000>
<embed src="epass_left.swf"
swliveconnect="false" width="100%"
height="100%" quality="high"
salign=1m bgcolor=#000000 play="true"
loop="true" type="application/x-
shockwave-flash"
pluginspage="http://www.macromedia.
com/shockwave/download/index.cgi?P1_
Prod_Version=ShockwaveFlash">
</embed>
</object>
```

This code enables the animation to maintain its relative shape when scaled up or down as visitors change the size of the browser window. "When you stretch a browser with frames set at percentages, the Flash is glued to the walls of the frame area." The `salign` parameter establishes that each movie aligns to the middle of the browser, creating a wrap for the HTML-based content. The navigation elements in the bottom movie load HTML, text, graphics, Flash content, and other Shockwave elements.

The end result is impressive, but it ain't easy. "It takes time and troubleshooting to create a seamless interface," Ingram admits. "Flash still has some alignment issues, especially with frames. It's hard to line up patterns between frames. That's easier in HTML with a graphical background. But the power of Flash is so positive that we can live with a little crunchiness, and if you're careful as you cut apart the original, it looks like one large Flash piece with embedded video and dynamic content."

LAYER IT ON

Ingram relates early history: "Early on during the transition from FutureSplash to Flash, the handful of folks using it as the only presentation method placed all of their content into one big file. For Flash to become a standard delivery method, the user wanted a quick download, and 700K to 3MB didn't cut it." The solution was layers.

Thanks to Flash's layers system, you can load multiple movies inside of movies. "You can lay in something like 20 layers of movies," Ingram says. "But you've got to be careful: You can create a file that's too processor-intensive. We've built Flash animations that crash the system. A typical problem is a transparent gradient that's looping and moving. So we test all files to check out CPU usage. If it's too high, we remove potential problems one by one."

Go to the Ingram Labs site and you'll actually see several movies, although the loading process is mostly invisible. "First it loads index.swf (12.15)," notes Ingram, "then it loads frame.swf, which is a separate movie, and then you're at the home page, where the text portion and menu tab also load as separate movies.

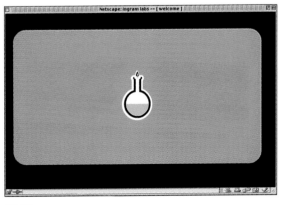

12.15

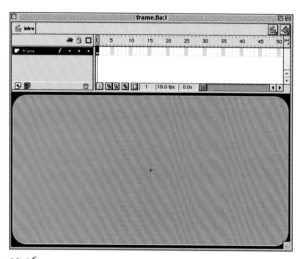

12.16

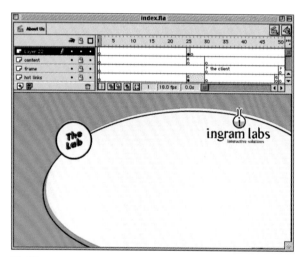

12.17

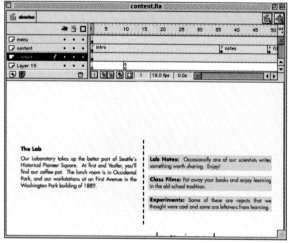

12.18

"Each section of the site has a Flash file sandwiched between the black frame and text file," he continues. "When you see the message 'loading,' it's loading separate text. We did that so we can update the text — instead of modifying the whole movie, we can retype one little piece. Also, it makes it so that the user doesn't have to download the whole site before seeing one section. They load it as they need it."

To create this set of movies within movies, Ingram Labs staff took the following steps:

1. They created a border to frame the whole site (12.16).

2. They designed navigation in a separate flash file, making sure that all movies were the same dimension and frame rate (12.17).

3. They built the content files for the different sections of the site — five movies in all, including the introduction page (12.18).

4. They used the Load Movie action to load the different movies as needed. Movies 0, 1, and 5 load first (12.19).

"It's important to understand the basic technical parameters of how movies are referenced," Ingram stresses. "Each movie has a Load or Unload action, a URL, and a Location." The action determines whether the movie will load or unload. "One way to exit a section of the site is to unload a movie to reveal a background image or content," Ingram explains. The URL is the name and location of the file to be loaded, and the Location indicates the level a file loads into. "The background is always level 0, and each additional layer goes up in number. Loading a movie into a level that has a movie in it replaces the existing movie with the new one. We chose to load the black frame file (frame.swf) in level 5 in case we needed to load more movies later."

FAKING 3D FLASH

Ingram misses the many applications and effects plug-ins that enhance still images. "Without them, it's a challenge to overcome the visual effect limitations of Flash and make interfaces pop off of the screen." Until plug-in companies support Flash, "we have to become skilled illustrators again." Importing raster images from bitmap-based image editors isn't a viable option because of the resulting increase in file size and decrease in quality.

Ingram explains a technique Ingram Labs employs that he says imitates the 3D bevel and emboss effects possible with programs like Kai's Power Tools. "We weld together gradients for a 3D look that sets our designs apart from the flat-color model."

Atom Films' E-Pass project is one example of the 3D look. "We laid out a flat gray panel," Ingram begins. "We decided to create a semitransparent gradient across the top, kind of like a picture frame's top piece. We cut a 45-degree angle so it formed a corner, and then we copied the gradient and flipped it to piece together rest of frame. The end product looked like debossed, brushed metal." Ingram gives step-by-step instructions below.

1. Create the interface shape. We chose to build an interface with a stainless steel look, so the base color was light gray (12.20).

2. Using the box tool, choose or customize a gradient that meets your color and textural goals. We designed a semitransparent linear gradient that lets the base color show through for consistent tone over the whole surface (12.21).

3. Next, draw a box to cover the top panel and mold it to create the curvature that indicates a seam. Group the gradient. Copy that panel for the bottom and rotate more copies for the sides. Fit the gradient parts together, adjusting each shape to form beveled seams (12.22).

4. After you're satisfied with the beveled effect, you can "deboss" details by offsetting three layers — white, gray, and black — just enough that one edge looks highlighted and another shadowed. For the E-Pass project, we debossed speaker holes, blinking lights, and lettering (12.23).

"It's a pain," Ingram acknowledges, "but once you get the hang of it, it's screaming fast."

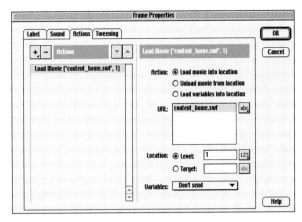

12.19

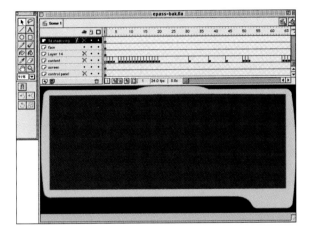

12.20

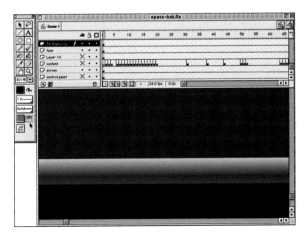

12.21

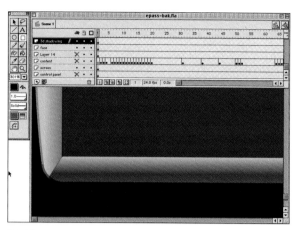

12.22

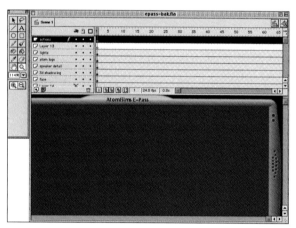

12.23

SEARCHABLE TEXT

As Ingram has pointed out, Flash is not without its drawbacks. But one charge against it — the lack of searchable text — is easy to overcome. "Since Flash files are embedded by HTML tags," Ingram says, "you can hide comments and descriptions in the HTML. When you export a Flash movie, you can click an option to include all the text in Flash text as HTML in your file. It will also save and write in text all the links in the Flash movie. So when search engine spiders hit your index pages, they'll see all that text."

SOUND OFF

One pleasure — and danger — of effective Flash files is sound. Sound can make your movie an even richer experience. The danger, of course, is the weight sound can add to previously svelte files.

"You've got to determine how much of a burden sound will add: The typical sound bit is the size of your Flash movie! But you need sound. You give a rich visual experience with Flash, but when there's no sound to back it, people start checking their volume controls. It's a natural reaction. People are used to TV and movies, where there are great sounds as well as great visuals. There are people out there who are as interested in the audio as the visual. Leaving them out is leaving out an opportunity to communicate."

Ingram offers tips for how to use sound wisely. "Sounds must be top quality, or they can be annoying," he cautions. "You don't want to send a user screaming for the volume control. We standardize all sounds to be 22Mhz with the highest quality possible for the desired file size. Now that Flash supports the MP3 format for compression, many of the previous file-size-versus-quality constraints aren't an issue. But for longer musical effects, it's still a good idea to use tightly tuned loops instead of streaming when possible.

"Find unique and appropriate sounds for button and motion effects," he continues. "Do your best not to use the sounds that came with Flash. They're too familiar to make much of an impact. I can't stand going to a site and hearing the same old sounds. Half the sounds I use are my mouth making noises. I can't find anything that makes better sounds. I record my voice into a mic and open a sound editor to warp the sound or speed it up."

Finally, "don't let the Flash defaults determine quality. You should test the sound. Check volumes on standard computers."

12.24

BUSINESS SENSE

In some circles, Flash has a rap as a creator of files that twirl, blink, make noise, but don't have real substance. Ingram is out to change that perception. "Flash doesn't have to be just a pretty show," he says. "That's got to change. Everybody's tired of static, brochureware Web sites. People expect sites to do stuff for them, not just sit there. It's the same way with Flash. It should benefit the clients' business. The only way we can make money off of Flash is to prove it's a viable business product."

That doesn't mean your movies have to sport pinstripes. Ingram Labs recently designed a site for Xircom (*www.xircom.com/flash/xircom-hiband.html*), a mobile communications company, built on sound and imagery that are far from the corporate boardroom (12.24, 12.25). Ingram describes the site as a "total techno-animated freaky thing. The experience is similar to a strobing TV video wall. We're calling it an interactive Web site trailer." Ingram says the site works because it "shows off Xircom's product with the display, and attracts people to dig further into the Web site for more information."

Form + function — imagine that!

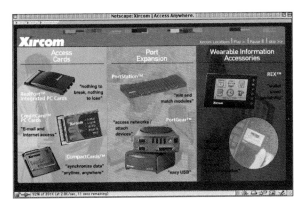

12.25

CHAPTER 13
FILMS AND VIDEO ON THE WEB

We all have fond memories of going to the movies, munching on popcorn, waiting for the house lights to dim, and watching the shimmering screen that transports us into times and places full of fantasy, excitement, and drama. A few short hours later, you shuffle out of the theater, eyes blinking as they adjust to the sudden brightness of the lobby or afternoon sidewalk light. Where had you been? To the ends of the universe and back.

Going to the movies is one of our favorite pastimes—but don't you hate it when the film that you wanted to see isn't playing in your neighborhood any longer and you have to wait for it to get to the video store? What about the classic black-and-white movies that flicker in our memories featuring Buster Keaton, Charlie Chaplin, and Mary Pickford (13.1)? Where can you go to see those classics? Pop the popcorn and point your browser to *www.afionline.org*, where you can see movies either in short QuickTime clips or as streaming-video feature films that play up to 20 minutes.

The American Film Institute (AFI) was founded in 1967 by an act of Congress to "advance and preserve the art of the moving image." At that time over half of all movies ever made in the United States had been lost due to environmental damage and sheer negligence. Film stock was deteriorating, nitrate films were literally burning up, and the lack of a comprehensive catalog of the American film was threatening even more losses. The American Film Institute, based in Los Angeles, California, is a graduate school with

Even though the screen is small, the audience we are reaching is huge.

DAN HARRIES

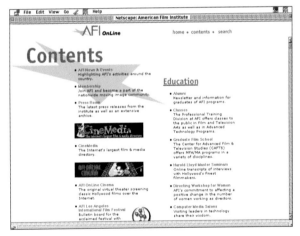

13.1

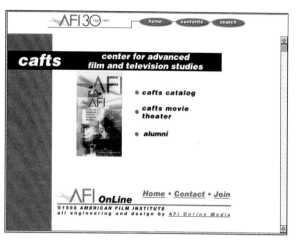

13.2

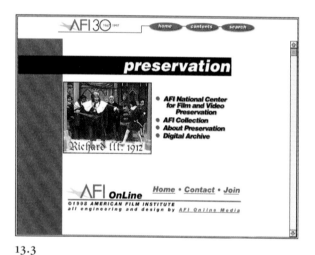

13.3

seven disciplines (13.2), a film preservation center (13.3 and 13.4), and a focal point for film aficionados from around the globe (13.5).

SMALL SCREEN, HUGE AUDIENCE

"One of the best ways to preserve a film is by having a lot of viewers see it," explains Dan Harries, former Director of Online Media at the AFI. Harries' team launched the AFI Web site in 1995. Within two years, more than half a million people were visiting the site every month, and in 1997 alone more than 500,000 people watched a movie. "In our OnLine Cinema (13.6), 85 percent of the audience have watched a movie from beginning to end. We're recapturing an audience for films that have rarely seen the light of a projector bulb in over half a century. The best thing is that film fans from all around the world are coming to the AFI site to learn more about a featured director, to see clips from the graduate students' work, or just to spend some time with the classics. In the area of film preservation, the AFI OnLine Cinema is an interesting juxtaposition that advances and preserves the classic films with the newest technology."

ARTIST:
Dan Harries

ORGANIZATION:
Formerly:
American Film Institute
2021 N. Western Ave.
Los Angeles, CA 90027
www.afionline.org
Currently:
Visual Culture and Media Department
Middlesex University
Cat Hill Campus
London EN4 8HT UK
Dan.harries@mdx.ax.uk

SYSTEM, MAC:
Power Mac 8500/180
Mac OS 8.0
2GB storage/48MB RAM

SYSTEM, PC:
Intergraph StudioZ

CONNECTIVITY, ISP:
T1

SERVER ENVIRONMENT:
Compaq NT

It would be great to watch a complete film at your computer anytime you wanted to—making the Internet not only your means of distribution but also your means of exhibition—but the present bandwidth limitations just don't make this feasible. On the other hand, including film clips on a Web site isn't very complex at all. In fact, the simplest type of movie can be a file that the viewer downloads to play whenever they want to. As more and more movies are accessible via the Web, we are actually developing an audience that needs, wants, and expects to see movies within the context of the online experience.

Very soon, you will see more instances where movies and interactivity are combined. As viewers watch a film, they will be able to click an actor's face and read a biography or listen to an interview with the director. At present, however, we are still in an incubation period as the codecs, file formats, and delivery systems get worked out. The cable companies are looking into delivering on-demand digital video via fiber optics in a way that will creatively combine the cable TV and Internet experience.

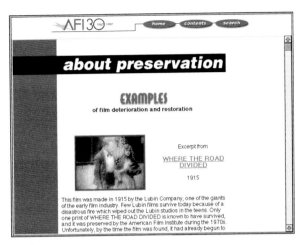

13.4

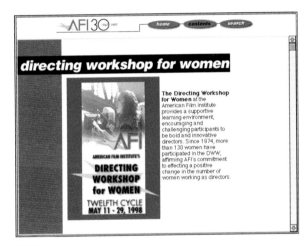

13.5

PERIPHERALS:
Radius 17-inch monitor and two external MicroNet 2GB hard drives for processing video

PRIMARY APPLICATIONS:
Adobe Premiere, Media Cleaner Pro, Movie Player, BBEdit, and Netscape

WORK HISTORY:
1992 — Ph.D. in film and television, UCLA.

1993 — Professor of Media. Griffith University in Brisbane, Queensland, Australia.

1994 — Designed and launched Cine-Media, the Internet's largest film and media directory.

1995 — Started the American Film Institute's Online Media Department. Designed and launched the Web site of the AFI in Los Angeles, California.

1997 — Launched the AFI OnLine Cinema featuring classic and contemporary movies.

1998 — Appointed head of Visual Culture and Media department, Middlesex University, London, UK.

FAVORITE MIDNIGHT SNACK:
Waffles with guava syrup

13.6

13.7

NOW SHOWING

"Before a movie goes online, we identify two primary factors: Who is the audience, and what is the function of the film going to be? These factors will influence the editing, digitizing, compression, and delivery method used. What experience do you want to deliver to your audience and what goals do the viewers have for watching these films? If a viewer goes to the trouble of either downloading a clip or getting the required plug-ins, then the movie he ends up seeing needs to be compelling, valuable, and fulfill his expectations.

"The two delivery methods that we feature on the AFI Web site are download and real-time viewing. Each type has its place, depending on the film and target audience. The simplest method is to have viewers download a QuickTime movie and watch it whenever they want to, as many times as they want to."

USING QUICKTIME

Today, location scouts and film production teams are using QuickTime clips to show casting and stock footage to producers and directors around the world. "The benefit of using QuickTime is that in the US alone 60 million computers already have it installed, most viewers won't have to download a separate plug-in, and the quality of a QuickTime clip is usually much better than the streaming video. The drawback is that the delay between the viewer deciding that they want to see a movie and the actual playing of the movie grows in direct relationship to increasing file size. To offset this delay, we use a progressive download scheme that lets the movie start to play before the entire file is done downloading."

USING STREAMING VIDEO

"The real-time movie experience screens the film in the context of the online experience. These clips are perfect for movie trailers, brief interviews, and often serve as teasers for film festivals. The longest films that we feature have a run length of up to 20 minutes and weigh in at 60MB per film. Using streaming video technology, we screen extended interviews or entire films. As the viewer watches the film, additional footage is being funneled to the browser in the background. The advantage to streaming video is that there is never an actual file downloaded to the viewer's hard drive, allowing more movies to go online since films cannot be downloaded, manipulated, or redistributed. The disadvantages of streaming video are that it requires server support, browser plug-ins, a very fast connection on a clear pipeline, and the quality isn't of the highest caliber — hey, it's a miracle that it's even getting there in the first place." The most common types of streaming video include RealMedia (*www.real.com*), VDO (*www.vdo.net*), and NetShow (*www.microsoft.com/theater/*).

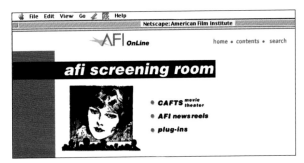

13.8

13.9

CHOOSING THE RIGHT FORMAT

Balancing the function of the film, goals of the Web site, and audience expectations with the pros and cons of QuickTime and streaming video form the foundation for the decision about which format to use. "I've noticed that a lot of Web sites are using videos to catch the viewer's attention when an animated GIF would work much more quickly and easily. We use animated GIFs in combination with our movies to create a setting or convey an atmosphere (13.7 – 13.9). Animated GIFs are a great way to start with motion imaging on a Web site."

FROM CELLULOID TO BITS AND BYTES

"We spend a lot of time shuttling back and forth with the video deck to find the best twenty seconds. We edit with the viewer in mind, looking for the twenty seconds that tell a story. It also helps to select clips that aren't full of frenetic detail and motion, since fine details don't come across well in the small frames that we use on the Web."

CAPTURE

QuickTime and streaming video are captured in the same way, either through a separate capture board or with any AV Power Macintosh 8100 or 8500 in combination with a standard video deck and simple RCA jack connections. "We digitize straight into Adobe Premiere, where we also edit, add simple transitions and titles, and then export to Media Cleaner Pro for fade-ins, fade-outs, and final compression. Our goal is to get the file as small as possible, maintain reasonable image and sound quality, give the viewer a 20-second clip, and come in with a 1.5 – 1.7MB movie file size."

Setting up the capture preferences correctly in Premiere is essential to getting a good video capture. "We use a letterbox format of 164×124 pixels. This gives the clip the accustomed movie theater aspect ratio. We capture at 15 frames per second and do not apply any compression to the incoming video (13.10). It is better to capture at the final pixel resolution of

the file and with the correct sound settings, rather than capturing, reworking, and sizing the file down later. If needed, we correct tonal problems, hue shifts, and contrast issues at the time of capture."

Desktop and digital video professionals often capture at full screen and size the image down in Media Cleaner Pro, but this creates files that are unwieldy. By capturing larger than the final size, you can crop off edge noise without making the video smaller than the final image. Also, by capturing at a larger size and scaling down, the video noise is reduced. For example, if you capture at 640×480 and scale down to 320×240, each pixel in the final image is an average of 4 original pixels. This averaging tends to smooth the image and reduce noise. However, all this being said, it is frequently difficult to capture at full screen because it requires much more hard drive space and a more tightly "tuned" system.

"Capture the audio at the highest quality setting of 44.1 Hz with 16-bit sound at mono, since streaming doesn't support stereo sound yet. We put an increased importance on sound — if the sound is really good, it will help compensate the experience of the video being jerky, fuzzy, or blurry — to a point! Viewers will put up with less image quality but will not tolerate poor sound. If the sound is ambient sound or background noise, less quality is required than for an interview where the sound is obviously more important."

Queue up the tape and capture the segment with a little bit of buffer at the beginning and end of the clip. Place the raw capture into Premiere's construction window and do any editing required (13.11). "One problem with Premiere is that it has so many easy-to-use transitions — spins, wipes, zooms, fades, peels, and dissolves. If you only have 20 seconds, you don't want to waste a lot of time with fancy transitions. Jump cuts and a simple fade-in at the beginning and a fade-out at the end are better. The opening and closing fades set the tone — analogous to the house lights going down in a real movie theater — making the film experience contained and special. We use Media Cleaner Pro to add the final fade-ins and outs."

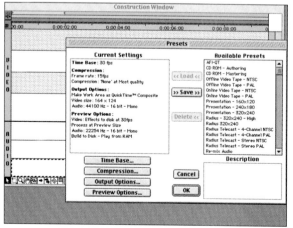

13.10

CLEANUP

After digitizing a video clip, it is necessary to prep it with file efficiency and format in mind. Harries uses Media Cleaner Pro, an encoder software, to add opening and closing fades, optimize color palettes, and do the final compression—all with a tab before/after interface which makes making decisions really intuitive. "If you are digitizing video for the first time, using the Media Cleaner Pro wizard is a great way to learn about the variables to take into consideration, such as the final media (CD-ROM, WWW, DVD) connection speed, playback options, and so on. The best thing about the wizard is that as you select a certain option it will remove conflicting options further along so that you create the best movie possible (13.12)."

Once the capture is done, do a preview in Premiere in RAM and export the file into Media Cleaner Pro or save it as a MOV file and open it with Media Cleaner Pro. "When you export the file into Media Cleaner Pro, Media Cleaner Pro has to be running in the background. This may sound odd at first, but it is actually very interesting since a preview in Premiere is just a map of the pieces, and exporting the map allows Media Cleaner Pro to construct the movie file from the map."

Video compression looks at image information in two ways—spatially and temporally. *Spatial* compression removes redundant information row by row. For example, a large expanse of blue sky will compress spatially very well. *Temporal* compression looks at a video frame by frame and removes the information that isn't moving. Imagine a person walking in front of a building. Because the person is moving, he will be left alone and because the building is not moving it will be temporally compressed.

Experimenting with settings and variables is crucial to making movies successful on the Web. This requires editorial decisions, testing, saving and comparing settings, and always checking the final movie on a PC with a 256-color monitor. "Although we do all of our digitizing and creative work on a Macintosh, the great majority of our audience is coming to the AFI Web site via a PC. Our general rule is: Make it look good on the PC and it will look great on the Mac."

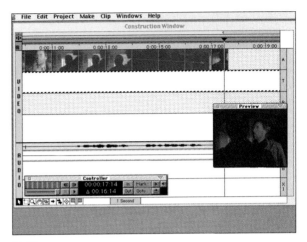

13.11

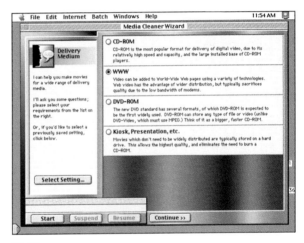

13.12

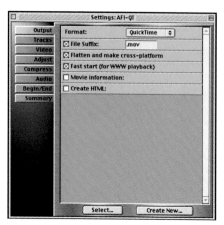

13.13

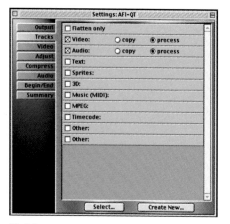

13.14

13.15

SETTINGS FOR QUICKTIME

Here's how the settings that Harries uses to create downloadable QuickTime movies (13.13) work:

- Set the output format to QuickTime and add the file suffix .MOV to the filename by checking the File Suffix box. It is important to add the file suffix so that the server knows how to handle the file.

- *Flattening* is the final pass applied to a compressed movie, which ensures that no edits remain in the movie.

- The Make cross-platform option enables both Macintosh and PCs to see the movies.

- The "Fast start" option enables the very important progressive download in which a movie will start playing before the entire file has been downloaded.

- Selecting Process means that the track will have all the adjustments and compression parameters applied to it prior to inclusion in the final output movie (13.14).

- Harries maintains his original pixel dimensions of 164 × 124 pixels (13.15).

- The compression used is very important to the final outcome of the movie quality. Cinepak is a commonly-used QuickTime codec and allows temporal and spatial compression, as well as data rate limiting (13.16)."

- "We like to play the movies at 15 frames per second, but if the file size becomes too big, we drop down to 10 frames per second."

- The *keyframe rate* is a safety net in case the movie doesn't download or play quickly enough, then at least every fifteenth frame will be displayed. Especially if you have a slow machine or connection that can't keep up playing the movie, the keyframes will play like a slide show.

■ After the actual pixel dimensions of the frame, the Data Rate Control option is the second most important determining factor that affects playback quality and speed. The *data rate* is the amount of information per second used to represent a movie. "A single-speed CD-ROM movie is usually made at a data rate of 100 Kbps and we try to keep the data rate between 65 and 100." This number does not refer to download speed, which is dependent on a users modem; rather, this is for playback.

■ "Although we capture the audio track at 44.1 kHz, we let Media Cleaner Pro take the audio track down to 22.050 kHz and still get very good results."

■ "Media Cleaner Pro does a great job at doing the fade-ins and outs, and we use the shortest increment possible of one second, fade to and from black (13.17)."

Once the settings are all determined, save the settings, export the file from Premiere into Media Cleaner Pro, and save the file. Notice the video and audio breakdown. By moving the tab slider to the left and right you can see how the settings are going to effect the final output (13.18).

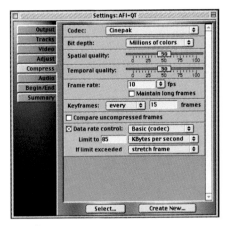

13.16

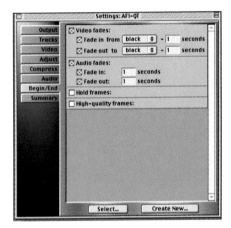

13.17

HTML FOR QUICKTIME

The HTML required to embed a QuickTime file that shows the control strip and starts playing when the download is complete is straightforward:

```
<EMBED src="name_of_movie.mov"
WIDTH=164 HEIGHT=124 AUTOPLAY=true
CONTROLLER=true LOOP=false PLUG-
INSPAGE="http://quicktime.apple.com/"
ALIGN="MIDDLE">
```

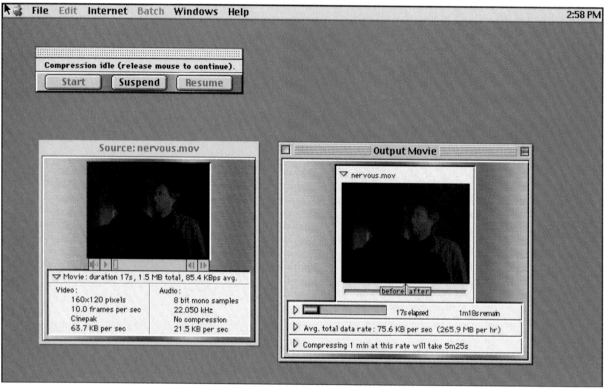

13.18

13.19

BEHIND THE SCENES

When you see a movie you like on the Web, download it, open it in Movie Player, and Get Info to see all the information you will ever need—video tracks (13.19), frame rates, data rates, audio information (13.20), width/height, bit-depth, and so on (13.21). It's a great way to learn. "We rarely use Movie Player to play videos, but we do use it to analyze our clips all the time."

13.20

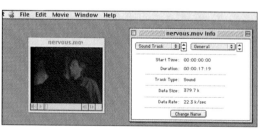

13.21

STREAMING VIDEO

"We use streaming video for films up to 20 minutes in length, long enough to screen graduate projects, short films, and in-depth interviews. The difference between a 20-second QuickTime clip and a 20-minute streaming video is huge, but we often grapple with the decision as to which one to use. The quality of the QuickTime movies with progressive download is much higher than the streaming video movies, but the time it takes to download a file can be too long for some viewers. On the other hand, a 20-minute streaming-video movie can balloon to a 60MB file, but it starts to play within seconds."

Viewing a 20-minute movie requires that the server, server software, and the viewer's browser are configured to handle the demands of streaming video. Harries uses VDO Live — a true streaming, server-based online video architecture created by VDOnet. The biggest advantage to streaming video is that the file is never downloaded to the viewer's hard drive; rather, streaming video uses a buffer that feeds video data into memory — if there was a bandwidth transfer slowdown, enough data should be in the memory buffer to allow continuous play. "We use a VDO codec and server. VDO monitors the connection speed, and if the connection slows down, the server will reduce quality to continue sending frames — albeit blurred frames. If the data flow slows severely, the VDO server will send out a slide show based on your keyframe setting. That way the viewer will always be seeing something."

The capture workflow is similar to that just described here: video deck to Macintosh computer, into Premiere, capture clip, preview, and export to Media Cleaner Pro running the VDO settings in the list that follows. (When working with such large files, you'd do best to work with two external hard drives — one for the raw captures and the second for the built files.)

■ Output a VDOLive file that is 160 × 120 pixels (13.22 and 13.23).

■ Keyframe every 100 frames at a 15-frame-per-second frame rate (13.24).

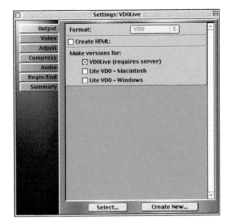

13.22

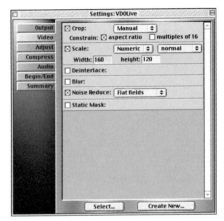

13.23

13.24

Media Cleaner Pro will automatically create an AVI file, which is required with streaming video. When viewing an AVI file in QuickTime, the bottom few rows of pixels may be blurred. This is irrelevant since it will not show up in the final presentation, so don't worry about it.

> **NOTE**
>
> Additional effective streaming video solutions include RealMedia by RealNetworks, Inc., (*www.real.com*) and Microsoft's NetShow (*www.microsoft.com/theater/*).

SERVING STREAMING VIDEO

Using VDOnet streaming isn't as simple or inexpensive as linking a QuickTime file in an HTML document. Serving streaming video requires specialized server software that monitors the streaming process, and the viewer must have the appropriate browser plug-ins installed. When a viewer accesses a streaming video file, the VDO protocol in the HTML document redirects the viewer's browser to access the VDO server that has the desired movie file (13.25). Simultaneously, on the viewer's machine, a 3K homing file is created that establishes the IP address that communicates with the VDO server. Using browser cache, the movie immediately begins to screen without ever downloading any of the video.

13.25

13.27

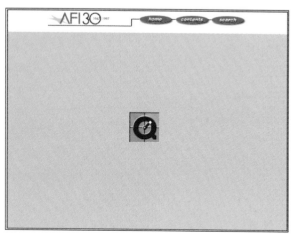

13.26

13.28

To embed a VDO file into your Web page use the following code:

```
<EMBED SRC="name_of_movie.vdo"
WIDTH=166 HEIGHT=129 STRETCH=TRUE
AUTOSTART=TRUE ALIGN=MIDDLE>
```

FROM NICKELODEON TO MULTIPLEX

The context in which both QuickTime clips and streaming-video movies are presented influences the viewer's experience tremendously. Creating the viewing environment combines HTML, page design, and deciding how much control the viewer has over playback.

The simplest method is to embed a QuickTime movie into an HTML file just like any other image. When the viewer accesses the clip, it comes up in a gray default browser page (13.26), and the viewer waits for the entire QuickTime movie to download before the movie plays. With all that gray space around the movie, the clip looks much smaller than it really is (13.27).

The second method used is to have the movie clip play in a separate mini-browser. This keeps the viewer within the context of your Web site and in the online experience. In the example pictured here (13.28), the viewer can read about Robert Wise and Orson Welles and then click See a Clip to watch a scene from *The Magnificent Ambersons.*

Constructing a context for the movie draws the viewer into the moviegoing experience. For example, before you can go into the AFI OnLine Cinema, you see the cinema entrance, enter, and click the usher (13.29) before taking your seat. The surrounding environment (13.30), beautifully designed by Todd Hughes, the AFI's online media designer, gives the movie clip a grandeur that an isolated QuickTime postage stamp just doesn't have. As the movie starts to play, the viewer has the feeling of being in a classic theater.

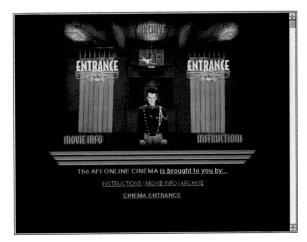

13.29

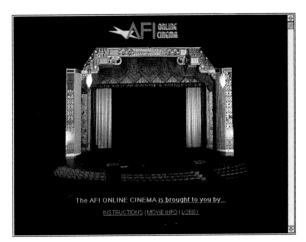

13.30

IN HONOR OF ROBERT WISE

In 1998, the AFI honored Robert Wise (13.31) with the Life Achievement Award. The AFI Web site has numerous Web pages that feature interviews, film clips, and photo galleries in his honor. Robert Wise directed and won the Oscar for *West Side Story*, and on the AFI Web site you can read about the film's production and how he solved the problem of imparting the feeling that the young lovers were by themselves when they were actually on a swirling school dance floor. After reading about how the problem was solved, you can watch the clip and see the final results.

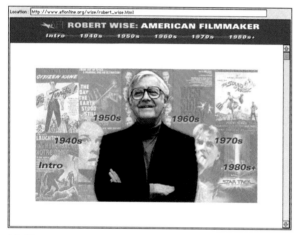

13.31

Strikingly, the frame for the movie clips, again designed by Todd Hughes, is an animated GIF that mimics the flickering light coming out of a projectionist's window in a crowded theater. This sets the tone perfectly for classic American films such as *West Side Story*, *The Sound of Music*, and *The Day the Earth Stood Still*. The GIF animation projectionist is made up of three separate GIF files put back together in a table with the movie clip in the center. (13.32 – 13.34)

USING JAVASCRIPT

A variation on the concept of setting the stage is to use JavaScript to target the film to go into a specific frame. The AFI was featured on the morning news program *Good Morning America* (13.35). "The spot was four minutes long, and we edited the highlights and created nine separate QuickTime movies for the best sections. The viewers can choose which clip they want to see, and the JavaScript tells the clip to play within the television frame (13.36 and 13.37)."

FINALLY, WITH OR WITHOUT BUTTER?

"When you go to the movies, you are not responsible for when the movie starts or stops. In our online cinema, we have hidden the controls of the clips since they connote 'computer-ness' and distract the viewer

13.32

13.33

13.34

from the entertainment experience. It may be a small cinema, but we are trying to create a complete experience!"

Make sure the viewer has to click to see a movie. "Never embed a movie on a page that starts to download without letting the viewer decide whether he or she wants to see the clip. Technology makes watching movies on the Web possible, but it is still slow, and the unassuming viewer will become very irritated as the browser slows to an imperceptible crawl. Always design the interface so the viewer makes a decision to watch a movie by clicking on a play, select, or load button."

The most important question to ask before putting any video online is, "Is this compelling content?" The technology is fascinating, but it shouldn't usurp a good story or a well-crafted film production. Kevin Thomas, film critic from the *Los Angeles Times*, reviewed the revival of Buster Keaton's *The Boat*, which the AFI featured in the OnLine Cinema. In the review, he did comment on the fact that the film was on a computer, but within a few minutes he became so enamored with the story that he forgot he was watching it on a computer monitor: "How does it look on a computer screen, at about 2 by 2½ inches, framed by a gorgeous, colorful, though over-lit, Art Deco proscenium? The answer is surprisingly good. Ever at odds with the absurdities of the material universe, Keaton and his cool, deadpan humor come

across just fine in miniature." At the same time, it's hard to imagine anything but a silent short film, running roughly 22 minutes, working in this format. The classic two-reelers are relatively free of intertitles; they have a strong, clear visual style, and their appeal and meaning, as Miss [Lillian] Gish said, really is universal.

In the end, "we're inventing the medium as we work with it, and the reality is that movies online are still small, jerky, and blurry. But even though the screen is small, the audience we are reaching is huge." If only AFI could deliver popcorn through the computer, we'd be set — click here for extra butter!

13.36

13.35

13.37

CHAPTER 14
IMMERSIVE ONLINE IMAGING

When you look at a photograph, do you ever wonder what was behind the photographer or just outside the image frame? Wouldn't it be fascinating if, when viewers came to your Web site, they could interact with a photograph? For example, moving through a scene, walking around an object such as a car or a sculpture, or visiting a museum, strolling freely from room to room. If your creative curiosity is piqued by any of these possibilities, then *Immersive Imaging* will intrigue, excite, and literally open new horizons for you and your images on the Web.

David Falstrup, CEO of eVox Productions, has been working with Immersive Imaging, or VR photography, since May of 1995. In the beginning, Immersive Imaging was called *QuickTime Virtual Reality* (QTVR). But times change, and since virtual reality connotes goggles and wired gloves, which Immersive Imaging does not require, the new term was created to reflect the concept that viewers can pan and zoom to "immerse" themselves in the photograph. Professionals in the field also use the terms *VR photography* and *QuickTime VR* to mean the same thing: interactive photographic images based upon Apple's QuickTime virtual-reality technology. Although the technology and format was developed by Apple Computer, both Macintosh and PC users can see and create cross-platform VR photographs.

Putting semantics aside, viewers that come to *www.evox.com* (14.1) can look around the newest Volkswagen Beetle (14.2 – 14.4), see the first interactive television commercial for Intel (14.5 – 14.7), or

Immersive Imaging is about photography, and anyone with a 35mm camera, a tripod, and stitching software can start experimenting with it.

DAVID FALSTRUP

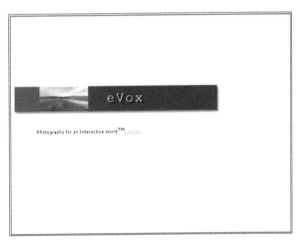

14.1

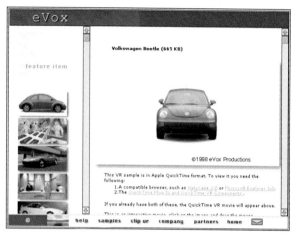

14.2

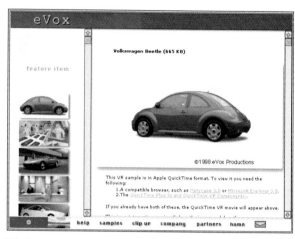

14.4

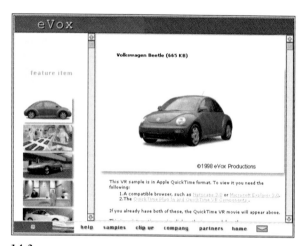

14.3

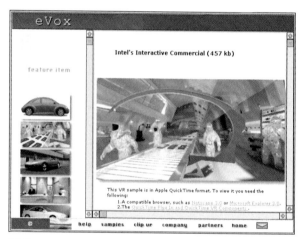

14.5

ARTIST:
David Falstrup

ORGANIZATION:
eVox Productions Headquarters
20432 South Santa Fe Ave., # J
Long Beach, CA 90810
310/605-1400 phone
310/605-1429 fax
Other locations:
New York, NY
Detroit, MI
London, England
Rancho Dominguez, CA
www.evox.com
david@evox.com

SYSTEM, MAC:
Apple Power PC G3
4GB storage/200MB RAM

SYSTEM, PC:
Dell 266 Pentium
4GB storage/128MB RAM

CONNECTIVITY, ISP:
T1 and ISDN
Several Mac and PC servers

PERIPHERALS:
More than 30 digital cameras, custom
motion control and lighting rigs, large
turntables, cycloramas, and eggshells

visit Monument Valley (14.8) and Lake Powell (14.9). As Falstrup explains, "The viewer can decide where they look in the scene, and this interaction with the image gives the viewer 'ownership' over their experience. Most importantly, Immersive Imaging is about photography, and anyone with a 35mm camera, a tripod, and stitching software can start experimenting with it. The best thing about doing VR photography now is that the software has become much easier to use. We used to have to write code to stitch images together with Macintosh Programmer's Workbench (MPW). Now we can drag the photographs into a folder and the software stitches them together for us."

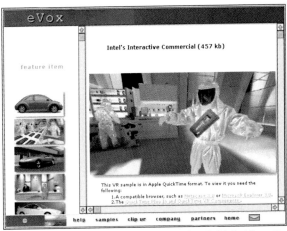

14.7

Pentium II is a registered trademark of the Intel Corporation.

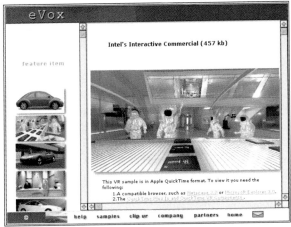

14.6

Pentium II is a registered trademark of the Intel Corporation.

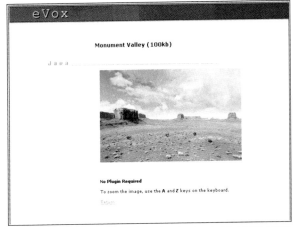

14.8

Pentium II is a registered trademark of the Intel Corporation.

PRIMARY APPLICATIONS:

Apple QTVR Authoring Studio 1.0, Live Picture Real VR Studio, IPIX Builder, Adobe Photoshop and After Effects, Macromedia Dreamweaver and Flash, DeBabelizer 1.6, IBM HotMedia, Netscape and Internet Explorer versions 2, 3, and 4

WORK HISTORY:

1981 — Engineering Science degree from the University of Exeter, England; came to the U.S. and headed west. Became an aerospace engineer.

1983 — First start-up venture converting aerospace technology into products for formula one racing.

1987 — Turnaround consulting projects in U.S. and Europe, including analysis of Chrysler's strategic plan for Lee Iaccoca.

1989 — General management, strategic planning, and consulting.

1989 — Masters of Management degree from Northwestern University's J.L. Kellogg Graduate School of Management and Certificate in Advanced International Business Management from the Copenhagen School of Business.

1994 — Introduced to multimedia. Recognized the need for a focused service company.

1995 — Attended the first Apple Developer University for QTVR. Founded eVox Productions in Long Beach, CA, a VR photography studio focusing on automotive and other high-end clients.

1998 — Opened second studio in New York, expanding into fashion work.

1999 — Opened London operations and eVox Imaging Factory in Los Angeles.

2000 — Opening eVox Vehicle Imaging Factory and expanded New York operations

FAVORITE THRILL:

Sailing on San Fransisco Bay in a 40-knot wind.

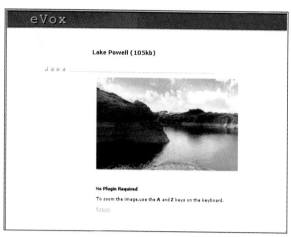

14.9

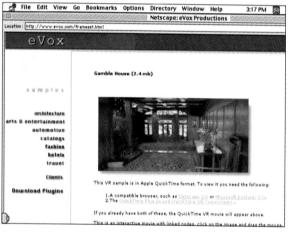

14.10

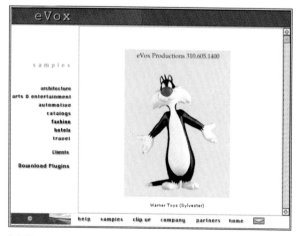

14.11

IMMERSIVE IMAGING FLAVORS

"There are different types of Immersive Imaging. The first one is the *interactive panorama*, in which the viewpoint is from the center out and the viewer can explore a 360-degree environment, such as the Gamble House Museum in Pasadena, California (14.10). The second type of Immersive Imaging is the *interactive object movie*, in which the viewer sees an object and can examine it from different points of view, as seen in the work that we have done for Warner Toys (14.11 – 14.13). In a nutshell, Immersive Imaging starts by photographing a scene, object, or person in a full 360 degrees, either processing and scanning the film or acquiring the digital camera files, and then stitching the images together with software by Apple or Live Picture. Once the image is on the Web, viewers can choose where they look — up or down, left or right, they can go in for a closer look or 'step back' to enjoy the scenery — all with the click and drag of the mouse. We also partner with IPIX to create BubbleView images (photographs mapped inside a sphere), IBM HotMedia, and Macromedia Flash. On our Web site, we have a VR photography comparison chart and links to many VR technology providers (14.14)."

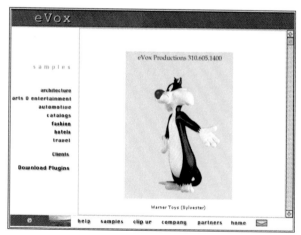

14.12

INTERACTIVE PANORAMAS

Interactive panoramas are ideal for both interior and exterior shots, such as tours of museums or interesting architectural sites, movie sets, and natural landscapes. "For the Park Hyatt Hotel in Tokyo, we created an extensive interactive tour (14.15). The viewer can 'walk' through the lobby, go up to the rooms (14.16), see the breathtaking view from the presidential suite (14.17), or check out the banquet (14.18), wedding, and spa facilities that the hotel offers. When the viewer comes to the Web site (*www.parkhyatttokyo.com*), they can either download the entire tour, which is a huge 24MB, or go on a freeform online tour to visit the areas that they are specifically interested in. In the full 24MB version, the viewer can move from one area to the next by clicking on the hot spots that we've added. For example, when the viewer is in the presidential suite, they can start in the living room (14.19), move into the dining room (14.20), the study (14.21), or even see the opulent marble baths."

"The interactive panoramas begin with the camera in the center of the environment being photographed. The photographer 'is shooting from the inside out.' Depending on how wide your lens is, take

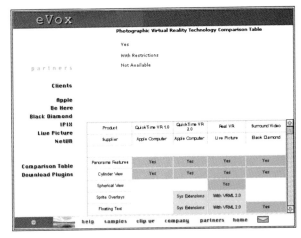

14.14

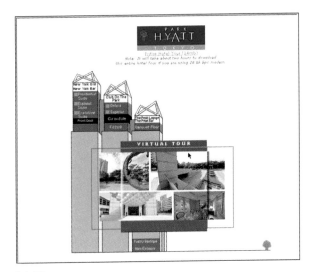

14.15

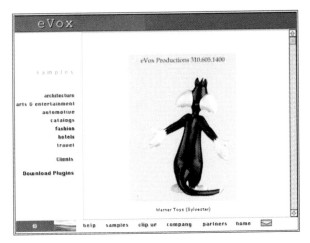

14.13

14.16

14.17

14.18

14.19

14.20

12 – 16 overlapping pictures to complete the 360-degree circle of view which will later be stitched together with the QTVR Authoring Studio 1.0 or Live Picture's Photo Vista or Reality Studio to create a single 360-degree image." The most important factors to take into consideration when shooting for professional interactive panoramas are as follows:

■ Work with a panoramic tripod head that can be moved in exact increments.

■ Rotate the camera on the nodal point of the lens. The nodal point of the lens is the specific point where light rays intersect on the image plane and the image flips. Aligning the camera on the nodal point will minimize the appearance that the elements in the picture are sliding when the viewer pans.

■ Work with a wide-angle, flat-field rectilinear lens — such as a Nikkor 15mm or Sigma 14mm.

■ Allow for 25– 40 percent overlap between images, enabling the stitching software to create seamless images (14.22).

14.21

14.22

■ Keep exposure consistent. Set the exposure manually so that the auto exposure of the camera doesn't change the f-stop, which influences the images' depth of field and impacts the software's capability to stitch the images back together in postproduction. If the light range varies a lot, bracket the exposures. Take a set of images for the light parts of the image and a set for the dark parts of the image. After the shoot, you can merge the files in Photoshop to create one set of images that are well-exposed for both the highlights and shadows. "When we photographed the hotel dining room, the sky in the windows was much brighter than the furniture in the room, so we shot the scene twice, exposing once for the room interior and once for the sky, and merged the shots in Photoshop (14.23)."

■ When using film, work with color negative film because it has greater exposure latitude in regard to lighting and exposure.

■ Shooting in a portrait orientation gives the image visual height.

■ Photographing the correct number of frames simplifies the stitching process. Table 14.1 lists the most common lens formats for 35mm cameras, and Table 14.2 lists consumer digital cameras and how many images to take.

14.23

You can learn about Immersive Imaging with much simpler tools, including consumer digital cameras such as the Apple QuickTake 200 or Kodak DC 210, a standard tripod that you've marked in equal increments, and Live Picture's Photo Vista software.

TABLE 14-1	DETERMINING THE NUMBER OF PHOTOGRAPHS FOR 35MM CAMERA LENSES	
LENS FOCAL LENGTH	PORTRAIT	LANDSCAPE
14mm	8	6
15mm	8	6
16mm	8	6
16mm Fisheye	8	4
18mm	8	8
20mm	10	8
24mm	12	8
28mm	14	8
35mm	16	12
50mm	24	16

TABLE 14-2   DETERMINING THE NUMBER OF PHOTOGRAPHS FOR CONSUMER DIGITAL CAMERAS

CAMERA	PORTRAIT	LANDSCAPE
Apple QuickTake 200	18	12
Canon PowerShot 600N	12	8
Epson PhotoPC 500	18	14
Fuji DC 300	16	10
Kodak DC-50	18	12
Kodak DC-120	18	12
Kodak DC-210	4	8
Olympus D-200L or D-300L	16	12
Polaroid PCD-2000	18	12

Note: Use widest zoom lens setting possible.

Into the Driver's Seat

A straightforward interactive panoramic image is interesting, but eVox pushes the technology further by combining studio shots, natural landscapes or computer-generated 3D environments, and sound to create one-of-a-kind viewing experiences. eVox has worked with over 45 international automobile manufacturers including Toyota, Volkswagen, Ford, Ferrari,

Mazda, KIA, and many others. The production begins with the photographer shooting the 360-degree image of the inside of the car. The car is shot in the studio with a green-screen background to simplify and increase the accuracy of the masking process. After the film is processed and scanned onto Kodak Photo CD, the individual images are acquired into Photoshop, where they are retouched, enhanced, and the windows are masked. Then the car image is layered on top of the landscape image and, by using the Offset filter set to wrap around, eVox can see how the landscape fits into the scene. Once position and relationship are set, the layered file is flattened, saved as a PICT file, and brought into QTVR Authoring Studio where the two edges are stitched together. This creates the illusion that a car which was shot and lit in a professional studio is really outdoors on a seaside cliff or in a remote desert (14.24). As viewers move around the interior of the car, they see the landscape changing just as if they were in a car outdoors. In VR panoramas that are combined with object movies, the viewer can open the glove compartment, fold down the seats, honk the horn, and even start the engine — everything but drive away with the Aston Martin pictured here (14.25)!

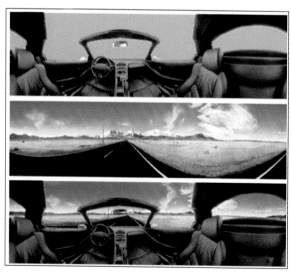

14.24

14.25

Going Deeper

By adding sound and interactivity to immersive images, the viewer is invited to explore and experience the car, scene, or product more intimately. With the addition of nodes or hot spots, the viewer can move from one point of view to another within the panoramic scene. "Museums and artists use interactive panoramas to document exhibitions, allowing the viewer to pan around the exhibit. And when the viewer sees a painting that they are interested in, they can click on the hot spot to see a high-resolution version, read about the artist, or be linked to another Web site. We use hot spots to give the viewer more information. For example, in a tour we did of the Hard Rock Cafe (14.26), you can walk into the entry way (14.27), look around in 360 degrees, and then click on a hot spot that takes you further into the restaurant (14.28 – 14.29). Interactive panoramas with hot spots can really add up in file size, so we use them mostly on CDs and interactive kiosks and less on the Web.

"One more thing that we like to do with the panoramic images is to make large photographic quality prints with them. We've created panoramas that are up to 100MB large, which allow us to make prints up to eight feet wide with the Durst Lambda 130 direct digital printer at Infinite Photo and Imaging in Arlington, Virginia (*www.infinitephoto.com*). The prints are really quite spectacular (14.30 – 14.31)."

14.26

14.27

14.28

14.29

14.30

INTERACTIVE OBJECT MOVIES

The second type of Immersive Imaging is the interactive object movie, in which the object is in the center of the image and the viewer can move around it, looking at it from different vantage points. The object can be as small as a single rose or as large as a Toyota van. "For the smaller objects, we use virtual object rigs in which the object is clamped in midair and the camera is rotated around it, taking a picture every 10 to 20 degrees. The decision to use 10- or 20-degree increments depends on how smooth you want the rotation of the final movie to be. For larger objects such as cars, we place the object onto one of several 20- to 40-foot turntables, which are similar to a lazy susan. The camera is stationary and we actually rotate the object in ten degree increments."

Object movies range from simple spins, in which the object is photographed from one point of view, to multi-row object movies, in which the object is photographed from various perspectives while it is spun. "It all depends on how many points of view you want to give the viewer. For some products, such as the Heineken bottle (14.32), a simple spin is all that is needed (14.33). Often, the client wants the viewer to be able to look at the product from any point of view. We'll shoot the object in a grid pattern (14.34 and 14.35) and stitch the set of images together with the Apple QTVR Authoring Studio software. The final result is a file in which the viewer uses the mouse to move the object and look at any side of it—in this case the Nike sneaker (14.36–14.39)."

14.31

14.32

14.33

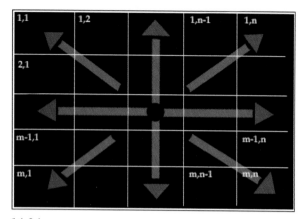

14.34

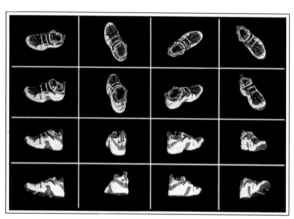

14.35

14.36

14.37

14.38

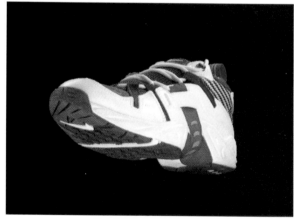

14.39

After acquiring the individual images, creating the required masks, and saving the images as PICT files with Photoshop, the files are imported into Adobe After Effects, where the object images are composited with the desired background or environment. Using the Apple Media Developer Kit, eVox adds interactivity and the capability to spin, zoom, and pan the object with the Navigable Movie Player and then exports the file as a QuickTime movie.

More Than Objects

"Immersive Imaging isn't limited to static objects or empty spaces. We use it to do fashion work and training videos. The fashion work that we are doing for Boo.com, Jhane Barnes, and others allows viewers to browse the clothing selection and see how the clothing looks on a 'real' model versus just seeing the clothing from one side (14.40 – 14.43).

"In the self-defense training video, the viewer can scrub back and forth watching the moves of the teachers from many points of view. Shooting moving jujitsu fighters in 360 degrees was accomplished by having the teachers go through their moves a number of times on the turntable that we moved in 10-degree increments. After the instructors had done the jujitsu move a few times, we had all the frames needed to create a 360-degree view of how to flip an assailant. The advantage to using interactive object movies is that the viewer can study each move from different angles and at the pace that they choose (14.44 – 14.49).

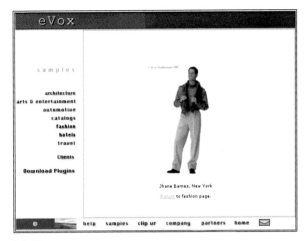

14.41

14.42

14.43

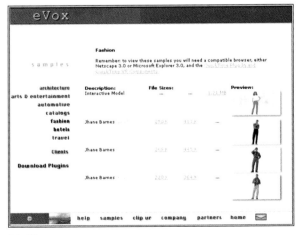

14.40

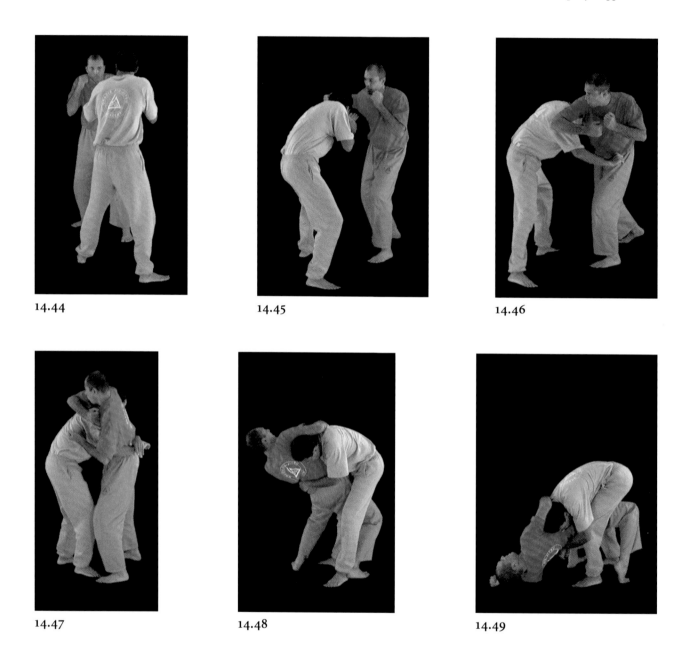

14.44

14.45

14.46

14.47

14.48

14.49

"When you're shooting outside in environments where there are people, it is always better to shoot an extra set of images. That way, if someone walks into the image, you have the ability to replace frames as needed. What usually happens is that a person will be on the edge of one frame and they will have moved out of the scene by the time you shoot the next shot. This causes 'ghosting' where you see part of a person. In the European street scene, you can see the 'ghost'

in the first image (14.50), which we removed to create the second clean image (14.51).

"Among the most interesting work we do, is when we combine interactive panoramic and object movies. In an interactive VR photograph, the viewer would be walking through a museum and see a sculpture that interests them. They would be able to zoom in on the sculpture and look at it from all different sides. The interactivity and dimensionality of these views is fascinating. Right now the bandwidth really isn't there to allow for these large files, but in the future, virtual Web shoppers will be able to walk down the aisles of a virtual store, take a product off the shelf, and turn it around to get a closer look!"

THE IMMERSIVE PHOTO STUDIO

Walking into the photo studio of eVox Productions is just like walking into any other high-end photo studio: huge banks of soft lights, a photographer directing the assistant, the client's coffee and snack table are all there. The picture is complete. It is only upon a closer look that you notice that the bright yellow Ferrari is on a room-sized turntable and that the assistant is moving the car in 10-degree increments with the photographer shooting one exposure at each turn with a high-resolution digital camera.

Either film or digital capture can be used to photograph images for Immersive Imaging production. In the studio, eVox uses several different digital cameras, including the Kodak DCS 460, PhaseOne, and the new Nikon D1. On location, they usually use a digital panoramic scanning camera, such as the Panoscan. When that's too cumbersome, they shoot to film. eVox used to work with a Seitz RoundShot, which is a medium-format 120mm strip camera that rotates a full 360 degrees. As the exposure is being made, the camera spins and simultaneously the film is transported across the slit that functions as the curtain in traditional 35mm cameras. One advantage to using the RoundShot is that exposures can be made as quickly as one second, allowing you to freeze motion. Another advantage is that the image is on one piece of film, which simplifies scanning and stitching (14.52). The processed film is then scanned onto Kodak Photo CD and input into the QTVR Authoring Studio for distortion correction, stitching, adding hot spots, and final image processing. As you can see by the warped ceiling, the original image is distorted by camera optics. This is the nature of taking a three-dimensional reality and flattening it onto a two-dimensional surface (14.53). The QTVR software resolves this distortion automatically (14.54), analyzing the image as if it was to be laid out on a grid (14.55).

14.50

14.51

14.52

14.53

14.54

AFTER THE SHOOT

Working in Immersive Imaging requires a combination of good photography, solid lighting skills, and the knowledge to work with digital postproduction tools. When shooting film, eVox has the film processed and scanned onto Kodak Photo CD, after which the files are acquired and brought into Photoshop for cropping, color correction, and retouching (14.56). "We color correct one image with an image adjustment layer (14.57) and then drag that adjustment layer onto all the other images, guaranteeing that all the images have undergone the same color correction." As you can see, the top row has had the image-adjustment layer applied, and the bottom two rows still need correction (14.58). "At this point, we don't do finely detailed image retouching since the stitching process may or may not actually cover up the problem areas." The next step is to save the files in PICT format and launch the Apple QTVR Authoring Studio.

In the QTVR Authoring Studio, select Panorama Maker, which creates one long PICT file, or Panorama Stitcher, which creates a long PICT file and a QTVR movie. Then import the PICT files (14.59). The software deskews (14.60), stitches, compresses, and previews the immersive image (14.61).

Here are the most important settings to consider when creating VR photography with Apple QTVR Authoring Studio:

- **Compression:** eVox uses JPEG compression set to High.
- **Colors:** "We always use millions of colors to maintain photographic quality."
- **Blending:** eVox uses Gaussian blending, which applies a Gaussian Blur filter. This preserves the contrast of the original image, balances image transitions, and minimizes the smearing that may occur when using narrow or normal blending settings.

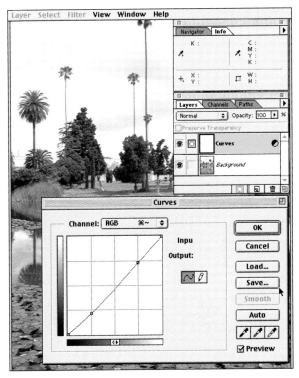

14.57

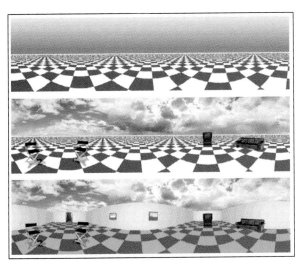

14.55

14.58

14.56

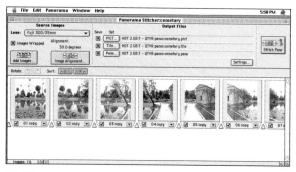

14.59

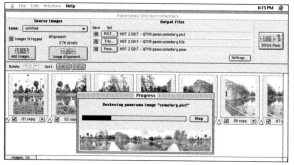

14.60

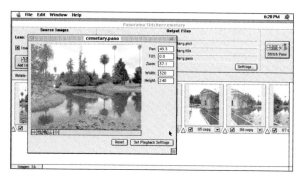

14.61

Once the Panorama Maker or Panorama Stitcher is done, you can bring the long PICT file into Photoshop to retouch frame edges and image blemishes, or to fine-tune exposure. In the working example, the PICT file was brought into Photoshop to clean up the bridge (14.62 and 14.63) and improve the sky (14.64). Then the PICT file was again brought into Apple QTVR Authoring Studio and was stitched together. Remember to use one of the three filename extensions that Netscape Navigator recognizes (.mov, .moov, and .qt) when naming the final panorama or object movie.

14.62

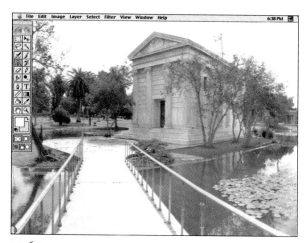

14.63

"In our work for the Gamble House (14.65), we used Photoshop to improve the ceiling and window density (14.66) before stitching the image together."

Interactive object movies often require that each individual frame is first brought into Photoshop to crop (14.67) and separate the object from the studio environment or object rig by cutting a mask (14.68) for each frame.

14.64

14.65

14.66

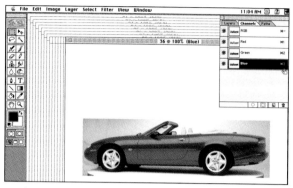

14.67

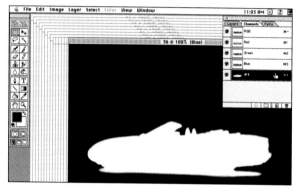

14.68

VR PHOTOGRAPHY ON THE WEB

As with other graphics on the Web, final image size is the most important determining factor to consider when preparing immersive images for Web viewing. A number of places, along the VR photography work-flow, influence final file size: whether you use film and Photo CD or consumer digital cameras as the initial input; at what resolution the individual Photo CD files are acquired; using Photoshop's image size to downsize the files before stitching the panorama or object movie; opening the long PICT file that the Apple QTVR Authoring Studio makes and sizing it down in Photoshop; or using higher compression rates than the recommended JPEG with high settings. "The final file size depends upon the final use for the image, and we work to balance the image-quality-versus-bandwidth issues. The problem with using very low resolution images is that the viewer can't zoom in to see the image details." In the images seen here, the better quality is from a 1.7MB VR movie (14.69), and the low-quality image is from a 132K movie (14.70). "On the eVox Web site, we give the viewer the choice to look at low-, medium-, or high-resolution VR photos.

"Working with film and Kodak Photo CD scans gives us the option to build a number of different resolution files from one photo shoot," as seen in Table 14-3.

TABLE 14-3   PHOTO CD RESOLUTION CHOICES

RESOLUTION	FILE SIZE	STITCHED FILE	MOVIE SIZE
384 × 256 Low-res	288K	1.1MB	260K
768 × 512 Medium-res	1.1MB	5.4MB	490K
1,536 × 1,024 High-res	4.5MB	19MB	1.8MB
3,072 × 2,048 Super Hi-res	18MB	70MB	5.3MB

14.69

14.70

EMBEDDING VR PHOTOGRAPHY WITH HTML

Adding immersive images to a Web site is straightforward. The simplest and crudest method is to use the `<A>` tag, which will open the movie into an empty gray window. To display the movie in context, use the `<EMBED>` tag as follows: `<EMBED SRC=yourqtvr.mov HEIGHT=320 WIDTH=240>`. Replace the name `yourqvtr.mov` with the name of your movie, and the values for width and height attributes with your movie window dimensions.

The QuickTime plug-in displays QTVR movies with the controller off by default. In order to show it, add the `CONTROLLER` parameter to your `<EMBED>` tag like so: `<EMBED SRC=yourqtvr.mov HEIGHT=320 WIDTH=240 CONTROLLER=TRUE>`. If you use values for `WIDTH` and `HEIGHT` other than those of the movie, the plug-in will scale the movie. If the controller is showing, it can appear cropped. To avoid this, use the `SCALE` parameter with the value "`ToFit`".

Several parameters control the appearance of the QTVR movie when it is displayed for the first time, including `PAN`, `TILT`, and `FOV`.

- `PAN`: The default setting for when a VR photograph opens centered on the left side of the original image. If you would like to specify a specific starting point use the `PAN` tag `PAN=xxx`, where **xxx** is the number of pixels you want the opening image moved to the left.
- `TILT`: The default setting for when a VR photograph opens centered on the middle (of left side) of the original image. You can have the viewer looking up or down by using the `TILT` tag `TILT=xxx`, where the **xxx** is any number between -42.5 and 42.5 — the negative numbers look down and the positive numbers look up.
- `FOV`: The field of view attribute is where you can define how zoomed in or out the initial opening scene is: `FOV=xxx`, where **xxx** is 5.0 (zoomed in all the way) to 85.0 (zoomed all the way out).

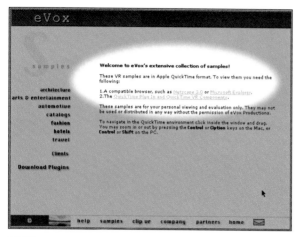

14.71

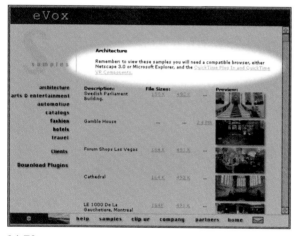

14.72

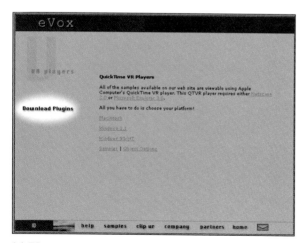

14.73

Since QuickTime movie files tend to be large, they are not cached by default. In a case where caching is desired, you can set CACHE=TRUE. Additional information regarding playback options can be found at the Apple Web site dedicated to Immersive Imaging (*www.apple.com/quicktime/authoring/embed.html*).

It is polite to let the viewer know that they are about to look at a VR photograph, since time and plug-ins are required to view them. Most Macintosh computers and Netscape Navigator 3.0 and later have the required QuickTime system extensions loaded, and Windows users can download the extensions from the Apple site (*www.apple.com/quicktime/qtvr/index. html*). "We let the viewers know that they are about to enter a page that has VR photography and how to interact, pan, and zoom in the image (14.71). In fact, we let them know twice (14.72) and also provide the links to download the appropriate plug-ins (14.73). Downloading a VR photograph takes some time, and

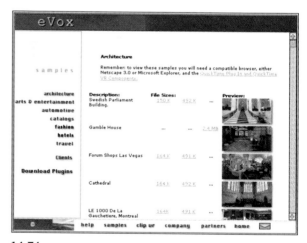

14.74

we give the viewer three resolution choices depending upon their connection speed and quality needs (14.74). When the viewer accesses the VR photograph, at first they see a grid, and as the grid fills in, they can pan and zoom before the download is complete (14.75 and 14.76). Once the image is in the browser cache, the viewer can spin, zoom, and look at the VR photograph (in this case, the Swedish Parliament) as often as they like (14.77 and 14.78).

Working in QTVR requires a combination of photography and lighting skills with digital postproduction finesse. Falstrup emphasizes that creating high-quality immersive images is 50 percent photographic and 50 percent digital. When the eVox production team works together, the sum is always better than the parts. If you want to give the viewer more of the picture, incorporating immersive images into your Web site will definitely put a new spin on your photography and the impact of your Web site.

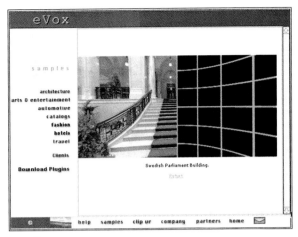

14.76

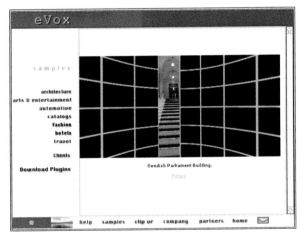

14.75

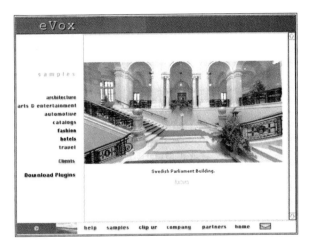

14.77

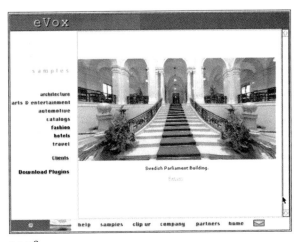

14.78

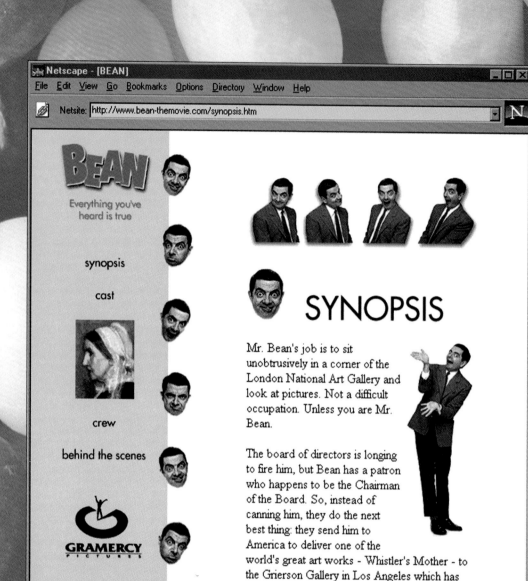

BEAN

Everything you've
heard is true

synopsis

cast

crew

behind the scenes

GRAMERCY
PICTURES

SYNOPSIS

Mr. Bean's job is to sit
unobtrusively in a corner of the
London National Art Gallery and
look at pictures. Not a difficult
occupation. Unless you are Mr.
Bean.

The board of directors is longing
to fire him, but Bean has a patron
who happens to be the Chairman
of the Board. So, instead of
canning him, they do the next
best thing: they send him to
America to deliver one of the
world's great art works - Whistler's Mother - to
the Grierson Gallery in Los Angeles which has
just purchased the painting for an astounding $50
million. The London Gallery will tell the Los
Angeles Gallery that the courier is Mr. Bean, a
renowned authority on the painting who will stay
there to lecture about the art work. Perhaps they
hope that once the Americans discover he is a
fraud, they will kill him. Even if only in
self-defense.

Netscape - [BEAN]

File Edit View Go Bookmarks Options Directory Window Help

Netsite: http://www.bean-themovie.com/synopsis.htm

Document: Done

CHAPTER 15

ANNOUNCING YOUR WEB SITE

SYNOPSIS

ob is to sit
y in a corner of the
onal Art Gallery and
res. Not a difficult
Unless you are Mr.

Y ou might question what Eric Ward is doing in this book. He's not a graphic artist. He's not a designer. Perhaps most telling, he's the only person featured in this book who doesn't list Photoshop among the tools he uses on a daily basis. "I wouldn't recognize Photoshop if you set it right in front of me. I'm a little embarrassed to admit this, but I know nothing about graphics. Nothing. When I was first putting together my site, I paid college students to create my graphics." The good news is, Ward chose good people to help him. "The college kid who I hired back in 1993 is now the creative director at CyberGold."

And yet Ward maintains that what he does is an art. Ward's business? Web site promotion. We're not talking about a guy who blasts a company's URL willy-nilly to a billion different search engines and says to his client, "There you go, consider yourself a player." Ward methodically matches each client's site with the people and places most likely to be interested in it. And he's been at it longer than anyone in the business.

"When I went back to college in '92, I saw the Internet for the first time. It was completely the domain of academia. There weren't any graphical browsers yet. But when Mosaic became available and suddenly the Internet had graphics, I knew it was all going to change. I hate to say this, but I could tell right away that business and commerce were going to take over the Web in a big way. I didn't know how long it would take or when it would happen, but I knew it was just a matter of time."

You need to take a holistic approach. Look at your Web site as a whole, based on its quality and content, and find the outlets that need to know about it.

ERIC WARD

Like any business entity, an online presence doesn't serve any purpose if nobody knows it's there. So having cut his teeth in traditional marketing, Ward quickly saw that the forthcoming professional Web sites were going to need his services. "Seven years ago, I went to an ISP that had just opened up in Knoxville, Tennessee. At this time, they probably had four or five corporate companies that had built some kind of Web presence. I told them I wanted to start a business promoting Web sites. All I really wanted to know was whether they thought my plan was feasible or not. But instead they said, 'Hell, if you can do that, we'll hire you to announce all our clients. We're having to do that now and it's a pain in the neck.' That's when I knew it was going to work. If the first ISP I talked to responded this enthusiastically, I had no doubt that my services were going to be needed."

So the question remains: What is a non-designer doing in a book about Web design? The answer is very simple. Ward knows how to unlock the door between you and your intended audience. After spending hours upon hours and weeks upon weeks establishing a Web presence, most of us don't have a clue about how we should go about announcing ourselves to the world. And let's face it, there's no point in launching your personal vision onto the million-lane information superhighway only to pile up and stall a few feet from the entrance ramp.

Eric Ward knows how to keep the traffic moving. And after all is said and done, this may be the most important art of them all.

\<META> TAGS AND SEARCH ENGINES

Not surprisingly, Ward doesn't condone the build-it-and-they-will-come philosophy. "I'm sorry, but the simple fact that you have a Web site isn't news. Everybody has a Web site. If you came to me and told me your company didn't have a site, now that would be remarkable."

Okay, so you can't hang up a sign and hope that the world decides to stop by for a visit. But what do you do? Should you put a ton of \<META> tags in your pages (15.1) so that the almighty search-engine "spiders" snag you and put you in their databases (15.2)? "A lot of people think \<META> tags were invented for the benefit of AltaVista and Infoseek. But when \<META> tags first came into use, there weren't any search engines. \<META> names and keywords are just ways of identifying your documents, so you can keep track of what all the different pages inside your site are doing. Then along came the automated search engines, and the \<META> tags became a convenient way for the engines to categorize sites.

ARTIST:
Eric Ward

ORGANIZATION:
The WardGroup
Knoxville, Tennessee
423/637-2438
www.netpost.com
netpost@netpost.com

SYSTEM:
Dell Dimension 486/300MHz
Windows 95
8GB storage/64MB RAM

CONNECTIVITY:
56 Kbps modem

PERIPHERALS:
Dell 17-inch monitor

PRIMARY APPLICATIONS:
Netscape Communicator, Microsoft Access, EWAN (Telnet client), and Microsoft Office

WORK HISTORY:
1986 — Published Knoxville-based franchise of *Travel Host* magazine, which gets distributed in hotels.

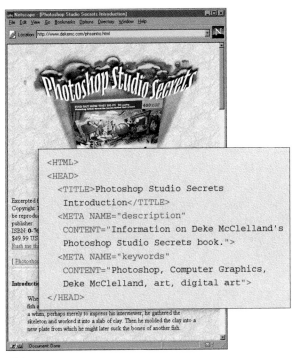

15.1

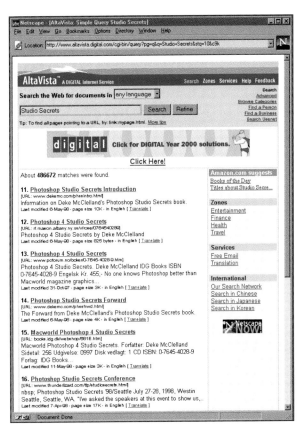

15.2

<u>1991</u> — After employer went bankrupt, took night courses at University of Tennessee.

<u>1992</u> — Turned on computer for first time and discovered potential of Internet through the eyes of a marketing person.

<u>1993</u> — The WardGroup was born when local ISP began forwarding all its clients who needed promotion.

<u>1994</u> — Asked Yahoo to create a new category for site-promotion businesses, now grown to include hundreds of companies.

<u>1997</u> — Named in *Websight* magazine's list of the 100 most influential people on the Internet.

FAVORITE TOM HANKS MOVIE:

Joe Versus the Volcano ("I relate to the beginning where he's stuck in this depressing job.")

15.3

15.4

"As a publicity tool, ⟨META⟩ tags are most useful if your site includes a lot of artistically designed pages that are nothing more than a series of graphics. If there's no text on a page, it becomes literally invisible to the search engine. All you've got is a bunch of ⟨IMG SRC=X⟩, which tells the search engine absolutely nothing about what your page has to offer. In this case, ⟨META⟩ tags become crucial. In the absence of any text in your HTML document, the ⟨META⟩ description and keyword tags are all AltaVista and others have to go off of."

Two of Ward's clients, coolshopping.com and Gramercy Pictures, are cases in point. The home pages for *www.coolshopping.com* (15.3) and *www. bean-themovie.com* (15.4) both feature lone GIF images against solid-colored backgrounds. A look at the source code for the coolshopping.com page shows an extensive list of ⟨META⟩ descriptions and keywords that are likely to help a search engine digest the site. The description text appears verbatim in the AltaVista hit (15.5). Like the movie it promotes, the *Bean* site source code is a little more peculiar (15.6). Although the ⟨META⟩ description is undeniably funny, it's less successful in conveying a sense of what the sight is about. As a result, it takes some effort to locate this site through AltaVista.

In fact, in every search we performed on the movie *Bean*, the first 40 or 50 hits were exclusively third-party reviews of the movie. Ward guesses that Gramercy wasn't very concerned with the search engines. "These movie sites generally come out a week or two before the movie premieres. Since the search engines take two to six weeks to list a site, they really don't drive much of the movie-going traffic."

But the movie was going to be out in six weeks. Shouldn't the designers have worked harder to massage the ⟨META⟩ tags so the site would get the first spot on a search? "Well, yes and no. I think these movie sites tend to be too focused on the cinema experience. They should be thinking longer term. How can they use the site to roll out the movie on Pay Per View? What happens when it comes out on video? I don't think the studios are exploiting the sites to their full advantage.

"But let's say that they actually did shoot for number one. Maybe the *Bean* ⟨META⟩ tags — strange as they are—were exactly what the search engines wanted. Maybe they had the first spot for a week or so and then they dropped to number 207 after that. Then maybe they massaged the code some more and got up to number three, only to be knocked down again a few days later. How long are you supposed to keep doing this? My feeling is, it's not a game you can win, so why even try?

"The fact is, you can spend thousands of hours trying to be number one with AltaVista. A lot of people do. But there's no point. First of all, search engines are fickle, so there's no telling what they want. But also, you have no secrets, because everyone out there has access to your HTML code. If you somehow manage to figure out the right keywords to come up high on a search, another person can go to your site and look at your source code and steal it. So if you decide you're going to tweak your code to come up high on a search, keep in mind that you're going to have to do it eight hours a day, 365 days a year, and everything you do can be stolen by your competitors because there's no way to stop them unless you spend a fortune in time and money building bait-and-switch pages. It becomes your own version of Dante's *Inferno*—a hell with many levels of madness. It's insane.

"<META> tags are a good tool, but they're just one of many. And hard as you might try, you can't leverage a search engine when 10,000 other sites are doing the same thing. I like to tell people, instead of massaging your HTML code, you're better off massaging the Webmaster at Infoseek. It's a joke, but it's true. The manual ways are better."

SUBMITTING TO THE DIRECTORIES

In addition to making your site accessible to automated search engines, Ward advocates that you make manual submissions to Web directories. Just so we're all on the same page, what's the difference? "Search engines all rely on spiders to automatically crawl around and investigate Web pages. The spiders generate an enormous index. When you enter a few words and hit Enter, the search engine looks through its index and comes back with a few hundred or thousand results. There are no humans involved.

```
<HTML>
<HEAD>
   <TITLE>coolshopping.com</TITLE>
   <META NAME="description"
   CONTENT="The ultimate source for ultra-cool
   shopping sites, including cool shopping
   site of the day, coolblue heat soap opera,
   chat, personals, online cards.
   Handpicked by the coolteam.">
   <META NAME="keywords"
   CONTENT="shopping,cool,shop,mall,submit,
   award,advertise,gifts,fashion,jewelery,
   software,cds,art,books,toys,banner,flowers,
   videos,travel,clothes,clothing,hardware,
   contests,sports,crafts,pets,accessories,
   children,kids,food,coffee,cigar
   collectibles,gourmet,gallery">
</HEAD>
```

15.5

> coolshopping.com
> [URL: www.coolshopping.com/]
> The ultimate source for ultra-cool shopping sites, including cool shopping site of the day, coolblue heat soap opera, chat, personals, online cards.
> Last modified 3-Mar-98 · page size 4K · in English

```
<HTML>
<HEAD>
   <TITLE>BEAN</TITLE>
   <META NAME="description"
   CONTENT="What's that, you say?
   You don't know Bean from bean?
   You're Bean-challenged?
   Well, now is the time to experience
   the Bean essence, the Bean allure,
   the eau de Bean.">
   <META NAME = "keywords"
   CONTENT= "Gramercy Pictures, PolyGram,
   EmeraldNet, ROWAN ATKINSON, MEL SMITH,
   TIM BEVAN, ERIC FELLNER, PETER
   BENNETT-JONES, RICHARD CURTIS, ROBIN
   DRISCOLL, PETER MACNICOL, PAMELA
   REED, HARRIS YULIN, JOHNNY GALECKI,
   ANDREW LAWRENCE, TRICIA VESSEY,
   BURT REYNOLDS">
</HEAD>
```

15.6

> BEAN
> [URL: bean-the-movie.com/]
> What's that, you say? You don't know Bean from bean? You're Bean-challenged? Well, now is the time to experience , the Bean essence, the Bean allure, the
> Last modified 17-Oct-97 · page size 939 bytes

AVOIDING THE APPEARANCE OF SPAM

There are lots of clever tricks for getting the attention of search engines. But Ward generally advises against them. Most of the tricks have been used to death by spammers, giving them a bad name with the search engines.

"There's a lot of <META> tag abuse going on. People add <META> tags that have nothing to do with what their sites are really about. Like a soft drink manufacturer might list the names of its competitors in its description field. Then when you search for Pepsi, you also get hits for Coke. That's not a real-life example, of course, but it's indicative of the kind of thing that happens all the time.

"There are so many different techniques for spamming, it's awful. For example, let's say you use a white background for your Web page. Some sites will then include a bunch of text on the page and color it white. The white text blends into the white background so the user can't see it. But the search engine can see the text just fine."

See, now to us, that sounds like a hot tip, especially for artists with very little text on their pages. "Well, in theory, there's nothing wrong with including invisible text so long as it's an honest description of your page. But there are search engines that will disqualify a page for it. The search engine figures invisible text means you're trying to pull a fast one so, bang, you're eliminated."

The search engine doesn't know if you're playing fair. It just knows that this trick is used by spammers, so you're guilty by association. "These are machines. They don't know clever from crooked. So the safest thing is to steer clear of the tricks."

"Directories rely on human beings. Unlike the search engines, they don't try to index every single site on the planet. They just go for the best sites. But directories also tend to be a better vehicle for promoting your site. Yahoo in particular is an immensely popular site. Its categories are predefined and well organized. So instead of sifting through hundreds or thousands of matches, as you do with a search engine, users can get to the sites they're looking for in a matter of a few clicks.

"The problem with Yahoo is that something like one third of the people who apply to be listed never get in. And it can take months to get a listing. But it's well worth the effort. If you make submissions to all the directories, you're bound to get on a few of them. And it doesn't hurt if you have a killer site. When it comes to directories, quality counts."

TIPTOE THROUGH THE YAHOO

Yahoo does a good job of documenting how you should go about making a submission. But speaking from experience, the more right-brained among us sometimes have problems following even the simplest of left-brained instructions. So we thought it might be helpful to watch over Ward's shoulder as he makes a directory submission for a real client, coolshopping.com (15.7).

"The client came to me with the idea of launching a site that was designed to be a directory of nothing but really high-end shopping-related Web sites. There are a billion people out there who will sell you stuff over the Web, but who's doing some really unique or unusual things? The idea behind coolshopping.com was to be a port of entry to the best shopping sites out there."

Before making your submissions, Ward recommends that you put together a brief text-only document that lists your name, URL, e-mail address, and other specifics, along with a few brief descriptions of your site. "It's good to include separate 15-, 25-, 50-, and 70-word site summaries. That way, they can just lift the summary that matches the length requested by the directory. By preparing in advance, you don't have to type the same information over and over every time you make a submission.

"Next I go to Yahoo (*www.yahoo.com*). It's not like Yahoo's the only directory out there, but it's a darn fine starting point. Then I type *shopping directories* into the Search field and hit Enter. I'm just doing some research here — I don't know if I'll find anything or not. I get a total of five category matches along with a bunch of internal Yahoo site matches (15.8). I want the categories because I need to announce a site that's not part of Yahoo. So now I'm scanning the list for a good category. I like the sound of the first one, *Business and Economy: Companies: Shopping Centers: Shopping: Directories*. I'm thinking this category might make sense.

"So I click on the category name. Yahoo takes me to the category, where I see a whole list of shopping directories, and sure enough, midway down is *cool-shopping.com* (15.9). But let's say I'm submitting the site for the first time. I've found this category and I'm thinking this is the one for me. At the very bottom of the page is a link that says 'Suggest a Site.' And there begins the process."

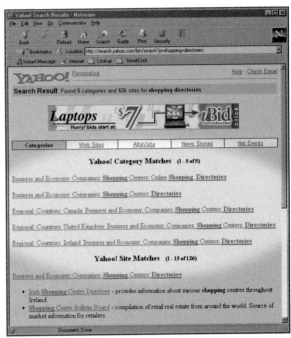

15.8   *Text and artwork copyright © 1998 by Yahoo!, Inc. All rights reserved.*

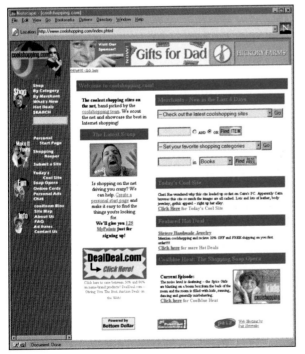

15.7

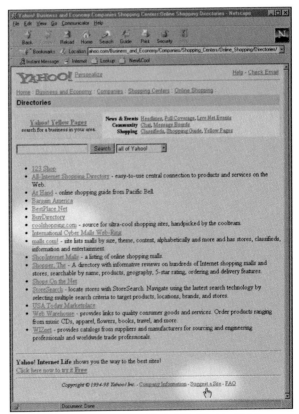

15.9   *Text and artwork copyright © 1998 by Yahoo!, Inc. All rights reserved.*

"From here, I'm asked for a bunch of different pieces of information. I open that text-only document that I created earlier. Then I just sit there and copy and paste from it. If you're organized up front, it takes maybe five minutes to go through the whole process."

It may be a few weeks or months before your site shows up on Yahoo. And even then, it may not show up in the category you suggested. "That's the funny thing about Yahoo—just because you say you want to submit your site somewhere doesn't mean that's where it's going to end up. There are human reviewers here and they make the decisions."

SEARCH ENGINE SUBMISSION

What about the automated search engines? Do they permit manual submissions? "Oh, yeah, you can and you should. Search engines rely on spiders, but it's still a good idea to show the spiders where to go. If you go to AltaVista (*www.altavista.com*), you'll see a link near the bottom that says 'Add a URL.' Just go ahead and click on it.

"Now you see how easy submissions can be. Yahoo and AltaVista represent opposite ends of the submission difficulty spectrum. Where Yahoo has five or six screens of options, AltaVista just asks for one thing—your URL. That's it. Every few months, AltaVista will go out and fetch your site and index it automatically according to the text in your HTML files. It doesn't need or permit any more input from you."

INDUSTRY-SPECIFIC DIRECTORIES

Yahoo and AltaVista aren't the only games in town. "Yahoo offers a great directory for other directories and search engines that you should definitely look into. But you have to go deep into Yahoo to get to it.

"Starting at the top of the Yahoo hierarchy—right after you enter *www.yahoo.com*—click on the Computers & Internet category. Then click on World Wide Web@, then Searching the Web. Now you've burrowed pretty far into the Yahoo directory system and you've discovered a mother lode of promotion information (15.10). You can see in this list that there are more than a hundred search engines, even more Web directories, and a bunch of articles comparing search engines. It's everything anybody could ever want for announcing a Web site.

"So if I were new to announcing Web sites, I would come to this page and click on the Web Directories link. Suddenly, I have this amazing list of the kinds of places I want to be submitting to (15.11). Keep in mind, not every one of these fits every kind of site, but you can definitely find a handful that are right up your alley.

"If you scroll through this list of directories, you start to see some familiar ones. But there are a lot of industry-specific directories as well. Like here's one called Achoo (*www.achoo.com*), the directory of Internet health-care sites (15.12). If you're a graphic designer and you're building a site for a hospital, an HMO, a private practice, or anyone else in the health-care profession, you need to submit them to Achoo. I used this directory when I was consulting with the American Medical Association (15.13). It was an obvious marriage. Once you know where to look, it's just a matter of common sense."

PUTTING A FACE WITH A NAME

"Often, a directory will present you with a specific person who you should e-mail. Then you know precisely who the arbitrator is. This is often the case with some directories and Web guides, like the fine collection of edited Web guides that are part of About.com (*www.about.com*, 15.14). Incidentally, I have to say, About.com is the top network of subject specific Web guides I have ever seen. It's really an awesome collection of sites.

"So let's say I want to promote Gramercy's *Bean* site (15.15). I'd click on the Entertainment link. Now I'm thinking, do they have anything about movies? And I see a heading called *Movies* with a category called *Hollywood Movies/Reviews*. So I click there and I'm presented at this point with the About.com discussion of Hollywood movies.

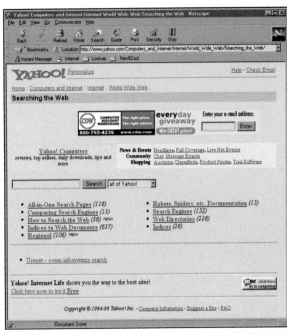

15.10

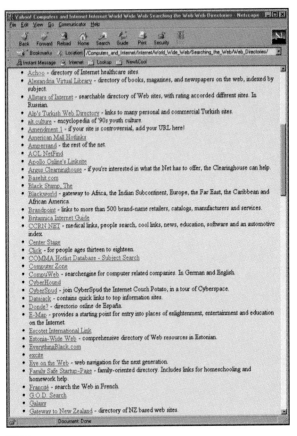

15.11

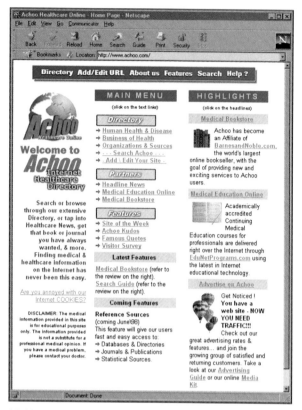

15.12

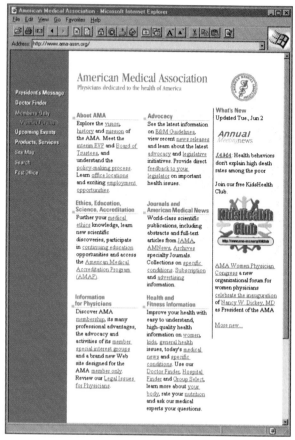

15.13

"Right at the top of the page is a name, J.Sperling Reich, that serves as a link to his e-mail (15.16). If I were promoting this site today, I would certainly want to submit *Bean* to him. See that NetLinks section on the left? Movie Sites (A-K) — there you go. *Bean* would definitely need to be submitted there."

PROMOTING OUTSIDE THE BOX

There's no denying that the tools we've explored so far are indispensable when it comes to promoting a Web site. But Ward insists that real creativity comes into play when you start thinking beyond the two walls of search engines and directories. "This is where the art comes in. You need to take a holistic approach. Look at your Web site as a whole, based on its quality and content, and find the outlets that need to know

about it. Only then can you come up with announcement angles that will give your site the competitive edge it deserves.

"There are two basic lessons I've learned in my years promoting Web sites. First, every site has a very specific audience. There are people out there who want to see it. There are services that want to classify it. There are writers, reporters, and editors who want to cover it. Your goal should be to connect your site with all of those things, with all those outlets that make sense and want to know about it. Figure out exactly who you're trying to appeal to, then go out and hunt down the sites that can do you the most good.

"Second, a Web site is more than just a URL. A lot of people think too small. They think, 'Okay, I've got this Web site and here's the URL for it. Now I need to submit the URL to all these places.' That's fine, but it's

15.15

15.14

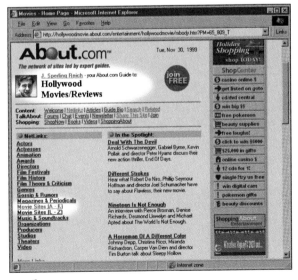

15.16

not enough. Think of your URL as a front door to all kinds of different content. Let's say at *www.site-x.com*, not only do I find a Web site that talks about what you do for a living and the services you offer, but I find out that you also publish a monthly Web zine on the art of Web site design. Well, that zine itself is promotable. It has its own URL. It might be *www.site-x.com/artweb* or whatever you call it. There are directories of Web zines out there like Zine Rack (*www.zinerack.com*, 15.17). Here's a place that doesn't care about Web sites, it just wants to know about Web zines. It divides those up and categorizes them by topic. If you went there now and did a search for graphic design for the Internet, you might find that there are 40 Web zines. In other words, your zine is an added hook to draw people to your site.

"Or let's say you sponsor an e-mail discussion group. It's not Web based, it's just plain old e-mail. Every time one person in the group sends an e-mail, everyone gets it. So you sponsor a discussion group about Web design tips, and it's just for people to share

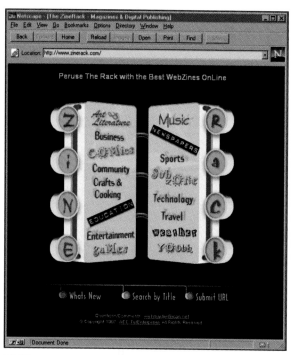

15.17

tips back and forth, nothing else. You're the moderator, so every post that gets sent goes to you first and then you decide if you want to release it to the entire group. There are list-serve programs that let you do exactly that. You have a little button at your Web site for people to sign up for the discussion group, and suddenly you have people signing up left and right.

"Again, that discussion group is separately promotable. In other words, there are directories and guides and editors, writers, and reporters who do nothing but highlight the best e-mail discussion groups. So there's another element of *www.site-x.com* that's promotable.

"Then let's say you're also an expert at Shockwave or some other authoring tool that lets you add cool elements to your Web site. There are about ten Web sites that do nothing but highlight cool Shockwave applications, with a Shockwave App of the Day.

"I could follow this same kind of concept through a dozen different elements of your Web site. You have to think beyond your URL and develop elements that are separately promotable. If you don't have any elements like this, you may want to consider adding them. The idea is to have as many separately promotable elements as possible."

SPEAKING TO THE ZINES

We asked Ward to walk us through a few specific examples of sites he's promoted that demonstrate the holistic approach at work. The first that came to mind was a specialized section of The Weather Channel's site christened Breaking Weather (*www.weather.com/breaking_weather*, 15.18).

"The Weather Channel has had a Web site up for a long time. But they came to me and said, 'We're building a major new section within our Web site dedicated to breaking weather. And we're going to launch this section of the site right at the beginning of the hurricane season.' In other words, they timed the launch of a topical site with a real-world event, which gave me that much more reason to think I could get it covered."

SEARCHING FOR DOMINANCE

According to Ward, one of the best ways to set up your site as the foremost authority in an area is to implement a search engine. "I know, a lot of people think it's counterintuitive. I once had this client, a boating manufacturer. I told them, 'You know, there's no search engine for the boating industry. But by God, there will be — it's just a matter of when. Why don't you guys use Swish or one of these other free tools to put together a search engine now while there are only 30 or 40 boating Web sites out there? You'll grow with it and eventually you'll be known as the source. You'll also have a vehicle for attracting banner ads.'"

"Well, they said, 'Oh. that's nuts! Why would we want to do that? You can't sell any boats that way. A search engine would just help people leave our site!'"

"No pun intended, but they missed the boat. These elements I'm mentioning, they become an extension of your Web presence. It's more than, 'Hey, come to my Web site and buy my product.' Instead it's 'Come use the search engine that I sponsor to help find what you're looking for.' Suddenly you have regular traffic, repeat customers, people who think of your company's name before any of the others. You control that market."

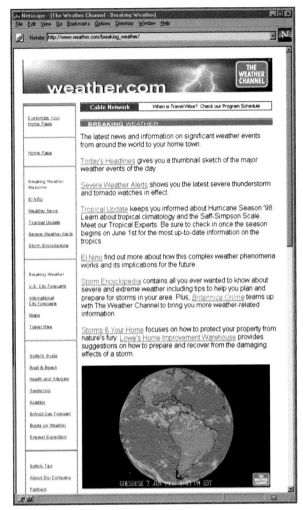

15.18

"Now, because this is an additional element of an existing Web site, the search engine and directory submissions have most likely already been done. I'm fairly certain that *www.weather.com* is already widely indexed. But there are sites out there that are interested in events as opposed to entire sites. For example, Netsurfer Digest (*www.netsurf.com/nsd*) is a Web-zine that comes out every two weeks and it highlights Web launches and happenings. They're looking for sites that make news. Because Breaking Weather is timed to a specific weather pattern, Netsurfer Digest is a perfect place to make an announcement."

TIMING IS EVERYTHING

Ward suggests that timing can be a crucial factor in how your Web site is received. "The Breaking Weather page brings up an important point: Just because your Web site is done doesn't mean you should be eager to get the thing out the door. You might consider, when's the best time to launch? What else is happening that might bring a little added excitement to my site? If you can find an event that gives your site greater relevance, you'll be rewarded for it."

So how does Ward go about submitting a partial site to a Web zine? "Along the left side of the Netsurfer Digest index page is a link that says 'Contact.' Clicking on that link takes you to a page of editorial contacts. Midway down, you see where it says 'Submit Networthy Items' (15.19). Click on that e-mail link and away you go."

So what does Ward include in his e-mail? A press release? "Well, I'll go ahead and distribute my client's press releases, yes. But press releases don't always get read. So I try to make my notes as personal as possible. I might say, 'Hey, the Weather Channel is launching a new portion of its site this week timed with the beginning of hurricane season. The company-issued press release is below. Feel free to read it, but here are some things that I think are particularly cool about this launch.' Then I'd list a few items. Certainly, you can automate e-mail to send out a million press releases in one chunk. But it's a waste. That kind of mail gets thrown away. It misses the human element—and I have to say, even over the Internet, the human element is extremely important.

"Obviously, Netsurfer Digest is just one example of the literally hundreds and hundreds of Web zines that exist. But it demonstrates a point: the Breaking Weather page isn't a brand new Web site, it's an extension of an existing site. But it's still a newsworthy Web launch, in my opinion, and there are people out there who will take it seriously and give it the attention it deserves."

GIVING PEOPLE A REASON TO STOP BY

Often, Ward's client is the one who comes up with the idea that makes it all work. "One of my favorite clients was Norbest (*www.norbest.com*, 15.20). Norbest is a turkey manufacturing co-op. They have all these turkey farmers market their turkeys under the name of Norbest. So you would think they'd be really boring. It's like, my God, how do you promote a turkey Web page?

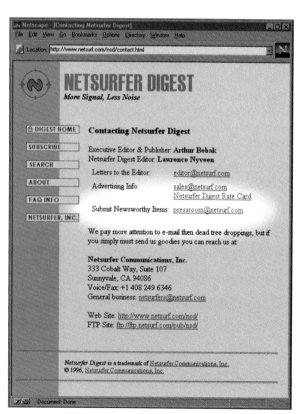

15.19

15.20

"Well, they launched a section of their site filled with Thanksgiving recipes and tips (15.21), all based on a diner motif. It was extremely clever. An editor friend at *USA Today* highlighted the site in the print edition. In many print publications, there's something about the Web each month. I tend to stay away from those because the odds of coverage are so small. But here a turkey site makes it into *USA Today*. This site attracted a lot of attention."

BRINGING NEW ATTENTION TO AN OLD SITE

"Another favorite of mine is the Acme Pet site (*www.acmepet.com*, 15.22). This is a community site for pet lovers of all kinds. If you have a pet, you can go there and find out why Fifi has fleas or whatever. I really love this site. The sites I enjoy most are the ones that have nothing to do with the Web or technology. They're about a real topic, something that people care about. It demonstrates that the Web has a purpose other than to promote itself.

"When Acme Pet came to me, the site was already in every search engine and directory they could find. But they were looking for some new way to promote the site. So I asked them, 'Do you have any events or special promotions coming up?' And they said, 'Well, we got a Halloween party where we're asking people to submit pictures of their dogs dressed up in Halloween costumes (15.23).' And I said, 'Damn that is so brilliant! If you were here, I'd kiss you. This is so insane that I can get you coverage. My editors will eat it up when I tell them that I have an online Halloween picture party for puppies.'

"I asked the site's creators to build a special page as an entryway into the contest. And they put a banner on their home page so that people would see that the contest was going on. And then I sent out a news release about a week before Halloween to all my appropriate online media contacts.

15.21   **15.22**

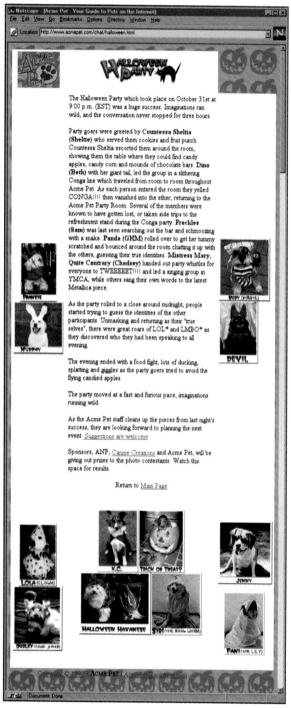

15.23

"But also, here's an event about pets. I know that there are online mailing lists for pet lovers. There are Usenet newsgroups for pet lovers. And each of those represent a place I could go to let people know about this costume contest.

"I was not trying to promote the Acme Pet Web site itself. But I knew by promoting the Halloween picture contest, I would do just that. The spillover would be that I would tell a lot of people about a site they hadn't seen yet."

DO IT RIGHT, DO IT YOURSELF

Earlier in this chapter, Ward mentions automating press releases through mass e-mailings. Can't you likewise automate search engine and directory submissions and save yourself a lot of headache? "Yes you can, but it won't save you any headaches. It would take me a heck of a lot of pages to explain all the pluses and minuses with automatic submission software. But it's basically like this: an auto-submitter tries to replicate the submission forms for Yahoo and all other search engines and directories. It tries to pass this information *en masse* to hundreds of forms at once. The program never actually goes to the Yahoo form, it uses its own version of the form and tries to make it fit.

"The first potential problem is that the auto-submit form may not exactly match the Yahoo form. It could be missing fields. The categories may not fit or they may not be offered at all. And the descriptions may be the wrong length. Second, some search engines and directories just flat-out don't like auto-submitters. If you're auto-submitting, then you're not seeing Yahoo's banner ads. I understand there are times when Infoseek refuses to take auto-submissions.

"The point is, if you use an auto-submission program, some sites will list your page, others will turn it down. And you'll never know why. Was it because you didn't give them what they needed, or was it because you used the auto-submission program? Instead of saving time, you've wasted it.

"If for whatever reason, you simply don't have enough time, then the best auto-submission program is SubmitIt (*www.submitit.com*). But I really urge you to do it yourself. You spend six months of your life putting together a Web site, right? So why would you believe you can announce it to the world in 30 seconds? Yeah, there are some things you can automate, and they might work okay, but announcing your Web site is just too important. If you're just willing to roll up your sleeves and spend some time at the keyboard, you can do a much better job than any machine."

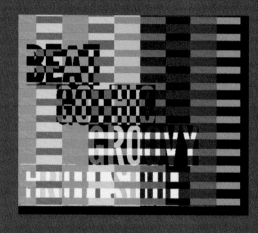

ABOUT THE CD-ROM

The CD-ROM at the back of this book gives us the opportunity to do something we can't always do inside the book—show as opposed to tell. Oh, sure, we can wax poetic about Neil Robertson's whimsical JavaScript rollovers or David Falstrup's creative use of QuickTime VR, but until you see a few examples for yourself, your socks will fail to be knocked off.

If you're having problems accessing the files and programs included on the CD, here's the skinny: Start by inserting the CD into your CD-ROM drive. On the Mac, the CD appears as a WebDesignSS 2ed icon on your desktop. Under Windows, you probably need to double-click on My Computer on your desktop to find the WebDesignSS 2ed icon.

In case you're wondering what that icon is, it's a cropped view of a globe trapped in an elaborate cable maze (A.1). Now you know the whole story.

Double-click the icon to open the CD-ROM. Depending on your platform, you will see one of two independent partitions, one for the Mac (A.2) and the other for the PC (A.3). (If you own Virtual PC on the Mac, you can check out the PC half of the CD from inside Windows.) While the Mac and PC partitions are similar, each contains a few extras that are exclusive to the respective platform.

The main item on the *Web Design Studio Secrets, 2nd Edition* CD is the Chapter Support Files folder. This folder contains support elements for many chapters in this book. For the most part, the chapter elements are self-explanatory, and many are referenced in the chapters themselves. If a folder contains

A.1

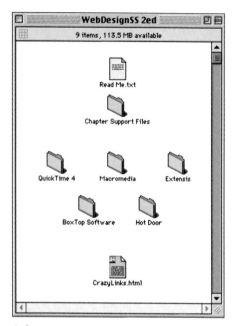

A.2

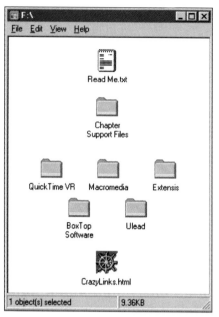

A.3

a sound file — in the AIFF format on the Mac or WAV on the PC — double-click the file to listen to the artist explain a topic in his or her own words. Beyond that, here are a few words of wisdom about the specific folders:

■ **Chap09 Goto:** If you're using a Mac, you can check out the Voyager demo, which was designed to sell Paramount on launching and promoting the UPN television network. The demo was never intended to appear on a book CD-ROM, so it isn't optimized for each and every machine, but it provides excellent insights into the production process. On the Mac and PC, you have access to the Phamis interactive kiosk (included with permission from IDX Systems Corporation). Double-click the Phamis icon to run the program. Granted, neither of these are Web sites, but this is a CD, and a CD deserves great multimedia.

■ **Chap11 Lopuck:** Double-click the rainforest.htm document to view a collection of animated GIF files. Double-click snow.htm to watch a Flash animation. (If you don't have the Flash Player installed on your system, you'll need to first run the Shockwave Installer program included in the Macromedia folder.)

■ **Chap12 Ingram:** Double-click the index.html file to view an extraordinary Flash-driven menu system. (If you don't have the Flash Player installed on your system, you'll need to first run the Shockwave Installer program included in the Macromedia folder.) When you're connected to the Internet, you can use the menus to access additional content online.

■ **Chap14 Falstrup:** To look at these marvelous VR files, your machine must be equipped with QuickTime VR. If it isn't, run the installer included in the QuickTime VR folder.

In addition to the Chapter Support Files folder, the CD contains free and demonstration software from a variety of top Web graphics vendors, including Apple, Macromedia (Portions Copyright © Macromedia. 1996-1998 All Rights Reserved.), Extensis, and BoxTop Software. Hot Door has provided a special Photoshop plug-in for Macintosh users, and Ulead has provided plug-ins and utilities for Windows folks. A typical demo runs for 15 to 30 days before expiring and inviting you to buy the fully functioning program, but some last for shorter periods. (One in particular, Hot Door Harmony, expires after 3 days. Erk!)

Finally, you'll find a file called CrazyLinks.html. Open this file in your favorite Web browser — or your not-so-favorite browser if you're feeling masochistic — to gain access to a plethora of Web sites that provide additional instruction, advice, and resources beyond the confines of this finite book (A.4). These links are so great, we must be crazy to offer them. At least, that's what we say in our infomercials.

CD TECHNICAL SUPPORT

If you have any problems getting the CD to work with your computer, it's very likely that some of your settings files or drivers are not working properly. For assistance, call IDG Books' technical support hotline at 1-800-762-2974. This is also the number to call if your CD is damaged.

A.4

INDEX

ABOUT THE AUTHORS

Deke McClelland is a contributing editor for *Macworld* and *Publish* magazines. He has authored more than 50 books on computer graphics and electronic publishing, and his work has been translated into more than 20 languages. He started his career as artistic director at the first service bureau in the United States.

Since winning the Ben Franklin Award for Best Computer Book of 1989, Deke has received two awards from the Society of Technical Communication (1994 and 1999), an American Society for Business Press Editors Award (1995), a Maggie from the Western Publications Society (1999), and a Cool2 Award from *Photo Electronic Imaging* magazine (1999). He is also a five-time recipient of the prestigious Computer Press Award. In 1999, the online column Book Bytes named Deke "Author of the Year" (*www.mymac.com*).

Deke is the author of the following books published by IDG Books Worldwide, Inc.: *Photoshop 5 Bible, Gold Edition; Macworld Photoshop 5 Bible; Photoshop 5 for Windows Bible;* and *Photoshop Studio Secrets, 2nd Edition.* He is also the author of *Real World Illustrator 8* and *Real World Digital Photography* from Peachpit Press. The first edition of *Photoshop Studio Secrets* won the Computer Press Award for the best advanced how-to book of 1997.

Katrin Eismann is an internationally recognized artist, educator, and author. In addition to *Web Design Studio Secrets*, she has coauthored *Photoshop Studio Secrets, 2nd Edition* and *Real World Digital Photography*. Katrin teaches creative digital imaging and digital photography throughout the United States and Europe. You can visit her Web site at *www.photoshopdiva.com*.

Terri Stone is an associate editor at *Macworld* magazine, covering print and Web design and multimedia. She was formerly the reviews editor at *Publish* magazine, where she also wrote articles about graphic and type design. She has created Web sites since 1995. This is her first book.

COLOPHON

This book was produced electronically in Foster City, California. Microsoft Word Version 7.0 was used for word processing; design and layout were produced using QuarkXPress 4.03 and Adobe Photoshop 4 on Power Macintosh computers. The typeface families used are Minion, Myriad Multiple Master, Prestige Elite, Symbol, Trajan, and Zapf Dingbats.

Acquisitions Editor: Michael Roney
Project Editors: Amy Thomas Buscaglia, Colleen Dowling
Technical Editor: Dan McClelland
Copy Editor: Ami Knox
Project Coordinators: Linda Marousek, Tom Debolski
Graphics and Production Specialist: Dina F Quan
Quality Control Specialist: Laura Taflinger
Book Designers: Margery Cantor, Cátálin Dulfu, Kurt Krames
Proofreading and Indexing: York Production Services
Cover Illustration: Larry S. Wilson

IDG BOOKS WORLDWIDE, INC. END-USER LICENSE AGREEMENT

READ THIS. You should carefully read these terms and conditions before opening the software packet(s) included with this book ("Book"). This is a license agreement ("Agreement") between you and IDG Books Worldwide, Inc. ("IDGB"). By opening the accompanying software packet(s), you acknowledge that you have read and accept the following terms and conditions. If you do not agree and do not want to be bound by such terms and conditions, promptly return the Book and the unopened software packet(s) to the place you obtained them for a full refund.

1. **License Grant.** IDGB grants to you (either an individual or entity) a nonexclusive license to use one copy of the enclosed software program(s) (collectively, the "Software") solely for your own personal or business purposes on a single computer (whether a standard computer or a workstation component of a multiuser network). The Software is in use on a computer when it is loaded into temporary memory (RAM) or installed into permanent memory (hard disk, CD-ROM, or other storage device). IDGB reserves all rights not expressly granted herein.

2. **Ownership.** IDGB is the owner of all right, title, and interest, including copyright, in and to the compilation of the Software recorded on the disk(s) or CD-ROM ("Software Media"). Copyright to the individual programs recorded on the Software Media is owned by the author or other authorized copyright owner of each program. Ownership of the Software and all proprietary rights relating thereto remain with IDGB and its licensers.

3. **Restrictions On Use and Transfer.**

(a) You may only (i) make one copy of the Software for backup or archival purposes, or (ii) transfer the Software to a single hard disk, provided that you keep the original for backup or archival purposes. You may not (i) rent or lease the Software, (ii) copy or reproduce the Software through a LAN or other network system or through any computer subscriber system or bulletin-board system, or (iii) modify, adapt, or create derivative works based on the Software.

(b) You may not reverse engineer, decompile, or disassemble the Software. You may transfer the Software and user documentation on a permanent basis, provided that the transferee agrees to accept the terms and conditions of this Agreement and you retain no copies. If the Software is an update or has been updated, any transfer must include the most recent update and all prior versions.

4. **Restrictions on Use of Individual Programs.** You must follow the individual requirements and restrictions detailed for each individual program in the Appendix of this Book. These limitations are also contained in the individual license agreements recorded on the Software Media. These limitations may include a requirement that after using the program for a specified period of time, the user must pay a registration fee or discontinue use. By opening the Software packet(s), you will be agreeing to abide by the licenses and restrictions for these individual programs that are detailed in the Appendix and on the Software Media. None of the material on this Software Media or listed in this Book may ever be redistributed, in original or modified form, for commercial purposes.

5. **Limited Warranty.**

(a) IDGB warrants that the Software and Software Media are free from defects in materials and workmanship under normal use for a period of sixty (60) days from the date of purchase of this Book. If IDGB receives notification within the warranty period of defects in materials or workmanship, IDGB will replace the defective Software Media.

(b) IDGB AND THE AUTHORS OF THE BOOK DISCLAIM ALL OTHER WARRANTIES, EXPRESS OR IMPLIED, INCLUDING WITHOUT LIMITATION IMPLIED WARRANTIES OF MERCHANTABILITY AND FITNESS FOR A PARTICULAR PURPOSE, WITH RESPECT TO THE SOFTWARE, THE PROGRAMS, THE SOURCE CODE CONTAINED THEREIN, AND/OR THE TECHNIQUES DESCRIBED IN THIS BOOK. IDGB DOES NOT WARRANT THAT THE FUNCTIONS CONTAINED IN THE SOFTWARE WILL MEET YOUR REQUIREMENTS OR THAT THE OPERATION OF THE SOFTWARE WILL BE ERROR FREE.

(c) This limited warranty gives you specific legal rights, and you may have other rights that vary from jurisdiction to jurisdiction.

6. Remedies.

(a) IDGB's entire liability and your exclusive remedy for defects in materials and workmanship shall be limited to replacement of the Software Media, which may be returned to IDGB with a copy of your receipt at the following address: Software Media Fulfillment Department, Attn.: *Web Design Studio Secrets, 2nd Edition*, IDG Books Worldwide, Inc., 10475 Crosspoint Blvd., Indianapolis, IN 46256, or call 1-800-762-2974. Please allow three to four weeks for delivery. This Limited Warranty is void if failure of the Software Media has resulted from accident, abuse, or misapplication. Any replacement Software Media will be warranted for the remainder of the original warranty period or thirty (30) days, whichever is longer.

(b) In no event shall IDGB or the authors be liable for any damages whatsoever (including without limitation damages for loss of business profits, business interruption, loss of business information, or any other pecuniary loss) arising from the use of or inability to use the Book or the Software, even if IDGB has been advised of the possibility of such damages.

(c) Because some jurisdictions do not allow the exclusion or limitation of liability for consequential or incidental damages, the above limitation or exclusion may not apply to you.

7. U.S. Government Restricted Rights. Use, duplication, or disclosure of the Software by the U.S. Government is subject to restrictions stated in paragraph (c)(1)(ii) of the Rights in Technical Data and Computer Software clause of DFARS 252.227-7013, and in subparagraphs (a) through (d) of the Commercial Computer — Restricted Rights clause at FAR 52.227-19, and in similar clauses in the NASA FAR supplement, when applicable.

8. General. This Agreement constitutes the entire understanding of the parties and revokes and supersedes all prior agreements, oral or written, between them and may not be modified or amended except in a writing signed by both parties hereto that specifically refers to this Agreement. This Agreement shall take precedence over any other documents that may be in conflict herewith. If any one or more provisions contained in this Agreement are held by any court or tribunal to be invalid, illegal, or otherwise unenforceable, each and every other provision shall remain in full force and effect.

Put a serious
dent
in your
workload with
Dreamweaver®
and Fireworks.®

Introducing Dreamweaver 3 and Fireworks 3

The newest versions of Dreamweaver and Fireworks work together to give you the power to create Web sites faster. Design buttons, animations and page comps in minutes with Fireworks 3. Mold your graphics and code into completed Web sites in record time with Dreamweaver 3. Streamline development with support for the content creation and Web application software you use. Together, Dreamweaver and Fireworks are one awesome team for rapid Web development.

www.macromedia.com

macromedia®

my2cents.idgbooks.com

CD-ROM INSTALLATION INSTRUCTIONS

Insert the CD into your CD-ROM drive. On the Mac, the CD appears as a WebDesignSS 2ed icon on your desktop. Under Windows, you probably need to double-click the My Computer icon on your desktop to find the WebDesignSS 2ed icon. In either case, the WebDesignSS 2ed icon features a cropped view of a globe trapped in an elaborate cable maze.

Double-click the icon to open the CD-ROM. Depending on your platform, you will see one of two independent partitions, one for the Mac and the other for the PC. If you own Virtual PC on the Mac, you can check out the PC half of the CD from inside Windows. While the Mac and PC partitions are similar, each contains a few extras that are exclusive to the respective platform.

The main item on the *Web Design Studio Secrets, 2nd Edition* CD is the Chapter Support Files folder. This folder contains support elements for many chapters in this book:

- Chap09 Goto
- Chap11 Lopuck
- Chap12 Ingram
- Chap14 Falstrup

In addition to the Chapter Support Files folder, the CD contains free and demonstration software from a variety of top Web graphics vendors.

Please read the appendix, "About the CD-ROM," for instructions on installing and copying files.